ENCOUNTERING AMERICA

HARPER  PERENNIAL

NEW YORK • LONDON • TORONTO • SYDNEY • NEW DELHI • AUCKLAND

ENCOUNTERING AMERICA

Humanistic Psychology,
Sixties Culture &
the Shaping of the Modern Self

JESSICA GROGAN

HARPER ⬤ PERENNIAL

ENCOUNTERING AMERICA. Copyright © 2013 by Jessica Grogan. All rights reserved. Printed in the United States of America. No part of this book may be used or reproduced in any manner whatsoever without written permission except in the case of brief quotations embodied in critical articles and reviews. For information address HarperCollins Publishers, 10 East 53rd Street, New York, NY 10022.

HarperCollins books may be purchased for educational, business, or sales promotional use. For information please write: Special Markets Department, HarperCollins Publishers, 10 East 53rd Street, New York, NY 10022.

FIRST EDITION

Designed by William Ruoto

Library of Congress Cataloging-in-Publication Data is available upon request.

ISBN 978-0-06-183476-9

13 14 15 16 17 ov/rrd 10 9 8 7 6 5 4 3 2 1

For Dan, Jolie, and Asa—the reasons for my striving

Contents

Introduction

This book tells the story of humanistic psychology, a movement that originated in the 1950s, formally emerged in the 1960s, and ignited, before burning out, in the 1970s. The angle of the story is intellectual and cultural; I care about both the intellectual theory and the cultural context that informed humanistic psychology, as well as the influence the movement had, in its own right, on both those realms. In telling this particular story, my purpose is to make people take seriously a movement that's been largely dismissed from the academic circles in which it arose and that's been gratuitously associated with the excesses of the 1960s and 1970s. I also hope to remind people of a truth to which humanistic psychologists were keenly attuned—that individuals in all their messy complexity should remain at the heart of psychological study and practice.

When I deliver this brief, cocktail-party explanation of the book to friends and colleagues, responses tend to fall into one of two categories. Some people focus on how little they know about humanistic psychology, aside from a vague recollection of a page of their Intro Psych text devoted to Carl Rogers and Abraham Maslow, and they suggest it's going to take concentrated work to convince them that some obsolete psychological theory could be relevant to their understanding of their lives and their culture at present. Others ask *what happened* to all the good stuff that was going on in the sixties in psychology (sensitivity training; encounter groups; progressive management; talk of human liberation, health, and growth), noting that it all just seemed to evaporate.

Defining humanistic psychology and defending its value is hard to do over wine and cheese, but I try to make a few basic points. First, that humanistic psychology was a collection of theories premised on the individual's innate tendency toward growth. Second, its theorists hoped to return human subjectivity, and human complexity, to the study and practice of psychology. Third, in resurrecting a dialogue that went back to the beginnings of psychology in America and the work of William James, humanistic psychologists breathed some life back into a discipline that had moved too far toward scientism and the medical model and that had strayed too far from its philosophical and theological roots in the fundamentals of human existence. And finally, although humanistic psychology was firmly rooted in intellectual and academic principles, it had its broadest impact on the wider culture, where it resonated in realms as diverse as executive management, psychedelic drug use, and civil rights.

Abraham Maslow, "the father of humanistic psychology," once asked himself in his journal how he would define the movement in one sentence. The answer he gave was grander than the one I've just given. It is, he wrote, "a move away from knowledge of things & lifeless objects as basis for all philosophy, economics, science, politics, etc. (because this has failed to help with the basic human problems) *toward* a centering upon human needs & fulfillment & aspirations as the fundamental basis from which to derive all the social institutions, philosophy, ethics, etc. I might use also for more sophisticated & hep people that it is a resacralizing of science, society, the person, etc."[1]

In every one of his attempts to articulate the goals of humanistic psychology, Maslow looked beyond ways to modify the methods of psychological research and practice. His ambition was vaster than that. By changing the way psychology approached the study of people, he hoped to incite a cultural paradigm shift. He wanted to transform our view of human nature on the most basic level. In doing this, he would make it the job of psychology to answer philosophical, moral, and existential questions that were central to human experience.

The questions that humanistic psychologists like Maslow hoped to answer were endemic to modern society and had been asked before in many ways. How can individuals maintain a sense of agency in an increasingly mechanized and technologized world? How can Americans achieve a sense of identity based on values distinct from those of both capitalism and Christianity (or other traditional religions)? What does it mean to be psychologically healthy, beyond not being mentally ill? How can individuals' unique and divergent experiences be quantified and meaningfully compared?

They also explored questions that were more universal in their scope: How can individuals find meaning in their lives? From where can they derive values?

These questions were particularly salient in the 1950s and 1960s, when humanistic psychologists were responding directly to deep cultural needs. Alienated by technological change, confused by the decline of traditional roles, unsettled by World War II and its consequences, and plagued by Cold War fears, many Americans found the positive and optimistic answers they provided compelling. This attraction was demonstrated, during the 1960s and 1970s, in high attendance rates at growth centers founded upon its theory, in widespread adoption of related techniques (like encounter groups and bodywork), and in the permeation of American culture with the language of human potential and encounter.

Although the specifics of our cultural moment may have changed, the issues with which humanistic psychologists were wrestling remain pressing. Instead of dishwashers and washing machines, we're struggling to integrate smart phones and iPads. Our Cold War fears have been replaced by terrorist threats and the specter of global warming. Even with our new forms of social connectivity, or perhaps because of them, our sense of community still feels terribly inadequate. While opening up many frontiers, globalization threatens us with a new sense of smallness. Within psychology, the dehumanizing tendencies of behaviorism and psychoanalysis have been displaced by the equally reductionistic approaches of psychopharmacology and neuroscience.

Well then, some ask, why should we look for insight into our current condition in a movement that so obviously failed to solve these problems the first time around? And not only did it fail, it disappeared. Humanistic psychology, they argue, was a fad of the sixties and seventies, no more relevant to our lives today than disco and bell-bottoms.

To the evaporation issue I tend to argue, depending on my mood, that the ideas and practices of humanistic psychology have dispersed so widely and thoroughly they've become virtually undetectable—they're the air we breathe. Or, when I'm feeling more cynical, I explain that these theories and techniques have been so distorted—exploited by business interests and invoked as a justification for drug abuse, infidelity, or narrow self-focus—they no longer embody the intentions or resemble the original forms from which they were born.

Many Americans have some understanding of the extent to which our contemporary culture is a "therapy culture," one in which we hold fast to notions of the self as changeable and

redeemable and in which we have largely replaced more traditional structures of religion and morality with the values of
therapy. They watch Oprah, they read self-help, and they might
even attend therapy instead of church. But it's less likely that
they understand the ways in which our twenty-first-century
existences, relationships, and choices owe a unique debt to humanistic psychology. Its language has seeped into our relationships, our self-expression, our self-talk. We speak regularly of
our "potential" and our need for "growth." We look for marriages to be growth-fostering, therapeutic. We may even ask of
our spouses the very things one could expect of a humanistic
psychotherapist (unconditional acceptance, impeccable emotional attunement, and empathy).

If we do go to therapy, we're likely to see the founding
ideas of humanistic psychology embodied, at least in part, by
our therapist. We sit in chairs or on couches, face-to-face. We
guide the sessions ourselves, receiving empathy and encouragement, and a minimal amount of direct instruction. We may call
our therapist by her first name, and we may even learn details of
her personal life (how many kids she has, for example, or what
kinds of lessons she's learned from her own marriage).

We may also, however, find a distorted form of humanistic
psychology in psychotherapy and in the wider culture. We may
find therapists who don't seem to do anything but listen; they
may seem almost passive in their acceptance of our flaws, of our
endless complaining, of the ways in which we repeat dysfunctional patterns in our lives. Rather than propelling us toward
growth, in the way Carl Rogers theorized and demonstrated,
they may enable our fixations. And rather than modeling a
healthy positive regard, they may merely display a begrudging
tolerance.

We encounter distortions of humanistic psychology in our daily lives, as well. Talk shows and self-help books, for example, often tout the importance of being true to our inner selves, even when it's at the expense of our families or our community. In defiance of the intentions of Maslow and others to reform society by improving individuals, these cultural voices may be so committed to affirming the individual that they ignore moral questions and encourage selfishness.

The distortion of the movement's founding principles is not a recent development. The moment of humanistic psychology's inception in 1962 was itself cytokinetic. As quickly as humanistic theorists put forth their ideas, they split in a hundred different directions. Even before the official creation of the movement, Maslow's ideas were adopted widely in management theory, often with the intention more of optimizing production and maximizing profit than of improving workers' lives. Almost as quickly as it was formed, humanistic psychology erupted into the human potential movement, a cultural outgrowth that quickly dispensed with its thoughtful academic foundations and the caution that had characterized the original theory. These wild detours, though, were the very roads that brought us to the vastly different configuration of culture and psychology we find today.

My cocktail-party answer is informative, particularly if you corner me long enough to extract a fuller explanation, but in one sense, it misses the macro. This is also the story of the relationship between culture and psychology in America as it evolved from the postwar to the Reagan eras. The narrative is dramatic and rocky; it snakes across a revolutionary period of intellectual experiment, through a phase of countercultural excess, and into a period of social conservatism that was nonetheless undeniably stamped by the legacy of what came before. It's the story of how figures like Abraham Maslow, Carl Rogers, and Rollo May resurrected the humanizing principles and productive paradoxes that were present at the birth of American psychology but were diluted by positivistic and scientistic pursuits. It traces their specific contributions—to psychotherapy and the philosophy of science—in relation to the broader field of psychology, assessing the ways in which the field expanded to absorb some of the interests of humanistic psychologists, while at the same time it contracted to reject others more strongly. American psychology was elevated by the insights of humanistic psychologists, damaged by their excesses, and, ultimately, forever changed.

1

The Problem of Psychological Health

"I'm trying to shake the ground beneath clinical psychology. It's too confident, too technological, too proud. But all its concepts are moot. What is 'cure'? 'Illness'? 'Health'? There should be more humility, more fear and trembling."

ABRAHAM MASLOW[1]

On December 6, 1967, psychologist Abraham Maslow doubled over in pain. He was having a massive coronary.

Maslow had been at the peak of his powers. One of the founders of a revolutionary movement called humanistic psychology, his writings had spoken to members of a culture in crisis, offering hope and direction. With their political, economic, and spiritual relevance, his insights had extended psychologists' already significant social role. He had theorized a more humane approach to managing workers, which had been adopted widely by corporate advocates of progressive management. He had advanced a utopian vision of a healed culture, of people at their best, that had informed clinical practice and academic research.

While in recovery in the ICU of a Cambridge-area hospital, Maslow was told that a mysterious malady he had experienced twenty years earlier had likely been a prior coronary. As a result, his heart was badly scarred. It would take years to recover from this most recent episode. If he lived "carefully," there was a small chance he could avoid another, likely fatal, heart attack.[2]

As he gazed out the window at the forbidding December sky, Maslow contemplated his prospects. In many ways, his life was complete. By his side was his wife, Bertha, whom he had loved, and loved well, since he was sixteen. Also beside him were his daughters, Ann and Ellen, whose very existences had propelled him to the height of his own. He had made many good friends who treasured his insights. With his extensive publications (four books and countless articles), he had reached millions. He was tenured at Brandeis and esteemed by his colleagues. In fact, he had just been nominated to serve as president of the American Psychological Association (APA).

He didn't feel finished, though. He imagined starting a new journal, *Assent*, which would encompass "the Utopian, the self-growth, the hope, the optimum."[3] He planned to complete an anthology of his work. He hoped to improve the lives of American workers by further disseminating his ideas for humane management throughout the corporate world. And when he looked at the gap between the influence he'd had and the transformative changes in the culture and politics of America that he'd dreamed his theories would bring about, he was disappointed.

America in 1967 was about as damaged as Maslow's heart. The day of his coronary alone was arguably the bloodiest in the history of the Vietnam War.[4] Protesters had set up permanent camps in Washington, DC, and engaged in frequent demonstrations across the country. Thirteen years after the *Brown v. Board of Education* decision, racial tensions were still appallingly high. Angry students, guided by Students for a Democratic Society (SDS), demonstrated for civil rights. At the same time, their rebellion had disrupted the hierarchy of universities across the country and, to Maslow's lights, undermined important structures of knowledge and respect. Meanwhile, American women were growing impatient with the government's inadequate attempts to raise their status. And, just five years after the Cuban Missile Crisis, citizens still quaked at the threat of nuclear war.

Rather than viewing the social problems of the 1960s as indicative of a negative cultural ethos, however, Maslow saw them as a mark of a healthy "clash of cultures."

"On one hand," he explained, "is the culture of courage and coping and fighting back and striving, which all imply hopefulness of a certain kind, or at least possibility, if not probability. Then, on the other hand, is a culture of despair, of hopelessness, of a theory of evil which has pervaded certain groups in our population."[5] Each conflict had arisen out of hope as much as out of despair.

Maslow himself rode the crest of the culture clash. His "humanistic psychology" promised an antidote to the sense of personal and cultural hopelessness that often seemed pervasive. It brought to the surface a latent optimism, premised on more than just material success and economic prosperity. His theory of self-actualization had earned him, in some sectors, the status of a guru and, in others, distinction as a supreme expert.

But the esteem he had gained by the late 1960s was predicated on more than just the congeniality of his theory with the cultural ethos. He had fulfilled the academy's expectations of him: plodding methodically through a PhD program at the University of Wisconsin in the early 1930s, through decades of experimental research and years of thankless teaching. He had published widely and systematically on topics like animal behavior, sexual dominance, and motivation. It wasn't until the 1950s that he began to write on the more unconventional topics of human fulfillment and self-actualization.

The Maslow who lay on the hospital bed recovering on that dreary day in 1967 was the Maslow who had been made in the 1950s. With the encouragement of a small coterie of like-minded scholars and well-funded businessmen, Maslow had tunneled to the core of his psychological passion—the achievement of human peaks, transcendent moments, well-lived lives. He had laid the foundation for the theory of self, and the psychological worldview, that would define American interests into the twenty-first century.

More than a little luck had come his way. Maslow's interests had ripened at a historical moment wide open to psychologists. In the 1950s, the field of psychology had earned a new kind of fame. Americans had agreed to let psychologists into nearly every facet of their lives.

In 1957, *Life* magazine's five-part series "The Age of Psychology in the U.S." bore the tagline: "Less than a Century Old, the Science of Human Behavior Permeates Our Whole Way of Life— At Work, in Love, in Sickness and in Health." Its opening paragraph enumerates the daily contacts Americans had with psychology: in advertising, popular media, industry, politics, warfare, education, and entertainment. This all-pervasiveness, argued author Ernest Havemann, was a unique product of the 1950s and "strictly American."

"By now," he wrote, "the U.S. has more psychologists and psychoanalysts, engaged in more types of inquiry and activity, than all the rest of the world put together. It certainly provides the biggest and most eager audience for psychology."[6]

American psychology had grown at an exorbitant rate in the years after World War II. This was, in part, because of the government's interest in assuaging cultural fears over the prevalence of "psychoneurotic" illness in returning servicemen.[7] As thousands of functionally impaired soldiers filtered back into the United States, psychological treatment programs reassured them (and an anxious population) that their problems were imminently fixable. The newly medicalized approach to diagnosis and treatment psychologists offered was a product of their success in aligning themselves with natural scientists. Through a (sometimes tenuous or superficial) connection to experimental research and empirical evidence, the psychologist had become a new kind of scientific expert—one who appeared to be uniquely qualified to address individual and cultural suffering.

In the late forties, the American need for psychologists, and psychotherapists in particular, outpaced the supply of professionals within the field. The *New York Times* estimated a demand for as many as 27,000 new clinical psychologists in 1949.[8] Prior to the war a "tiny handful" of psychologists had considered themselves "clinical," but after the war the APA made clinical training a mandatory component of graduate education in psychology.[9]

The perceived need for new therapists perpetuated the expansion of the field. The Rockefeller Foundation and other charitable trusts endowed university departments and research centers with monies for training new clinicians. In 1946, Congress passed the National Mental Health Act, appropriating greater funding for psychological research and education and creating the National Institute of Mental Health (NIMH), the soon-to-be center of American psychological research, which would receive considerably more government support in the years to come.[10]

In the years after 1945, psychotherapy entered the domain of functional people. "Psychotherapy for the normal," wrote historian Ellen Herman, "gained momentum not only because of the formal expansion of government services but because it meshed easily with cultural trends that made therapeutic help appear acceptable, even inviting, to ordinary people at midcentury." These trends included the continued breakdown of a sense of community, and heightened feelings of alienation derived from the growth of corporations and mass institutions. More people, and specifically more middle-class, educated people, participated directly in psychotherapy, as they began to view it as a means for finding personal and interpersonal meaning.[11]

Culturally, the psychological practitioner came to occupy an almost mythical status in the American imagination during the 1950s. As if they possessed a psychological X-ray vision, clinicians seemed able to unlock deep unconscious secrets, map and correct the insidious effects of childhood experiences, and eradicate destructive current behaviors. This conception was perpetuated by depictions of psychologists in film, theater, and popular media. According to Havemann, in the mid-1950s one movie out of every ten depicted a psychiatrist or psychiatric problem.

"Practitioners of psychology are too intriguing for their own good," he wrote. "Every scrap of information about them is eagerly gobbled up, whether authentic or not, so that a good deal of what the public has come to believe is utterly wrong."[12]

Much of the psychological theory that reached average Americans was a distortion of the theorist's original intentions. Lay popularizers of psychoanalysis, for example, tended to depict Freudian psychology as an individualized solution to loneliness, emptiness, and hopelessness in a society that in basic ways was sane. Although Freud himself had intended to oppose oppressive standards of morality and intrusive forms of governmental control, Freudian theory was often deployed in America to shore up the status quo and to pathologize individuals who departed from it.[13]

Popular articles about psychoanalysis focused almost exclusively on treatment, rarely dealing with theory in any meaningful way.[14] Even rarer was any mention of elements of psychoanalysis that undermined dominant cultural values. For example, although Freudian analysis was areligious, more than one mainstream article suggested that analysis could provide a more "rational basis" for religious beliefs.[15]

"Popularization crystallized a socially conservative image of psychoanalysis," wrote historian Nathan Hale, "from its identification of practitioners with dentists and businessmen to its vision of therapy as a tough, painful exercise that resulted as a rule in marital harmony, personal equilibrium, and vocational success."[16] Hale notes that the depictions of Freudianism in popular sources (ranging from *Life* magazine to *Scientific American*) reinforced and perpetuated stereotypes of analysts, patients, and treatment. Grossly simplified accounts of psychoanalysis consistently relied on the notion of catharsis. "In all these dramatic human interest stories," states Hale, "someone hears a forgotten memory that is dredged up, and suddenly somebody can walk, or talk if they are a hysterical mute."[17] With "monotonous regularity," treatment results in normalcy, happiness, success.[18]

American psychoanalysts were often complicit in this distortion. For one, they elevated the self over all other units of concern.[19] In the case of the ego psychologists, Freudian theory was revised to deemphasize intrapsychic conflict and instead construct the ego as "masterful and adaptive."[20] "The neo-Freudians exemplified Americanization," wrote one historian. "They watered down a radical depth psychology that hinted of liberation into a tepid doctrine of social meliorism."[21]

In addition to encouraging social adjustment, many American psychoanalysts sought to align Freudian theory with the general American insistence on individual satisfaction, fulfillment, and happiness. They emphasized Freud's concept of "optimal psychological functioning" at the expense of more central (and more disturbing) aspects of his theory. The theory of optimal functioning boiled down to the idea that an equilibrium between the individual psyche and the social environment, obtained through adaptation, was imperative for superior functioning. The achievement of this kind of psychic equilibrium marked the successful substitution of "hysterical misery" with "common unhappiness" (the goal of psychoanalysis), and the yielding of the chaotic and sometimes dangerous impulses of the id to the real demands of the social and cultural environment.[22] In this respect, adjustment was akin to health, and maladjustment was synonymous with neurosis.[23]

The popular preference for the doctrine of adjustment fueled the cycle of theoretical distortion and further implicated psychologists in the illusion of cultural harmony. Although he framed himself as a debunker of psychological myth, Ernest

Havemann betrayed himself as a popularizer. He was overly rosy: he saw the omnipresence of psychology as a net social gain. "Even those of us who never took a course in psychology," he wrote in the conclusion of his five-part *Life* series, "and never saw a psychoanalyst in the flesh are probably a little happier—a little more understanding of our wives and children, a little kinder to our associates, a little less given to superstition and prejudice about human nature. All of us, even myriads among us who have emotional problems ranging from the light to the serious, have far more hope for the future."[24] For Havemann, as for others, the story of psychology's victory, the "psychoanalyzation" of American life, thought, and institutions had a happy ending, which was itself premised on a pretense of American happiness.[25]

To Abe Maslow, this narrative of psychology had it exactly backwards. Whatever glimmers of promise and progress there were to be found in America in the 1950s—and the ever-optimistic Maslow identified many—American psychologists seemed constitutionally incapable of recognizing them as anything other than disturbances to tamp down. They were too negatively oriented, sickness-focused, problem-centered. They lacked, he argued, an imagination for people at their best, and for the ways they could aid in the amelioration of social problems. Their highest ambition, it seemed, was to rehabilitate fallen individuals to better conform to social expectations.

Maslow stood out in this dreary landscape. Though he had been reared in the tradition of "classical laboratory research" that tended to reduce humans to a set of stimuli and responses, he was irrepressibly compelled, by nature, to view people as resplendent.[26] He had begun to diverge from dominant theory under E. L. Thorndike's tutelage in the 1930s, but his original approach bloomed in the 1950s, when he began to forge a psychology of people at their best. His first article representing his new interests, "Self-Actualizing People: A Study of Psychological Health," was published in 1950 and responded to the pressing need to consider the "problem of psychological health."[27]

In this study, he attempted to identify the qualities of healthy, or "self-actualized," people, whom he defined as those making full use of their potentialities, talents, and capacities while opposing the social norms that got in their way.[28] He took as his subjects his own contemporaries (including anthropologist Ruth Benedict and Gestalt psychologist Max Wertheimer) and historical figures (including Abraham Lincoln, Thomas Jefferson, Albert Einstein, Eleanor Roosevelt, Jane Addams, William James, and Spinoza). Instead of using rigorous empirical methods to identify them (as he had in the culling of appropriate subjects for past research), he identified his cases largely through hunches, dividing them into categories of highly probable, probable, partial, and potential subjects. He obtained data on the subjects using comparably fuzzy methods: namely, holistic analysis and composite impressions derived from whatever exposure he had to the individuals (in person, secondhand, or in their written works).

Maslow's unconventional methods, he felt, had been born of necessity. Because of their underrepresentation in the general population, attempts to select his subjects more systematically had failed. Of the three thousand undergraduates he evaluated, only one was usable as a "possible" or "potential" case. More systematic data collection seemed impractical.

He met the inevitable scrutiny of his fellow researchers head-on, arguing for the validity of his study as a form of "pre-science." "I consider the problem of psychological health to be so pressing," he wrote, "that *any* leads, *any* suggestions, *any* bits of data, however moot, are endowed with a certain temporary value."[29] If nothing else, his impressions would provide a valuable starting point for future research in a field that was wide open.

Maslow's analysis led him to propose a list of fourteen "whole-characteristics" of self-actualizing people. He noticed that his subjects seemed to have more efficient perceptions of reality than others. In contrast to neurotics, self-actualizers seemed able to view reality effectively without the filter of their own fears, theories, hopes, anxieties, and expectations. They also seemed better at accepting themselves and others, without the burden of unnecessary guilt or defensiveness. This quality extended from a relative lack of aversions to specific foods to a high tolerance for the weaknesses of others.

Behaviorally, he wrote, self-actualizers tend to be spontaneous and able to move facilely from conventional to unconventional behavior in response to the demands of a situation. Their humor is unhostile, non-damaging to others. They are universally creative and generative.[30]

Maslow deemed self-actualizers, in their general approach to life, to be problem-centered rather than ego-centered, meaning outwardly directed toward a problem bigger than themselves. Their appreciation of the "basic goods of life" is continually fresh, thrilling, exciting.[31] Their attitude toward mankind is one of fellow feeling, characterized by deep sympathy, affection, and identification. They can both teach and learn from anyone.

Interpersonally, self-actualizers tend to have a small number of profound relationships, characterized by "more fusion, greater love, more perfect identification, more obliteration of the ego boundaries" than others would find possible.[32] This is a complement to their capacity for fusion with experience, as in the case of orgasm or mystical states.

However, Maslow observed that in spite of their deep and fundamental connection to mankind, self-actualizers also possess a capacity for detachment. They seem to appreciate solitude and appear not to depend upon the evaluations of others. In fact, their autonomy seems to place them "above the battle," independent in valuable ways from the wider culture and environment.[33]

In the conclusion of his study, Maslow noted that self-actualizers aren't perfect. In fact, they can be irritating, stubborn, alienating, and even ruthless. Their independence often makes them difficult to get along with. But this inherent lack of perfection is also what makes self-actualization a possibility rather than an unattainable ideal.[34]

Maslow's success in setting the bar of psychological health high, but not unrealistically so, was a key accomplishment of his study. He was attempting, admittedly imperfectly, to begin a long-in-coming conversation on the constituents of psychological health. He was opposing decades of illness-oriented theory that provided only a default definition of wellness as the absence of symptoms. And, through his questionably scientific methods, he was going out on an empirical limb to do so.

Throughout Maslow's study, he focused on the issue of nonconformity in self-actualizers. The ability to buck convention, to resist acculturation, to think independently, and to act autonomously were observations no doubt primed by the cultural context in which he generated them.

In advancing his description of self-actualizers, and in focusing on their independence from cultural expectations, Maslow was implicitly critical of the mandate for conformity that seemed to be descending upon the nation, and of the adjustment-oriented model of psychology that was structurally supporting it. He worried that by urging domestic solidarity in the face of the Cold War, American leaders were also calling for the erasure of important individual differences. But he wasn't alone in advancing this concern. In fact, his was one of many voices urging Americans to resist the hypnotic power of the herd mentality.

In the 1950s, several widely read cultural critics wrote in opposition to the idea that conformity represented a form of social harmony. Sociologist David Riesman, for example, argued in his 1950 book *The Lonely Crowd* that morality and autonomy were degraded when conformity commanded the preferences and expectations of individuals. By directing their gaze toward others, Riesman warned, average Americans (parents, teachers, and other leaders) sacrificed much of their generative influence to become enforcers of middle-class conformity.[35]

William H. Whyte also took on the idea of the damaging nature of conformity in his 1956 bestseller *The Organization Man*. Looking specifically at mass organization, Whyte charged corporations with promising a better life through time-saving devices (affordable cars, space travel, and fast food), that were actually premised on the degradation of the individual.[36]

While Riesman's book was intended as a descriptive sociological analysis, Whyte's was more polemical, indicting the organization and urging readers to fight it. By the end of the decade, social criticism was even less cautious. In *Growing Up Absurd* (1960), Paul Goodman attacked what he saw as the ugly imperative for conformity that had eclipsed America socially and politically. Criticizing even social scientists for their lack of interest in social change, Goodman argued that they were more concerned with societal adjustment—they sought only to "mop up the corners and iron out the kinks."[37]

Unlike typical social scientists, Goodman, Whyte, and Riesman found their work to be suddenly and unexpectedly popular.[38] Their success suggested the heightened interest of many Americans in the problem of conformity, but also more broadly in social and cultural problems, during the decade. It also hinted at the sense of urgency many Americans felt for putting their problems into words. As a *New York Times* journalist later noted of *The Lonely Crowd*, even those who hadn't read the book "were soon tossing around phrases like 'inner-directed' and 'other-directed.' "[39] The adoption of this language may have also served as a bulwark against insidious fear and anxiety, allowing individuals a means to externalize some of their struggles.

But if readers were looking to these books for a way to feel better, this kind of cultural criticism would only take them so far. It was, by nature, negatively oriented. It offered readers new paradigms for articulating their distress, or blaming someone for it, but rarely provided constructive directions for change, or for identifying individual or cultural strengths. This kind of writing, in fact, replicated the mistakes of psychologists; it was a form of diagnosis, aimed at naming pathology and identifying deficits.

• • •

Instead of mimicking these social scientists, who were acting as psychologists to the culture, a small group mainly comprised of actual psychologists took a different approach. In 1956, Clark Moustakas, a psychologist engaged in child development research at the Merrill-Palmer Institute, published a more positively oriented collection of essays on the topic of the self.[40]

Moustakas's collection, *The Self,* combined the positive insights of thinkers in a range of disciplines and aimed at providing a framework for investigating health.[41] By exploring positive attributes like creativity, expression, and self-actualization, and investigating human drives for growth, autonomy, and wholeness, the collection served two ends. First, the articles focused on inherent human strengths that could naturally oppose the influence of a sick society. Second, they offered a challenge to the pathology-oriented values of the human sciences, whose attention to individual problems had only reinforced notions of deviance and normality, allowing corporate and government interests to prevail.

In the spirit of Riesman, Whyte, and Goodman, the stated intention of the book was to question the aggrandized goal of adjustment that had saturated the culture and percolated into social science and psychiatry. Adjustment to and within society was certainly a reasonable goal, conceded Moustakas and his coauthors, and perhaps an unavoidable concern of psychology, but psychologists couldn't conscionably advocate adjustment in the absence of a consideration of the norms and standards to which one was being asked to adjust. Mental health couldn't be defined as default adjustment.

The authors seemed to agree that health was not likability, popularity, or belonging; rather, it was defined by independence, flexibility, and self-direction. Safe choices were actually sick choices, while healthy choices entailed taking creative risks. "While adjustment and stabilization are perhaps good because they cut pain," wrote the book's editor, "they are bad because development toward higher ideals, ordering, and creation ceases."[42]

Featured in the collection was a reprint of Maslow's break-through article "Self-Actualizing People: A Study of Psychological Health." Offering an alternative to the societal ideal Riesman had identified as the "other-directed" individual, Maslow's findings located the healthy individual somewhat apart from society, or at least from the norms that most people uncritically adopted as their own. He reminded those who had read him, and informed those unfamiliar with his theory, that self-actualizers were unique in their ability to remain dignified even in undignified surroundings, to repel the taint of what surrounded them. They succeeded because they stayed true to their intuitions, rather than depending on those around them to inform their interpretations.[43]

Maslow was the only author to publish two articles in *The Self.* His second, "Personality Problems and Personality Growth," identified the healthy individual as the potential redemption of the sick society. "Sick people are made by a sick culture; healthy people are made possible by a healthy culture," he wrote. "But it is just as true that sick individuals make their culture more sick and that healthy individuals make their culture more healthy. Improving individual health is one approach to making a better world."[44]

Health, however, argued Maslow, wasn't what most people seemed to think it was. It wasn't synonymous with happiness, popularity, and adjustment. Indeed, in a society that was off balance, health would manifest more in symptoms of unhappiness, alienation, and disrepute. Such symptoms could be healthy reactions to unhealthy situations.

"Which of the Nazis at Auschwitz or Dachau were healthy?" Maslow asked. "Those with the stricken conscience or those with a nice, clear happy conscience. [. . .] It seems quite clear that personality problems may sometimes be loud protests against the crushing of one's psychological bones, of one's true inner nature. What is sick then is *not* to protest while this crime is being committed."[45]

A key feature of the model of health psychologists like Maslow had begun to formulate was the notion that a healthy individual must stand apart from her culture. That she must transcend social expectations, and forge a path through the wilderness. Looking around at America in the 1950s, Maslow saw a virtual absence of true heroes and ideals from which to draw inspiration. "About all we have left," he wrote," is the well-adjusted man without any problems, a very pale and doubtful substitute."[46]

Maslow reflected the popular critique that the American entrepreneur, the innovator, the maverick had been replaced with "the man in the gray flannel suit." In 1955, Sloan Wilson's bestseller by that name had depicted this degradation of the American man's ideals, and explored the contrast they represented with the standards of bravery and valor that had characterized wartime. "The trick," antihero Thomas Rath tries to convince himself, "is to learn to believe that it's a disconnected world, a lunatic world, where what is true now was not true then; where Thou Shalt Not Kill and the fact that one has killed a great many men mean nothing, absolutely nothing, for now is the time to raise legitimate children, and make money, and dress properly, and be kind to one's wife, and admire one's boss, and learn not to worry, and think of oneself as what? That makes no difference, he thought—I'm just a man in a gray flannel suit. I must keep my suit neatly pressed like anyone else, for I am a very respectable young man."[47]

But Maslow—like Moustakas, who had assembled *The Self* with fervor—was unwilling to accept the man in the gray flannel suit as any kind of model, or as representative of the inevitable future. Maslow was optimistic about changes he perceived on the horizon. The publication of a rash of books like *The Self, The Organization Man*, and *The Lonely Crowd* was one clue that things were going to get better.

There were other hints that cultural change was dawning. In 1956 Elvis Presley appeared on *The Ed Sullivan Show*, defying conventional forms with his rock and roll and his swinging hips; *Rebel Without a Cause* played in local theaters, challenging the staid values of prior generations; and Allen Ginsberg published "Howl," rejecting literary convention and traditional sexual mores. Observing these moments, Maslow saw an opening for individuals to begin to think more autonomously, to question dominant values.

"Perhaps we shall soon be able to use as our guide and model the fully growing and self-fulfilling human being," Maslow suggested with his characteristic optimism. This new guide would be a man in the process of self-actualizing, of tapping into his capabilities, of expressing his inner nature freely, rather than allowing it to be "warped, suppressed, or denied."[48]

With his exceptionally bright eyes fixed on the future, Maslow stood out, even among *The Self*'s illustrious contributors—a group that included Carl Jung and Jean-Paul Sartre. His passion was reflected in his prose, which was confident bordering on grandiose. He ended his second article by stating: "What *is* within our power in principle is the improvement of personality, the turn toward honesty, affection, self-respect, intellectual and aesthetic growth, acceptance of our own nature, and turning away from hypocrisy, from meanness, prejudice, cruelty, cowardice, and smallness."

This boldness sprang, in part, from his awareness of a swelling interest in his concerns, both among his academic and professional peers and in the culture at large. Maslow, a shameless promoter of his own ideas, was constantly scouring professional meetings for sympathetic souls, charming them not only with the power of his argumentation, but with his paternal smile and expressive eyes. In these early years, at least, Maslow relied as much or more on networking than on publishing to disseminate his ideas and to join them with other significant work for cross-pollination.

Maslow's determination and ardor was partially responsible for the fact that a movement based on this positively oriented cultural criticism found its home in psychology, rather than in sociology (Riesman's institutional home), education (Goodman and others), or philosophy. Psychologists seemed to flock to the topic in greater numbers—perhaps because their field had played such a central role in the problem of pathologizing the individual and acquitting the culture in the first place. Of the nineteen contributors to *The Self*, thirteen were psychologists, psychiatrists, or psychoanalysts.

Psychologists also comprised the majority of the mailing list that Maslow assembled in the late fifties. Intended to facilitate communication between like-minded individuals in different fields who hadn't been exposed to each other's work, the list served as a channel for the exchange of reprints and mimeographed materials.[49] The group, which Maslow deemed the "Creativeness, Autonomy, Self-Actualization, Love, Self, Being, Growth and Organismic People," was comprised of geographically dispersed intellectuals and professionals who shared a common frustration with the negative orientation of much of the work in the social and human sciences. Even more diverse than the list of contributors to *The Self*, Maslow's group included one or more mechanical engineers, biologists, chemists, economists, theologians, writers, and artists, as well as several education professors, anthropologists, and philosophers. Among the 175 individuals on the original list were cultural critics like David Riesman, Paul Goodman, and Lewis Mumford.[50]

Other noteworthy figures were psychoanalysts and psychologists who had been, in the decades that preceded, slowly chipping away at the narrow institutional commitments that dominated psychology and dictated cultural perceptions. Erich Fromm, Gordon Allport, Rollo May, Sidney Jourard, and Carl Rogers had all, by the late fifties, contributed books and articles that challenged the practice of isolating the individual from the culture, of constructing human nature in a negative light, and of overemphasizing pathology at the expense of a clear articulation of health.

Proposing the idea of the "pathology of normalcy" in his 1955 book *The Sane Society*, psychoanalyst Erich Fromm arraigned Western culture for locating adjustment problems in individuals rather than considering the "possible unadjustment of the culture itself."[51] A sane society, Fromm argued, corresponds to the needs of man.[52] Rather than being bound by culture, these needs are universal, "valid for all men."[53] They relate

to man's primary drive to answer the problem of his own existence, rather than to his need to act out his libidinal urges.
Fromm's model of mental health was the "productive orientation," in which an individual chose relatedness and love over
narcissism, creativeness over destructiveness, individuality over
herd conformity, and reason over irrationality.[54] At the core of
his theory was a generative view of human nature, in which
man was comprised of positive and negative passions and drives,
the expression of which was encouraged or limited by cultural
conditions. But even in this context, Fromm contended that
"man is his own creation."[55]

The Sane Society was representative of Fromm's work,
which, in the forties and fifties, had begun to forge a union
between psychological and sociocultural interests. Unlike most
psychoanalytic theory, his writing was explicitly political, attacking directly the structures of both Soviet communism and
Western capitalism. Beginning with *Escape from Freedom* in
1941, Fromm analyzed mental health in the context of a modern democratic system that offered individuals freedom *from*
negative strictures, like fascism and dictatorship, but didn't provide them with a positively formulated notion of freedom *for*
something. In *Man for Himself* (1947), he suggested that human
reason is powerful enough to combat these "irrational value systems."[56] The humanistic ethics and value judgments of the mature and integrated personality (the ideal leader and model),
Fromm felt, could restore a degree of "freedom for" that had
been largely absent from Western democratic systems.[57]

Throughout his work, Fromm contended that capitalism
is dehumanizing and alienating and that legal definitions of
freedom often obscure a lack of existential and emotional freedom. His approach to these problems was an optimistic and

humanistic one, in which individual possibility and potential are forced to contend with social and cultural limits, but need not be extinguished by them.[58]

Fromm's "productive orientation" resonated with Gordon Allport's notion of the "tolerant" or "mature" personality, which he explored throughout the fifties in his work on racial prejudice and religion, and which he described as constituting a blend of cultural adjustment and cultural transcendence. Allport characterized the tolerant personality as flexible and politically liberal, empathic, and accepting of ambiguity. It was a fundamentally "democratic" personality.[59]

Allport's conceptions of tolerance and maturity had emerged in the context of a postwar nation struggling, in new ways, with racial and religious prejudice. In 1946, he published *Controlling Group Prejudice*, covering a topic he again took up in 1948 in the pamphlet *ABC's of Scapegoating* and in 1954 with *The Nature of Prejudice*. Exploring American prejudice against Jews, and later against blacks and Roman Catholics, Allport theorized the polar concepts of prejudice and tolerance.[60]

Prejudice, he explained, is often a product of unreflective conformity, but it sometimes has a functional significance in the psychic economy of the individual, providing a shortcut to self-identification and a defense against social vulnerability.[61] In contrast, tolerance can occur neither by default nor by defense. A tolerant person's approval of his fellow men necessarily springs from a healthy orientation in many spheres—family, school, community, temperament. In its character, Allport's concept of tolerance was akin to Maslow's notion of self-actualization, defined by a comfort with ambiguity, an openness to new experience, a flexible style of categorization, and a high threshold for frustration.[62]

Maturity, for Allport, was characterized by an attitude of tolerance. It was most easily seen in the form of mature religious sentiment, which he described in his 1950 volume *The Individual and His Religion.* Mature religious sentiment, he explained, is characteristic of the person whose approach to religion is dynamic, open-minded, and able to encompass contradiction.[63]

Just as Maslow's description of the self-actualized individual assumed a certain amount of struggle, Allport and Fromm tempered their visions of the generative powers of a healthy personality with the necessity of realistically perceiving cultural and personal problems. That meant, for all three theorists, that a certain level of detachment from social and cultural circumstances was natural, as were appropriate shame, anxiety, sadness, and defensiveness. A healthy person would be disturbed by what he saw in the world that was sick, but he would be strong enough to separate himself sufficiently from the sickness to see it and imagine ways to remedy it. "The normal human being," Fromm argued, "is capable of relating himself to the world simultaneously by perceiving it as it is and by conceiving it enlivened and enriched by his own powers."[64]

Realism and insanity, according to these theorists, were actually closer to health than was passive adjustment, in part because of the active engagement of the self in the struggle with personal and cultural meaning and values. To experience psychological symptoms was to be fully human, engaged in active psychic struggles against the restrictions of a dysfunctional environment, rather than a passive vessel for repressive cultural norms. According to this logic, the ability to experience anxious and depressive symptoms, even twinges of insanity, might actually suggest the capacity to experience meaning—because of the intensity with which an individual suffered from a lack of it.

This sort of anxiety was like a fever, argued psychologist Rollo May, another member of Maslow's mailing list. From this perspective, people whose systems were not struggling with "infecting germs" were the ones without hope, the ones whose immune systems weren't reacting to the "age of anxiety."[65] Ironically, those with the strongest natural drive toward optimism were also the "hollow people," plagued by the problems of emptiness and loneliness, and struggling with the experience of neither knowing what they wanted nor what they felt.[66] In his 1953 book *Man's Search for Himself,* May contended that these "healthier" individuals were more likely to seek psychotherapy and psychoanalysis.

"By and large," he wrote, "they are the ones for whom the conventional pretenses and defenses of the society no longer work. Very often they are the more sensitive and gifted members of the society; they need to get help, broadly speaking, because they are less successful at rationalizing than the 'well-adjusted' citizen who is able for the time being to cover up his underlying conflicts."[67]

At the root of May's drive to explain why otherwise healthy individuals were struggling to thrive was his experience as a psychotherapist. Many of his patients had presented a pattern of repeatedly frustrated attempts to generate meaning and express themselves creatively in a culture that seemed more committed to conformity.

"The great danger of this situation of vacuity and powerlessness," May wrote, "is that it leads sooner or later to painful anxiety and despair, and ultimately, if it is not corrected, to futility and the blocking off of the most precious qualities of the human being. Its end results are the dwarfing and impoverishment of persons psychologically, or else surrender to some destructive authoritarianism."[68]

Rather than identifying qualities that healthy people should strive for, May noted that adaptation to the norm, and by extension emptiness, had itself become a goal.[69]

When the more politically minded critics in Maslow's network tried to step past their critiques and imagine what personal development might look like in a less damaged culture, they tended to run up against a wall. With acute perception they described the vacuum of American desire—in which those struggling for meaning didn't know what they wanted and felt, in which advertisers and corporations were left by default to fill the void with market-oriented drives—but their perspective was perhaps too broad, or too political, to construct in detail any plausible path toward a new way of being.

In his ten-year-retrospective foreword to *The Lonely Crowd*, Riesman wrote, "We sought in writing the last chapter on 'Autonomy and Utopia' to modify the emphasis on 'freedom from' and to give a picture of human relatedness that would be visionary without being too formal or sentimental. Our imaginations proved unequal to the task."[70]

Fromm, in weighing the relative significance of the sociological and the psychological, came to the conclusion that the task of transforming the world simply couldn't begin with the individual psyche. The only real solution was to discard capitalism in favor of "Humanistic Communitarian Socialism," and a new way of being would, presumably, follow from that. His utopia was nothing short of a society in which greed, exploitativeness, and narcissism find no reward, one that stimulates "its members to relate themselves to each other lovingly," one that "permits man to operate within manageable and observable dimensions," and one that encourages the "unfolding of reason."[71] He ultimately concluded, however, that atomic war and the destruction of industrial civilization seemed more likely.[72]

Psychologists (particularly those without commitments to other disciplines) had a more manageable task. Rather than remaking society from the top down, they would begin by reforming the individual. Both Allport and Maslow approached the problem from the perspective of individual modeling. Their formulations of the tolerant personality and the self-actualized person were attempts to articulate a realistic vision of health that could supplant both unattainable ideals and the default goal of adjustment. They would offer more vigorous alternatives to the "pale and doubtful" models to which Americans had been limited.

Psychologist Sidney Jourard, another member of Maslow's mailing list, synthesized many of these early efforts to define realistic ideals in his 1958 volume *Personal Adjustment*. Attempting to provide a value-driven model of health independent of the negative values of illness, Jourard detailed the importance of reality-tested beliefs, rational emotional responses, appropriate and gratifying sexual behavior, flexible and expressive interpersonal behavior, and active rather than passive love.[73]

Although Jourard's description had broad implications in terms of a cultural redefinition of health—what he termed an "alloplastic" adjustment of the environment—it was most concrete in its application to individuals. A rational cure, he argued, was not one in which symptoms were remediated, but one that involved a healthy "autoplastic" adjustment, an alteration of the entire self-structure, and the encouragement of personality development in the direction of optimum.[74] Jourard felt strongly that a therapist's values, and his point of view for regarding psychological suffering, would shape his attempts to treat it. Thus, the psychologist oriented toward health, rather than illness, was likely to have more success in helping individuals to transcend narrow cultural expectations.

Unlocking the capacity for self-actualization was the goal for humanistically oriented psychotherapists. Self-awareness, and a reality-based perception of one's problems, was just the first step. "The task of the therapist," wrote Jourard, "is to engage in those activities which will serve to thaw out the patient's adaptive capacities and remove the barriers to further autonomous growth toward health."[75] Jourard felt these ends could be accomplished by either altering the patient's environment (or encouraging him to move toward a "more health-provocative milieu") or by changing the patient's personality structure through the therapeutic relationship.[76]

Perhaps the most optimistic member of Maslow's mailing list, in terms of facilitating such change, was psychologist Carl Rogers. Rogers had begun to develop a proto-humanistic theory of psychotherapy in the 1930s and had emerged from his experience as a psychologist during World War II more convinced than ever that there was immense, and largely unrealized, potential in the therapeutic relationship. During the war, he, like Gordon Allport and many others, had performed psychological testing of military recruits, matching personnel to positions best suited to their personalities.[77] After the war, in 1946, he published *Counseling with Returned Servicemen*, in which he applied his notions of the saving power of a growth-producing therapeutic situation to the experience of shell-shocked war veterans.[78]

Intended, in part, to assist in the expedient training of counselors, the brief book advocated a form of counseling that demanded neither omniscience, expert status, nor extensive training on the part of the counselor. "The counselor's basic responsibility," wrote Rogers and his coauthor John Wallen, "is the establishment of an atmosphere or climate that frees the client from the forces hindering his growth, and that makes possible self-initiated development."[79] The emphasis in this form of therapy is on "the full use of the strength and capacity for growth within the client," rather than on the analytical powers of the therapist.[80]

The application of the concepts Rogers laid out was not limited to counseling with "psychoneurotic" soldiers. By treating the psychotherapeutic situation as a microcosm of the culture, Rogers believed one could remake the individual's environment, purging it of growth-inhibiting factors and infusing it with growth-producing elements. Rogers theorized in *Client-Centered Therapy* (1951) that, given an atmosphere of acceptance and respect, individuals would inherently strive for health.[81] He referred to this process as organismic "valuing" or "sensing," suggesting that individuals know what is good for them and innately endeavor to attain it.[82]

By framing his solution to the problems of war in psychotherapeutic terms, Rogers was benefiting from psychology's newfound cultural power as much as he was reinforcing it. What was particularly striking about the expansion of psychology in the 1950s, beyond the sheer numbers of practitioners and patients in psychotherapy, was the increasing ability of those in the field to influence the cultural dialogue. As Allport noted, in his 1955 introduction to *Becoming*, Americans seemed to be relying increasingly on psychological theory to address the pressing questions of the time—including those related to race and gender relations, industry, and education. He noted that everyone seemed to be speaking the language of psychology, from the "common man" who "now talks in the language of Freud and reads an ever mounting output of books in popular psychology," to the leaders of industry and the scholars in adjacent disciplines, including anthropology, sociology, and political science.[83]

Given the cultural power of psychology in the fifties, there may have been no better field from which to mount a "humanistic" critique of society's role in defining and delimiting mental health and illness. Experts on the human psyche were being taken more seriously than ever before. At the same time, though, psychologists faced many obstacles in assembling a unified critique. It was a crowded field, where much energy was wasted on internal struggles. Psychologists, psychiatrists, psychoanalysts, and social workers all laid claim to, and fought with each over, the mantle of psychological expert. Within academic psychology, it was the behaviorists who reigned, and amongst therapists it was the Freudians who were dominant.

It was also the case, for humanistic psychologists trying to insert themselves into the debate, that one of their primary critiques was of precisely the scientism that had had so much to do with the rise in psychology's popularity. As Allport observed in 1950, "psychology without a soul" was considered a "badge of distinction and pride," and seemed to be growing too fashionable for its own good."[84] Many Americans expected psychologists to be experts who spoke with the authority of science.

2

Common Ground

"When one turns to the magnificent edifice of the
physical sciences, and sees how it was reared; what
thousands of disinterested moral lives of men lie buried
in its mere foundations; what patience and postpone-
ment, what choking down of preference, what submis-
sion to the icy laws of outer fact are wrought into its
very stones and mortar; how absolutely impersonal it
stands in its vast augustness,—then how besotted and
contemptible seems every little sentimentalist who
comes blowing his voluntary smoke-wreaths, pretending
to decide things from out of his private dream!"

WILLIAM JAMES[1]

"The history of academic, 'scientific' psychology is
largely a saddening story of futility and of very careful
and painstaking exploration of one blind alley after
another."

ABRAHAM MASLOW[2]

In the 1950s, Harvard Psychological Clinic director Henry
Murray formulated several handwritten lists of the pros and
cons of American psychology. The cons invariably outweighed

the pros. In one such list, titled "unfortunate characteristics of psychology/psychoanalysis," Murray included reductive analysis (the tendency to factor out complex human data in favor of straightforward conclusions), and described the field as "illness-oriented, enemy-oriented, wrong-oriented, distress-oriented-not joy (hope, goodness) oriented." He noted that it contains "no synthesis, no words for synthesis," excludes talk of values, refuses to evaluate alternative ways of living, and accentuates patients' narcissism. Of psychologists and psychoanalysts, he noted that their training had made them obtuse—ignorant of values, opposed to culture, and dismissive of religion. Their thin substitute for these vital institutions, he argued, was the self.[3]

His list of the advantages of psychology was shorter and less passionate. Psychology, he wrote, could serve as a lens of objectivity, providing impartial detachment and freedom from presumptions and rigid evaluations. Psychological methods could facilitate the analysis of abnormal, or even abhorrent, behavior without the burden of condemnation. They could also enable psychologists to form evaluations on many levels, assessing their own culture, other cultures, themselves, their friends, and the field of psychology itself.[4]

Even favorable descriptions of American psychology hinted at the field's problems. One historian described American psychology in the first half of the century as, "rough, direct, highly practical, aggressively ambitious and self-assured."[5] As a young field concerned with the elusive problems of human experience, it had little basis upon which to justify any of these qualities.

• • •

American psychology was saddled, from the start, with a fundamental structural conflict. Although committed to being a precise science, it took as its subject the messy and complicated data of human existence—data that would resist, at every turn, attempts at straightforward quantification. Psychologists have historically divided over how to address this conflict. Some have attempted to be more radically empirical, hoping to factor out the complexity. Others have tried to be squarely pragmatic, addressing things like treatment outcomes without presuming to understand their etiology. Only a few have attempted to study people in their totality, seeking to arrive at scientific truths without running away from the full complexity of the human organism.

The historical evasion of psychology's central paradox is the reason humanistic psychology finally coalesced in the late 1950s. But as a theoretical orientation, it wasn't entirely new. It was rooted in the struggles of the father of American psychology himself—William James—and it was built on the work that was done, in the decades that followed, by a few of his followers who were willing to look squarely at the inadequate attempts of psychologists of divergent schools and treat the subject of their inquiry (the person!) in her totality.

James himself initially subscribed to an atomistic approach. When he took the helm in forging the "New Psychology" in the late nineteenth century, he recognized the need for narrowing the field's scope to produce more reliable techniques and to arrive at more valid conclusions. In his seminal two-volume text *The Principles of Psychology*, published in 1890, he carved out a new realm for the discipline, isolating it from neighboring fields. Although psychology ought to study "every sort of mental activity," he argued, the field was forced by necessity to limit its subject matter.[6]

"The study of the harmful in mental life," he wrote, "has been made the subject of a special branch called 'Psychiatry.'"[7] Psychology, then, would confine itself to the conscious processes of sensations, thought, and the tendency to action. "In order not to be unwieldy," he conceded, "every such science has to stick to its own arbitrarily-selected problems, and to ignore all others."[8]

In issuing this foundational pronouncement, James was consciously steering the field away from the psychological practices that predated it.

American psychology's inheritance was the overly speculative pursuits of mental philosophy and the clumsy practices of nineteenth-century psychiatry. As the academic stewards of psychological inquiry, mental philosophers had, for decades, wrangled over abstract questions of dualism versus monism (Is the mind reducible to the brain, or is it composed of independent properties that emerge from the brain?), and materialism versus metaphysics (Is even consciousness reducible to matter, or is there something beyond?). At the same time, though, they tackled the practical topics that would come to define modern psychology, including intellect (attention, memory, reasoning, imagination, and consciousness) and sensibility (emotion, affections, motives, desires, and instincts). Although mental philosophers approached their subject with the "spirit of empirical inquiry," most professors studied the mind with the intention of divining the intentions of God's creation. They had been trained in seminaries, which had provided the only graduate education prior to the Civil War.[9]

American psychiatry, a medical specialty concerned with the treatment of mental illness, also rested on theological foundations. The dominant mode of psychiatric treatment was a combination of "moral therapy," based on religious ideas of self-control, and physical treatment, similarly premised on notions of purging and punishment.[10] Psychiatrists prescribed treatments like hydrotherapy (which consisted of a range of treatments from continuous hot or cold baths to a virtual mummification in cold, wet sheets), and bloodletting with leeches, the goal of which was to restore homeostatic equilibrium. A body in balance, it was thought, translated to a mind in balance. Rather than aiming to understand the causes of mental illness, or the categories, most psychiatrists spent their time in asylums, restraining, placating, and, ideally, rehabilitating the mentally ill.[11]

In generating a fresh perspective on human psychology, James benefited from the fact that he had been trained neither in mental philosophy nor in psychiatry. He was an outsider, with a medical degree and a background in physiology.

James also benefited from the unique historical moment at which he entered academia. He straddled the transition from the classical university system (a one-curriculum system with undifferentiated departments, which rewarded professors for the breadth rather than the depth of their knowledge and stressed the accumulation of factual knowledge) to the modern university system (an organization of differentiated disciplines that was modeled on European, particularly German, educational systems in which scholars were free to guide their own scientific inquiry and were encouraged to display creativity in their pursuits).[12]

Under the classical college model, James became a professor of psychology (psychology and philosophy were synonymous at the time) at Harvard. "I drifted into psychology and philosophy from a sort of fatality," he wrote. "I never had any philosophic instruction, the first lecture on psychology I ever heard being the first I ever gave."[13]

Although the classical model granted James the fluidity to enter the field of psychology, had it persisted it would have likely stifled the kind of creative thought and scientific probing that would prove central to psychological inquiry. Fortunately, James didn't have to wait long for the restrictions to abate. In 1876, Johns Hopkins established the first American graduate school, ushering in a new era of disciplinary specialization. American universities introduced to their academic programs scientific research and professional education—both of which had formerly been relegated to extra-academic spheres funded by the American government.[14]

In this new academic environment, which embodied the atomistic approach writ large, psychological research flourished. The first American psychological laboratory was established at Johns Hopkins University in 1883; J. McKeen Cattell became the first professor of psychology at the University of Pennsylvania in 1888; and the American Psychological Association (APA) was established in 1892.[15] Distinct departments of psychology proliferated, almost every one of which committed itself to emulating the natural sciences and to extricating psychological study from metaphysical concerns.[16]

The birth of the APA was a seminal moment in the solidification of modern American psychology's identity. From the beginning, the association prioritized the interests of the academic researcher over those of the clinical practitioner.[17] Its members erected standards to limit the number of practitioners to those who had met certification requirements and to reward all forms of research that embraced the scientific method. They upheld a uniquely American model of positivism, an epistemological perspective that maintained that the scientific method was the best approach for understanding human experience.

American psychologists were like Germans in this way, but they took it one step further, moving the field in the direction of a more rigid scientism. The prevailing paradigm for psychological research held that the natural sciences provided the only valid model for accessing truth; only through quantification could we really understand anything at all.

This shift aligned perfectly with the modern interests of the Progressive Era, a period that spanned from the 1890s to the 1920s. During this time, an interest in efficient scientific management, with the goal of effective social reform, provided the impetus for the proliferation of social science departments. Progressive interests were also partially responsible for the new cultural esteem afforded the scientific "expert," for increased specialization and professional technologization, and for the severing of philosophical considerations, and religious and metaphysical questions, from scientific disciplines like psychology.[18] In industry, academics, and politics, the distillation of complex problems to their component parts, and the systematic testing of potential solutions, was an approach that tended, during the era, to eclipse more holistic methods.

In America, the foundational scientific approach to psychology was an atomistic one, not suited to the consideration of philosophical questions and cultural concerns. It recommended the extraction of psychological states, personality traits, behavioral responses, and sensory perceptions from the intricate matrix of individual history, subjective experience, and interpersonal relations. It attempted to draw conclusions by isolating variables through experimental methods. Outcome-based psychological inquiry epitomized this atomism, focusing on behavior and expression without studying etiology. By factoring out internal motivations and emotional states, outcome-based scientists hoped to bypass the messiness of mentalism entirely, assuming that specific, rather than general, truths about people are the most for which we can hope.

Although he was himself instrumental in effecting the isolation of psychological concerns, James could never really stomach the separation of mental experience from its broader context. He was, from the first, uneasy about the reductive analysis that Henry Murray later identified as resulting from it.

In 1909, in opposition to his own statements in *Principles*, James identified the need for a humanistic psychology, one that employed phenomenological methods to capture subjective experience. He asserted: "The world of concrete personal experience [. . .] is multitudinous beyond imagination, tangled, muddy, painful and perplexed. The world to which your philosophy professor introduces you is simple, clean and noble. The contradictions of real life are absent from it."[19]

James's concerns reflected his personal struggles with religion and philosophy. He was "neurasthenic" and, during one of his episodes of religious questioning and severe depression, was so impaired as to be unable to rise from his bed for weeks. He was haunted by existential questions over the nature of the soul and the self; spiritual questions surrounding free will and the afterlife; and scientific questions of the feasibility of mental science.[20] Looking back on his contribution in *Principles*, he judged the classic text to be "a loathsome, distended, putrified, dropsical mass, testifying to nothing but two facts: first, that there is no such thing as a *science* of Psychology, and second, that W. J. is an incapable."[21]

James rued the hubris with which he and his peers had shorn the field of its ancestral lineage in their attempt to make it more practical and more scientifically precise. They had, he felt, doomed it to fail when they'd accepted the premise of logical positivism—the idea that psychologists, like biologists and physicists, could uncover verifiable "truths" about human behavior through a combination of empiricism and rationalism.

James's later work took on problems he had first excluded from the study of psychology. Although he remained committed to the scientific paradigm he set forth in *Principles*, he selectively explored religious experience and belief, as well as noetic and mystical states, attempting to characterize ineffable subjective experience.[22] In *The Varieties of Religious Experience* (1902), he described a wide variety of spiritual and psychological experiences, attempting to broaden psychological and religious understanding, rather than to empirically limit the categories or narrow the analysis.[23]

James's career itself embodied the tension between atomism and holism that came to define the field of psychology. Although it was hard to effectively integrate narrow inquiry focused on discrete mental events with holistic inquiry that didn't attempt to divide mental events from their context, James managed to seriously consider both. A rarity, James was at once a positivist and a phenomenologist, distrustful of binary solutions and ever pursuing "productive paradoxes."[24] He possessed an ability to fruitfully integrate conflict, or at least to acknowledge it and admit when his powers of reason were insufficient to the task of resolving it. Faced with the same difficulties, many of his successors failed to live up to James's example.

G. Stanley Hall was a perfect example. James's student and the first American to receive a PhD in Clinical Psychology (in 1878), Hall was deeply conflicted, even confused, about his religious and scientific sensibilities. Rather than seeking to practice science that somehow honored his spiritual impulses, however, Hall sublimated spiritual questions into the pursuit of rigorous positivism. He took a stand against philosophically informed models of psychology, which had been built, he believed, "not by the patient attitude of the scientist but by the speculative urge of the philosopher to grasp the whole of things."[25] His position was supported by many younger experimentalists, who desired to adhere strictly to the scientific method, eliminating all metaphysical and philosophical questions from consideration.[26]

The generation of American psychologists who followed James tended to reject philosophical speculation and turn from mentalist to exclusively physicalist explanations (meaning they rejected perception and introspection as valid topics of inquiry, and relegated their concerns to observable properties and processes). Psychologists like Edward Lee Thorndike (1874–1949), John B. Watson (1878–1958), and Harry Harlow (1905–1981) prioritized physiology and behavioral study, and chose to ignore philosophical questions and potential clinical applications.[27] In so doing, they created a climate favorable for the ascendance of behaviorist concerns.

Although they took different tacks, James's successors shared common qualities. Collectively, they elevated experimentalism over other priorities. They advocated the study of animal behavior as a guide for understanding humans, and they systematically dismissed transpersonal concerns, like spirituality and mysticism. They represented, in a way that was perhaps a bit unsettling to James in his final years (he died in 1910), the realization of the kind of narrowing of the realm of psychological inquiry that James had advocated in the *Principles of Psychology*.

In fact, much of the work of experimental pioneers was a direct product of James's work. Edward Thorndike, for example, credited his decision to pursue doctoral study to *Principles*. He began his work under James, first studying the behavioral responsiveness to facial expressions in young children, but soon shifting, for practical purposes, to the study of instinctive and intelligent behavior in chickens and cats.[28] Among his most notable psychological postulates was the law of effect (published in 1905), which states that positively reinforced responses are more likely to occur again than negatively- or non-reinforced responses. He was also a pioneer in aptitude-based psychological testing.[29]

In 1911, Thorndike published his own influential book, *Animal Intelligence*, signifying the official shift in academic psychology toward behavioral concerns and marking the triumph of atomism. In the preface, he describes his experimental reportage as marking "the change from books of general argumentation on the basis of common experience interpreted in terms of the faculty psychology, to monographs reporting detailed and often highly technical experiments interpreted in terms of original and acquired connections between situation and response."[30]

The years 1911 and 1912, in particular, marked a major shift in the content of American psychological research. While proceedings from the APA conference of 1911 were dominated by broad-ranging discussions of consciousness, the subsequent year's conference consisted almost exclusively of physicalist studies focused on observed behavior.[31] Representative of this behaviorist shift, Thorndike himself served as the president of the APA in 1912.

In 1913, John B. Watson published "Psychology as the Behaviorist Views It." This "behaviorist manifesto," as it came to be known, marked the formalization of behaviorism as a school of American psychology.[32] In his manifesto, Watson wrote: "Psychology as the behaviorist views it is a purely objective experimental branch of natural science. Its theoretical goal is the prediction and control of behavior. Introspection forms no essential part of its methods, nor is the scientific value of its data dependent upon the readiness with which they lend themselves to interpretation in terms of consciousness."[33]

Watson believed that the field had to leave behind mentalist emphases to secure its scientific status, arguing that psychology should "discard all reference to consciousness," and that it "need no longer delude itself into thinking that it is making mental states the object of observation."[34]

Watson was, even among his behavioristically inclined colleagues, at the extreme. Thorndike, for instance, opposed the use of introspection as a means of understanding consciousness, but did not, like Watson, renounce the study of consciousness altogether.[35] The nuance of this kind of debate, though, rarely penetrated beyond academic circles. Specialization had ensured that the real ideological battles were won and lost only by the people trained to converse in this kind of esoteric rhetoric.

This is not to say the theories of the new psychologists didn't reach the American public. They often did. In the years after the birth of behaviorism, successful academics like Thorndike often gave public lectures, sat for newspaper interviews, and, as the century progressed, made national radio appearances in the interest of educating the public about psychology.[36]

As would continue to be the case with the discipline throughout the twentieth century, however, it was the more extreme and less balanced attitudes of psychologists like Watson that got the public's attention. Watson's work on children in particular seemed to enthrall Americans, and he responded to the interest by publishing popular articles and, in 1928, a book on child rearing in which he presented a radical standpoint.

"It is a serious question in my mind," he wrote, "whether there should be individual homes for children—or even whether children should know their own parents. There are undoubtedly much more scientific ways of bringing up children which will probably mean finer and happier children."[37]

He also famously proclaimed that if given a dozen healthy infants, and complete control over their environment, he could raise any one at random to be anything, ranging from a doctor or lawyer to a beggar or thief.[38] This apparently scientific power was simultaneously compelling and horrifying to Americans, whose residual religious and moral interests were at odds with such determinism.

It is perhaps surprising that psychoanalysis first appealed to psychologists, and to Americans in general, for some of the same reasons as behaviorism. It tended toward atomism. Freud literally reduced the cluttered psyche to component parts and human development to fixed and linear stages. Freudian theory was a product of highly rationalized Enlightenment thought, aimed intently at the deduction of singular truths. And it followed the habits of science, eschewing theological musings, abstract philosophical speculation, and the taint of subjective report. In the words of one critic, "Science became Freud's faith, psychoanalysis his sect. Whatever illusions other men might or might not possess, his illusion was science."[39]

Freud pursued his theory of psychoanalysis with a positivistic zeal, wrought from the formative influences of his medical school mentors (a physiologist, a brain anatomist, and an internist).[40] Although he recognized that psychoanalysis was a young science requiring further testing, the acquisition of more data, and additional experimentation, he conceived of it as nothing but scientific.

In contrast to James, who felt ultimately that men must surpass the limitations of science to capture the more elusive aspects of "reality itself," Freud thought men should exclusively adopt a grounded, scientific worldview. James was eventually convinced, relatively late in his career, that "Humbug is humbug, even though it bear the scientific name, and the total expression of human experience, as I view it objectively, invincibly urges me beyond the narrow 'scientific' bounds. Assuredly, the real world is of a different temperament—more intimately built than physical science allows."[41] While Freud agreed it was possible to perform bad science, and felt it was the job of other scientists to discredit it, he believed resolutely that it was only within scientific boundaries that anything at all could be understood.[42]

In spite of the fact that Freud's scientific approach to psychology (composed of case histories, self-analysis, clinical reports, and the rare experiment) violated some of the basic premises of the new experimental psychology, Freud was initially received by academic psychologists with approbation. William James told Freud during his visit to America in 1909 that "The future of psychology belongs to your work."[43] Even behaviorists supported Freud. Watson himself was an early champion, Thorndike conceded to psychoanalysis the realm of abnormal psychology, and G. Stanley Hall embraced Freudian notions of child development with fervor. As Thorndike's biographer explains, "The automatisms of Freudian views of life, the anticonsciousness of the theory of the unconscious, the biological determinism of sexuality, and infancy considered the emphatic period of life" all aligned harmoniously with behaviorism.[44]

By the 1920s, Freud had fallen from favor in American academic circles.[45] His approach was atomistic, but in a way that relied on a radical inductive leap rather than a clear and careful scientific path. He was positivistic, but the truths he uncovered didn't seem earned, lacking as they were in reproducible experimental data, in the isolation of specific factors, and in the exclusion of subjective reports and personal biases.

At the same time, though, Freud had reached new heights of popular appeal. The aroma of atomistic science, the scent of systematic thought, was sweet enough for the American public to swarm to. Within ten years of his first visit to the United States, psychoanalysis had crowded out mention of all other forms of applied psychology in the popular press. Freud's theory of the unconscious (the neatly divided psyche), his explorations of childhood sexuality (structured in discrete developmental stages), and his revolutionary ideas of talk therapy (backed by the pseudoscientific bases of medicine and scientific-seeming case studies) helped Americans transition from the traditional, Victorian values that defined the nineteenth century to the more liberal, modern values that would characterize the twentieth. His ideas were transmitted, beginning in the 1920s, through popular books, newspapers, films, and public lectures. By the 1940s, most of the literate public was familiar with Freud's ideas on the unconscious, defense mechanisms, psychological conflict, and the link between dreams and repression.[46] His theories broadly informed child-rearing advice, progressive education, and criminology.

Freud's theories and techniques created both a small cult of analysis (comprised mainly of writers, intellectuals, and artists who were compelled by Freud's colorful explanations of the psyche) and an actual market for analysis (constituted by mostly prosperous, educated clients who possessed the requisite verbal skills).[47] Psychoanalysis quickly came to monopolize psychiatric practice and would, for decades to come, represent the dominant influence on psychotherapy in the United States. This triumph suggested the alignment of American popular and academic culture in the first half of the twentieth century with the clarity and precision of atomism.

3

Higher, Better Leaders

"Human freedom involves our capacity to pause between the stimulus and response and, in that pause, to choose the one response toward which we wish to throw our weight."

ROLLO MAY[1]

Poised between the atomistic extremes of behaviorism and psychoanalysis, Abraham Maslow and Carl Rogers entered the world of psychology. In the course of their training they were nourished by both theories and came to value the scientific claims of each. They prized the representative theorists' systematic approaches, their attempts to forge repeatable techniques, their interest in uncovering the common features of human experience. But when they were professionally sophisticated enough to forge their own theories, charting courses distinct from those of their teachers, they independently concluded that a central premise of both Freud and the behaviorists—the idea that atomism equals science, while holism is thoroughly unscientific—was misguided. Ultimately, it was the reductive nature of both theories, rather than the specific content of either, that Rogers and Maslow came to reject in favor of what they perceived to be a fuller, though still scientific, treatment of the individual.

As a psychologist who viewed himself foremost as a scientist, Rogers had much in common with Freud. His training in psychometrics, however, spurred him to evaluate more systematically the varied constituents of individual experience and made him suspicious of Freud's explication of unmeasurable concepts (the id, superego, ego, defense mechanisms, and various childhood complexes). He rejected outright his sharp division of the psyche and his reduction of individual experience to the childhood fixations that arose at preset stages of development. At the same time, though, Rogers came to value Freud, and to count him as an influence on his own later theory. The nondirective method of psychotherapy he was to develop would borrow from Freud "in its concepts of repression and release, in its stress on catharsis and insight." The psychotherapy he came to practice, too, benefited as a response to what he deemed to be Freud's successes (patient-guided sessions, his therapeutic interview procedure, and his interest in internal psychological dynamics) and failures (intractable therapist-patient hierarchies, policies of emotional nondisclosure, and an overemphasis on the past).[2]

Maslow, too, related to Freud as a fellow scientist, though not the kind he wished to emulate. He rejected the *structure* of Freud's work, but at the same time he valued its products.[3] He was drawn to the concepts of repression, defense, resistance, and dream analysis as frames for understanding the psychical barriers to self-actualization.[4] He borrowed generously from psychoanalysis, but acknowledged a more specific debt to the theories of the neo-Freudians he encountered in New York City, most of whom had discarded Freud's atomistic approach. From Karen Horney, he took the synthesis of cultural values with the individual aspects of character, self-esteem, and emotional well-being. Because of Erich Fromm, he deepened his humanitarian commitments, passion for social justice, and sense of utopian possibility. And from Alfred Adler, whom he sought out as a postdoctoral mentor, he derived the interest in superiority strivings that informed much of his work on dominance, at the same time that he gleaned ideas about human holism and social context, and enhanced his innate optimism and appetite for reform.[5]

While both Maslow and Rogers drew inspiration from psychoanalysts, as academic psychologists they had more direct contact with behaviorists. And though they were temperamentally inclined toward a more holistic psychology that opposed adjustment-driven models, they found behaviorism—as embodied in mentors like Thorndike and Harlow—at least initially more appealing. It aligned better with the scientific bases upon which they were trained. Its laboratory procedures were utterly scientific, quantifiable, repeatable. And it seemed to have launched psychology to a new height of respectability, effectively raising it from pseudo-scientific status to that of an actual science. What's more, behaviorism's potential to affect behavioral change through experimentation opened up endless possibilities for larger social reforms.

Although Rogers never subscribed to behaviorism per se, he considered one of its founding fathers, E. L. Thorndike, an influential mentor. As a doctoral student at Columbia University's Teachers College, he took a stimulating class with Thorndike and drew inspiration from his impeccable experimental methods and aptitude for quantification and measurement. As a young father, he incorporated elements of Watsonian behaviorism into his parenting, adhering to strict schedules and withholding, at times, emotional and physical support. And as a scientific researcher, he emulated the careful, experimental methods he saw behaviorists practice.[6]

In contrast to Rogers's piecemeal absorption of behavioristic emphases, Maslow became (for a time) a full-fledged convert. As a budding young psychologist in the 1920s, who viewed behaviorism as "an explosion of excitement," he wasn't initially bothered by its inherent atomism.

"Bertha [Maslow's new bride] came to pick me up at New York's 42nd Street library," he recalled, "and I was dancing down Fifth Avenue with exuberance. I embarrassed her, but I was so excited about Watson's behaviorist program. It was beautiful."

Even if its methods were narrow, he saw behaviorism's implications as potentially transcendent. "I was confident," he explained, "that here was a real road to travel: solving one problem after another and changing the world."[7]

In evoking this utopian vision, Maslow was referring, in part, to Watson's claim that science could offer a degree of control suited to remaking the world. If nature didn't matter, and nurture was king, things like criminality and violence could be eliminated from a culture committed to producing healthier, more successful individuals. Evil, Maslow came to believe, didn't arise from people, but from the negative effects of pathological environments on people. Far from viewing the psychological laboratory as a hopelessly miniaturized version of the real world, Maslow saw it as an incubator for the seeds of real social change.[8]

Maslow's exuberance landed him, in the early 1930s, in Harry Harlow's laboratory at the University of Wisconsin, where he studied learning in primates. Harlow's research was both experimental and observational. It was also comparative; he attempted to make generalizations about humans based on evolutionary deductions about related primates.[9] Maslow's first article, coauthored with Harlow in 1932, appeared in the *Journal of Comparative Psychology* and was titled "Delayed Reaction Test on Primates from the Lemur to the Orangutan."[10] It jump-started his career. He published four others that same year alone—three in the esteemed *Journal of Comparative Psychology* and one in the well-known *Journal of Social Psychology*.

Continuing to study with Harlow, and intent on basing his career on monkey research, Maslow performed further observational studies on Harlow's primates related to food preferences. He ultimately wrote a dissertation on sexual behavior and social dominance in monkeys.[11] Although Maslow hesitated to apply his findings to humans, the dissertation had been inspired, in part, by his discovery (in 1933) of Freudian and Adlerian theories of sex and dominance. His research, in turn, sparked his interest in exploring the idea that sexual behavior in humans was directly related to social power.[12]

How he intended to change the world with his monkey research is a bit unclear. Perhaps it was unclear to him, as well, as his passion for this work was soon eroded by a swath of holistic influences. Maslow continued reading deeply in areas other than experimental psychology. He studied embryology, read Ludwig von Bertalanffy's articulation of systems theory, immersed himself in Bertrand Russell and English philosophy in general, and then fell in love with Alfred North Whitehead's vitalism and Henri Bergson's process philosophy. According to

Maslow, "Their writings destroyed behaviorism for me without my recognizing it."[13]

Still unaware of the ideological change overtaking him, and of the ways his newly complexified understanding of human psychology would undermine the reductive orientation of his behavioristic program, Maslow decided to study at Columbia under Thorndike, focusing on human sexuality. Coincidentally, he settled in New York at the same time that many impressive European theorists, including Erich Fromm, Karen Horney, and Alfred Adler, were illuminating the New York intellectual scene with their expansive cultural and social theories.[14]

In these theorists, Maslow found abundant fuel for the fire his reading had ignited. He later credited Gestalt psychologist Max Wertheimer, in particular, with catalyzing his shift toward a more holistic, humanistic form of psychology. In a 1962 discussion with students at the New School for Social Research in New York, Maslow explained that his true education "began when I came from the Midwest, as an experimental psychologist, to the seminars of Max Wertheimer, who all alone [at the New School] formed the best psychology department in the world."[15] In 1942, Maslow had attended Wertheimer's course "Being and Doing," where he began to rethink the methodology of his comparative research, which failed to consider personal values, and didn't recognize the importance of subjective experience, individual freedom, and autonomous choice.[16]

In seizing on Gestalt psychology, Maslow broke from the atomistic approaches that had defined his career to that point and tied himself instead to a long tradition of holistic European theory. Gestalt had derived from romanticism, which, in the late eighteenth and early nineteenth centuries, had attuned philosophers, artists, and writers to the primacy of the individual will and the importance of subjectivity. But Gestalt (or holistic) concerns reached far beyond the humanities or the arts, appearing as well in the natural sciences. In the field of biology, for example, scientist Hans Driesch sought to reanimate vitalism (the doctrine that life has an immaterial component that cannot be explained scientifically) in 1905. And embryologist Ludwig von Bertalanffy focused on the holistic consideration of living processes from the 1920s onward.[17]

Gestalt methods offered psychologists a paradigm that was liberating. It allowed them to enter realms of inquiry that behaviorists had declared off-limits and freed them to consider the kinds of qualitative data that served as the cornerstones of human existence.[18] Psychologist Wolfgang Köhler later described Gestalt theory, in his presidential address to the APA, as a "great wave of relief—as though we were escaping from a prison. The prison was psychology as taught in the universities when we were still students."[19]

Köhler and others made plain that the choice between holism and atomism was not synonymous with the choice between science and philosophy. Gestalt was inclusive of both. It was a philosophical approach that informed the collection and evaluation of data, and deepened human analyses, directing researchers and therapists to look at contextual factors in evaluating a subject or a patient. According to the Gestaltists concerned with psychotherapy, for example, an understanding of individuals' depression could not be gained without information about their behavioral appearance, prior history (History of abuse? Happy childhood?), current circumstances (Had they recently lost a job? Were they grieving?), and subjective experience (Did they experience their current state as markedly different from prior states? Just how sad did they actually feel?).

Experimentally, Gestalt psychology signified an approach to scientific inquiry that began with data collection attained from the direct report of experience. It then moved to the collection of qualitative data gathered through observation and, finally, to the acquisition of quantitative data derived from demonstration and experiment. When Max Wertheimer studied visual perception, for example, he first presented individuals with a visual picture on a stroboscope, and then noted not only their subjective visual perceptions, but also their "subjective behaviors," including eye movement and "posture of attention."[20] From there, he went on to manipulate the input from the stroboscope and to chart their reactions. The aim of these methods was to include the contextually relevant factors that were consistently omitted from other forms of scientific inquiry.[21]

When Maslow encountered Gestalt psychologists like Koffka, Wertheimer, and Köhler at the New School in the 1930s and 1940s, he felt an instant connection and esteemed them as "the center of the psychological universe."[22] He was a bit ahead of his time, in this regard. As Kurt Koffka wrote in the foundational text of Gestalt psychology: "In America the climate is chiefly practical; the here and now, the immediate present with its needs, holds the centre of the state, thereby relegating the problems essential to German mentality to the realm of the useless and non-existing. In science this attitude makes for positivism, an overvaluation of mere facts and devaluation of very abstract speculations, a high regard for science, accurate and earthbound, and an aversion, sometimes bordering on contempt for metaphysics that tries to escape from the welter of mere facts into a loftier realm of ideas and ideals."[23] Gestalt was not at home in this climate.

For Maslow, personal and historical circumstances intervened to cement his break from behaviorism and to deepen his openness to holistic theories like Gestalt—most seminally the birth of his first child, and the full realization of his horror at the Holocaust.

Throughout his studies and research pursuits, Maslow had maintained a passionate investment in his family, prioritizing them above his work. It was through his family, in fact, that he experienced his first peak experience (defined in his own theory as a life-changing moment of self-transcendence). He explained, "When my first baby was born, that was the thunderclap that settled things. I looked at this tiny, mysterious thing and felt so stupid. I felt small, weak, and feeble. I'd say that anyone who's had a baby couldn't be a behaviorist."[24] Maslow's baby, Ann, humbled him because of the purity of her goodness. She had not a mean bone in her body, not a single ill intention. And her goodness had not been conditioned; it sprung forth at the moment of her birth in a way that transcended any learning, good or bad, that would take place in the course of her life.

Ann destroyed Maslow's illusions about behaviorism from one direction, while Hitler dismantled them from another. From 1939 to 1941, as newspapers began to cover more fully the German shooting operations in Poland and the Soviet Union, it became increasingly difficult to avoid wrestling, in some form, with painful moral questions about the nature of evil. One could choose only to look at the problem "from below" or "from above."

To look from above, for Malsow, meant to be realistic about the existence of evil, but to place it in context. A compassionate man, Maslow argued, would see evil as an ignorant, thoughtless, and fearful fumbling toward otherwise good ends (in Adler's words, toward mistaken goals). To view evil from below, he said, meant to pathologize it, externalize it, dehumanize it.

By temperament, Maslow looked from above, with an orientation toward understanding. A day after the bombing of Pearl Harbor, Maslow encountered a small pro-war parade and responded with what he would come to view as a seminal insight: "I was driving home and my car was stopped by a poor, pathetic parade. Boy Scouts and old uniforms and a flag and someone playing a flute off-key. As I watched, the tears began to run down my face. I felt we didn't understand—not Hitler, nor the Germans, nor Stalin, nor the Communists. We didn't understand any of them. I felt that if we could understand, then we could make progress. [. . .] That moment changed my whole life. Since then, I've devoted myself to developing a theory of human nature that could be tested by experiment and research. I wanted to prove that humans are capable of something grander than war, prejudice, and hatred. I wanted to make science consider all the people: the best specimen of mankind I could find."[25]

Seeing people as fully human, Maslow concluded, required psychologists to embrace the full range of human emotion and behavior, and to stop replacing "human" with average or normal. People were sad and hurt and mean and destructive and joyful and creative and kind. The only way to study them was to study them holistically—acknowledging and accepting this multiplicity, and thinking meaningfully about the values we would call upon in elevating the best in us without pretending the worst didn't exist.

• • •

The Gestalt approach did gain wider acceptance in America, though not until the 1950s, when the tangible, external threats of the Germans and Japanese subsided and much of our fear turned inward. Just as many intellectuals in war-ravaged and politically polarized post–World War I Germany had been drawn to a restorative science to help make sense of the ruin and resurrect for them a fraction of the culture's former grandeur, many Americans found consolation in a holistic approach after the Second World War.[26]

Gestalt theory had much to offer Americans. It opposed adjustment psychologies (and the mandate of social conformity) by emphasizing the significance of personal context and experience and affirming the value of the unique individual. It assuaged pragmatists by invoking the experimental method in the pursuit of basic philosophical questions.[27] And it contributed to the emergence of theories of health, premised on a positive view of human nature.

The work of German émigré Kurt Goldstein, in particular, resonated on all three counts. The humanistic concept of self-actualization came directly from his experience in the 1920s, when he worked as a neurologist at the Institute for Research into the Consequences of Brain Injuries in Frankfurt, treating soldiers who had incurred neurological injury during World War I. Goldstein had been impressed by the resiliency of the soldiers he treated. He concluded from his observations and inquiries that the manner in which they reorganized their functioning, compensating for deficits by developing strengths in other areas, was indicative of an intrinsic tendency toward wholeness in humans. Their continual striving, which entailed a certain amount of anxiety and vulnerability, demonstrated what he perceived as their inherent actualizing tendencies.[28]

Goldstein's work was part of a small but persistent current in psychology, one toward which Maslow increasingly turned, that pushed back against the taboos that positivists in general, and behaviorists in particular, had tried to establish against considering subjective reports and relying on personal deductions.

"The fallacy of the behaviorist's formula," wrote one early one critic of behaviorism, "lies in the omitted terms with the result that, were he consistent, his cupboard would be as bare as Mother Hubbard's; he smuggles in his provender from stores which he ignores."[29] The "folly of behaviorism," he argued, was the denial of "large areas of compelling fact."[30]

The main problem with behaviorism, as critics saw it, was that it distilled human experience to only the most quantifiable components. But the most interesting elements of individuals were also the most difficult to quantify. While it may have been easy to study visual perception or reaction time in a laboratory, it was next to impossible to look at an individual's dreams, desires, or emotional reality. Thus the more elusive, complicated, or multifaceted aspects of human experience were the first to be excluded from study.

By the 1950s, Maslow's divorce from behaviorism was final. He became one of these critics. "It was the beautiful program of Watson that brought me into psychology," he wrote in his journal. "But its fatal flaw is that it's good for the lab & in the lab, but you put it on & take it off like a lab coat. It's useless at home with your kids & wife & friends. It does not generate an image of man, a philosophy of life, a conception of human nature. It's not a guide to living, to values, to choices."[31]

Humanistic psychology was born out of dissatisfaction—with an academic climate dominated by scientism and behaviorism, and with a psychotherapeutic realm ruled by Freudian hierarchies, negative definitions of health, and medicalized notions of human suffering. At the same time, though, it grew from dogged optimism and uninhibited hopefulness.

Although the founders of humanistic psychology were more different than they were similar, they shared several things in common. They were born in the aughts (Rogers in 1902, Maslow in 1908, and May in 1909), sharing their infancy with psychology itself and inheriting its uneasiness with larger questions of meaning and values, while feeding on the culture's new lust for all things scientific. They were educated, in the 1920s, 1930s, and 1940s, at major research universities where the practice of psychotherapy was crowded out by experimental research and a singular interest in people's quantifiable behaviors. And their theories crystallized in the 1950s, in a culture that was agitated by Cold War fears and (the other side of the coin) insistent upon adjustment as a solution to individual woes.

They stood out, against these backdrops, like sore thumbs. They tended to question—in faculty meetings, in presentations, and in their own writing—principles and methods that earned almost unanimous agreement in departmental circles. Surprisingly, though, they didn't seem too grumpy about it. In fact, their peers consistently described them as sunnier, kinder, gentler, more flexible, and more original than other colleagues.[32]

Maslow's peers tended to praise him for his childlike enthusiasm, his unflagging curiosity, his ever-calm voice, his endearing smile. They saw in him something pure, something preserved from the taint of the chaotic world into which he'd been thrust, something childlike and wondrous.[33]

As the son of Russian immigrants who were sometimes hard to live with and harder still to please, and as a Jew growing up in Brooklyn in a neighborhood conducive to the flinging of rocks and ethnic slurs, Maslow learned to channel his passions into books. He practically lived in the library until high school, when he melded his intellectual interests with his latent leadership abilities as the officer of several academic clubs and the editor of his school's Latin magazine and physics newspaper. His proclivities, which included intellectual openness and a tenacious drive for self-betterment, ensured his resilience; he rebounded gracefully from failed studies at City College and Cornell, as well as from his disillusionment with behaviorism.[34]

In all his endeavors, Maslow's ambitions were capacious. When he courted behaviorism, he did so with all the ardor that would later infuse his humanistic psychology. And when he abandoned behaviorism, he rejected it with all the force that he had once used to support it. His colleague James Klee later remarked on the impressive nature of his change of heart, likening him to William James, who ultimately renounced the whole of psychology, calling it a "dirty little science." Klee saw parallels between their stature in the psychological world and the intellectual and emotional strength they had displayed in entirely overhauling their theoretical perspectives.[35]

After leaving Thorndike's laboratory in 1937, Maslow set out on his own course. As a young instructor at Brooklyn College, he opened himself up to other disciplines. Guided by his peers in anthropology, he tested his theories of dominance and sexuality across cultures. He adopted new theoretical frameworks, replacing a comparative orientation (that generalized from animals to man) with a paradigm of cultural relativism (that recognized the more subtle differences between men). "I realized," wrote Maslow in the late thirties, "that my test of dominance was a test of dominance-in-an-insecure-society."[36] Gradually his blind spots were revealed to him. With the press of World War II, Maslow abandoned his earlier commitments more cleanly, devoting himself instead to forging a more positive, and unconventional, theory of human motivation.

Within the wider world of psychology, Maslow's new orientation was an apostasy. It posed several immediate challenges. While he had grown accustomed to publishing easily in prestigious journals, he now found few journals willing to print his unorthodox new theories. His publication record remained strong; he published twenty-eight articles in the first decade, twenty-three in the second. But the reputation of the journals that would accept his articles declined sharply. His first study of healthy people, "Self-Actualizing People: A Study of Psychological Health," for example, was published in 1950 in a small journal that soon folded.[37]

Another challenge was the sense of professional isolation Maslow experienced. His colleagues at Brooklyn College favored experimental studies of learning, perception, and animal behavior, and didn't identify with his work.[38] In fact they all but blocked his application for tenure, delaying it several years.[39] His experience with his students mitigated his detachment somewhat. He loved teaching. At the same time, the demands at Brooklyn College were overly rigorous; he taught five courses each semester, with no hope of his course load ever being reduced.[40]

Being in New York, though, softened the blow. Maslow found the city full of intellectual excitement and drew inspiration from academics outside his department and college, most notably those he had met at the New School of Social Research in the 1930s. In 1951, when Maslow was offered a position at Brandeis University, in pastoral Waltham, Massachusetts, he was reluctant to leave.[41]

The move to Brandeis, in general, was risky. The university was not yet accredited and had just barely avoided bankruptcy (under the name of Middlesex University) before getting a new name and an infusion of funds from a Jewish group in 1946. It was premised on the dream of a group of Jewish investors to build their own nonsectarian university—a cause in which Maslow had little interest. The offer they made him, though, was one he couldn't refuse.[42]

Max Lerner, the head of social sciences, recognized Maslow's distinctive value. Although Lerner knew little to nothing about psychology, he promised Maslow the opportunity to create a program in any way that suited him. He could construct the department from the ground up, recruiting his own faculty and training graduate students as he wished. Lerner also wooed him with the promise of a more integrated intellectual community; at the time, Brandeis was entirely interdisciplinary, and there were no discrete departments.[43]

Maslow accepted the position at Brandeis not out of a fantasy of personal power, but because of his desire to propel psychology toward greatness. His administrative duties were overwhelming, particularly in terms of hiring, but he remained highly principled. He refused to hire faculty who validated his perspective out of obligation or deference, attempting, instead, to hire only truly gifted scholars, without regard to their age or approach.[44]

Although he was spread thin with his new administrative duties and his course load, Maslow managed to solidify his theory of self-actualization and higher needs in his early years at Brandeis. He published several articles based on earlier work, including "Higher Needs and Personality," "Love in Healthy People," "The Instinctoid Nature of Basic Needs," and "Deficiency Motivation and Growth Motivation." More significantly, though, he assembled a collection of his work in a 1954 book called *Motivation and Personality*, which expanded on the ideas he had briefly outlined in his 1943 article "A Theory of Human Motivation." At the heart of the book was his concept of the hierarchy of needs.[45]

The basic thrust of Maslow's motivation theory was that people are innately driven to reach their fullest potential, but to do so they must ascend through a series of "prepotent" needs. One set of needs, said Maslow, must be fulfilled in order for an individual to focus on the next set of needs. The first four levels of Maslow's hierarchy consisted of basic needs, beginning with the physiological: water, air, food, sleep, etc. "When our bellies are full and we are sheltered," explained Maslow, we move to the second level, turning "toward the problems of safety and security in the world. We want a good police force and good doctors. Then, we think of education, and we want good schools."[46] The third level of the pyramid contained "love" and "belonging" needs, and the fourth "esteem" needs (for respect from others and for self-respect). At the fifth and highest level were "being" needs. If the attainment of any one of the four basic needs were thwarted, an individual would fixate on that particular level, and possibly never reach the very highest needs, being needs, and would never achieve "self-actualization."

Maslow drew the term and concept of self-actualization from Kurt Goldstein, who had served as a mentor to him during his time in New York. Goldstein had been struck by the resiliency of the brain-injured soldiers with whom he worked, and he'd studied closely their ability to completely reorganize their functioning, compensating for deficits by developing strengths in other areas. He argued that self-actualization, the basic and singular drive for the organism to realize, to the maximal extent, its capabilities in the world, was the organism's "affirmative answer to the shocks of existence."[47] Rather than acting in the interest of self-preservation or tension reduction, the healthy, self-actualizing individual would offer creative, generative responses to the difficulties of life.

Maslow chose to use Goldstein's term in a more specific and limited fashion. "It refers," he wrote of his own interpretation, "to the desire for self-fulfillment, namely, to the tendency for [man] to become actualized in what he is potentially. This tendency might be phrased as the desire to become more and more what one is, to become everything that one is capable of becoming."[48]

Maslow described self-actualization in more depth in his chapters "Self-Actualizing People: A Study of Psychological Health" and "Love in Self-Actualizing People." In them he outlined the ideals of health, the heights toward which we are intrinsically motivated. Self-actualizing individuals, he wrote, are accepting of self, others, and nature. "They can accept their own human nature in the stoic style, with all its shortcomings, with all its discrepancies from the ideal image, without feeling concern." They are spontaneous and authentic; they focus on problems beyond their own; they savor privacy and solitude; and they appreciate the details of life with freshness and wonder. Their attributes are many; their liabilities are few. Still, Maslow did not wish to make them a caricature. On the negative side, he noted, they are capable of ruthlessness and coldness; they occasionally alienate others; they can be too kind; they often sacrifice social politeness to intense concentration; and they often feel shame, doubt, anxiety, and internal strife.[49] They are, quite interestingly, the very picture of Maslow himself—of everything one can glean from his journal entries, his personal memos, and the reflections of his friends.

Motivation and Personality became the crowning work of Maslow's career. It broadcast his concept of self-actualization, and his theory of the hierarchy of needs, to a wider audience than even the most prestigious academic journal could have. It earned him a national reputation that spread beyond psychology, penetrating business management, marketing, education, counseling, and psychotherapy. And it flooded him with offers for speaking engagements.[50]

He was pleased with the book's success, remarking, in January 1961, on the royalties and the still-increasing sales.[51] Though he had always had utter confidence in the book, counting it among the most significant works in psychology's history, he displayed the "nonneurotic" doubt typical of the self-actualized and remained apprehensive about his colleagues' view of it. The book was unconventional for an academic psychologist. In it, he argued against many of the assumptions that the field rested on: health as the absence of pathology, universal values, valid science as exclusively empirical science. Instead of offering original research, he appended an outline of more than a hundred prospects for future "humanistic" research—on topics like creativity, love, ecstasy, and mysticism.[52]

• • •

Like Maslow, Carl Rogers stood apart from the typical academic psychologist both personally and professionally. He listened better, was gentler, and was more soft-spoken. One of his colleagues described his amazing capacity for open communication: "He would sit forward and look you in the eyes."[53] Also like Maslow, he took professional risks, like the decision to publish full accounts of his therapy sessions, complete with very unscientific sounding "m-hms" and "uhs."

In contrast to Maslow, though, who was known for his ability to tolerate conflict, and even productively initiate it, Rogers rarely stirred things up in person. When he faced down the profession, he did it in writing—in careful, methodical prose, with insights that were so simple as to be difficult to refute.

Rogers's style was a product of his background. The son of Congregationalist Midwesterners, trained at the University of Wisconsin in agricultural science and Union Seminary in theology, he was pragmatic and thoughtful. When he turned to psychology in 1926, as a doctoral student at Columbia's Teachers College and a fellow at New York City's Institute for Child Guidance, he was guided by his own intuition to combine academic psychology's interest in measurement and assessment with the clinical interests of personality and emotion, writing a dissertation titled "Measuring Personality Adjustment in Children Nine to Thirteen."[54]

Instead of taking an academic post, Rogers worked from 1928 to 1939 at the Rochester Society for the Prevention of Cruelty to Children. There, he became even more pragmatic: witnessing the struggles of suffering children, he was singularly concerned with outcome. "Will it work?" he repeatedly asked.[55]

He quickly grew disenchanted with the standard diagnostic process, which relied heavily on intelligence testing and achievement, and developed instead the "component factor method," a multifaceted approach designed to consider a child's development and behavior holistically. With this method, children were rated on seven-point scales for eight factors: self-insight, physical factors, family emotional tone, economic and cultural factors, social experience, heredity, mentality, and education and supervision. Published in 1931 as the "Personal Adjustment Inventory," this assessment tool built on the insights of Freudians (who emphasized family factors and childhood development), sociologists (whose interests lay in schools and culture), psychiatrists (who were concerned with physical health and inherited traits), and of course psychologists (who insisted upon the repeatability and validity of measurement).[56]

Rogers's therapeutic approach at Rochester was environmentally oriented, focused on schools, foster homes, camps, and institutions.[57] But he gradually shifted to a model of intensive psychotherapy in which the therapeutic relationship itself acted as a growth-fostering home that could correct prior negative experiences and unleash the child's inherent drive toward health. Although Rogers had little practical training in psychotherapy, and found disappointingly few systematic accounts of effective practice, he surveyed techniques, rejecting manipulative approaches like hypnosis and favoring interpretive and expressive therapies. He aimed at enabling children to achieve insight, either through discussion and analysis or, with younger children, through play therapy.

In 1940 Rogers left applied work to return to academia. Though he lacked academic experience, his extensive publication record and clinical background allowed him to enter Ohio State as a full professor. At this level, he could immediately diverge from mainstream psychological research without first having to prove his legitimacy to a tenure board.

In 1942, he introduced a new model of therapy in *Counseling and Psychotherapy*, one that reflected his own inclinations. It was systematic, replicable, and explicit. He laid out what he took to be the basics of a therapeutic relationship: warmth and responsiveness, permissiveness regarding emotional expression, clearly defined limits, and freedom from persuasion and pressure.[58] He would later distill these characteristics down to the tenets of unconditional positive regard (an attitude of total acceptance), empathic understanding (consisting of warmth and attunement), and congruence (a lack of hierarchical doctor-patient boundaries and a sense of an open encounter between both parties).

Rogers's presentation of the fundamentals of nondirective counseling culminated in "The Case of Herbert Bryan," a verbatim account of eight sessions with a client that he included in the last 170 pages of the book. His main technique was empathic communication: a reflecting back of what Bryan was saying, not by using literal repetition, but by affirming his statements with imagination, acceptance, and understanding. When Bryan describes the physical experience of his anxiety, for example, Rogers links it to a deeper feeling of emasculation:

BRYAN: "When I walk, that is, when I'm feeling badly, I walk hunched over and sort of like I had a bellyache, which I actually do have, psychologically.

ROGERS: It just makes you more or less half a man, is
that it? And only half able to do your work—[59]

Bryan agrees to this interpretation, as he does to many of
Rogers's encapsulations. And, when he doesn't agree, Rogers
pulls back, fine-tuning his understanding and reframing his
statements to make them more accurate.

While the transcript was fascinating and its publication
groundbreaking, this unconventional move made Rogers inor-
dinately vulnerable. In piercing the shroud of mystery that surrounded psychotherapy, he risked the ire of psychotherapists
whose status depended, to a considerable degree, on the myth of
the psychological expert's magic powers. He threatened to make
them look common, simple, human. The things he said in the
sessions often reflected uncertainty, and he repeatedly fumbled
as he tried to understand Bryan and say the right thing.

His unconventional work was dismissed by most academic psychologists, who didn't seem to buy his claim that the
publication of complete accounts of psychotherapy represented
scientific progress. (The book wasn't even reviewed in academic
journals.) Somewhat surprisingly, though, clinical professionals
were not cowed; he was invited to give speeches and workshops,
and elected to offices in prestigious professional organizations.[60]

Rogers rode his professional esteem into the 1950s. Even
the academy had to acknowledge his value, particularly since he
continued to meet their requirements of systematic research and
frequent publication. Moving to the University of Chicago, again
as a full professor, he continued to systematize his therapeutic
techniques, performing outcome studies and publishing the results widely (nearly fifty articles from the mid-1940s to the mid-
1950s, in addition to three books). He served as president of the

APA, as well as several other organizations, and won numerous awards, including the APA's Distinguished Scientific Contribution Award. During the same time, he saw hundreds of articles and studies published on his nondirective method.[61]

It's not an exaggeration to say that by the late 1950s, Rogers's work had forever changed American psychotherapy. In 1957, the same year he accepted yet another academic post at the University of Wisconsin, *Time* devoted a full page to Rogers's theory, which was by then quite familiar to those in the profession. Referring to Rogers as a longtime "maverick," the author pitted him against psychoanalysts. Rogers's "manful" attempt at defining his technique ran as follows: "We see therapy as an experience, not in intellectual terms. We treat the client as a person, not an object to be manipulated and directed." In opposition, a neo-Freudian was reported to have contemptuously stated, "Rogers' method is unsystematic, undisciplined, and humanistic. Rogers doesn't analyze and doesn't diagnose. We have no common ground."[62]

Psychologists trained in the 1950s, most of whom had read Rogers's theory firsthand, inevitably possessed a more nuanced understanding of his approach. As a result, they didn't tend to see client-centered therapy and psychoanalysis as an either/or proposition. In fact, many found that it was not only possible, but also productive to incorporate portions of Rogers's theory into their own approach.

Although Tom Greening, a future Association of Humanistic Psychology president and *Journal of Humanistic Psychology* editor, already had some familiarity with Rogers when he joined a private practice in Los Angeles in 1958, his psychoanalytic training and academic coursework at the University of Michigan had rooted him in a pathology-oriented tradition. His gradual shift toward a more humanistic paradigm was compelled, in part, by the impression Rogers's concept of congruence had made on him, and by the notion of the I-Thou encounter (the highest form of communication, in which social roles are discarded in favor of an embrace of each participant's total uniqueness), which Rogers, along with theologian Martin Buber, had explored when they visited Greening's graduate school in 1957.

Greening's early style, and early debt to Rogers, are exemplified in one of his first psychotherapy cases. In 1959 he began treating "Carol," a functional but neurotic grade school teacher who was quickly becoming overweight, depressed, and suicidal. One night, she called him after ingesting a bottle of pills, frantically explaining that the ghost of her mother was reaching from her closet to drag her to hell. Although he was panicked, as a green therapist with no crisis training, he managed to offer her three things that she thanked him for twenty years later. He was fully present (in the I-Thou encounter sense), he kept his cool in the face of grave pathology (unconditional positive regard), and he held out a positive vision of a future beyond the painful present (a kind of humanistic hopefulness).[63]

It wasn't atypical, in the 1950s, to see traces of Rogers's theory even in the practice of psychotherapists like Greening who ascribed only a peripheral influence to him. Although psychoanalytic techniques still predominated in the 1950s, psychotherapy tended to be a hybrid of various theories. Patients weren't necessarily lying on couches anymore, or free-associating while their analysts silently evaluated them. And psychoanalysts, in general, tended to be less severe and reductionistic than strict Freudians had been.[64]

Clinical psychology programs housed diverse influences, as well. Although behaviorism was the rule, and all else the exception, places like the University of Michigan—where Greening received his doctorate—emphasized psychoanalysis in a way that was depth-oriented, holistic, and "meaningful."[65] This program stood in contrast to Greening's undergraduate institution, Yale, which was strongly behavioristic and where Greening had actually dropped out of a psychology class mid-year "in disgust" to take more literature courses.[66]

In the late 1950s, Greening, presumably in a way that was typical of other psychotherapists at the time, read much that fertilized the seeds Rogers and others had planted. He read Wilhelm Reich, a psychoanalytic body therapist who broke Freudian taboos on neutrality by sitting next to patients, touching them directly to relieve and increase awareness of tension, and answering their questions directly in an authentic shared dialogue.[67] He read Hellmuth Kaiser, who soon published the influential story "Emergency," a fictional account in which a psychotherapist pretends to be a patient in order to effectively treat a fellow psychotherapist (thereby turning the doctor-patient hierarchy on its head).[68] He read Theodor Reik's *Listening with a Third Ear*, a volume focused on encouraging psychoanalysts to develop a more human and holistic way of tuning in to a person, one in which the therapist makes use of her "unconscious feelers" and is not afraid of her sensitivities or flights of imagination.[69] And he read Rollo May's *Existence*, a collection of writings—some new, some in translation—that fused his prior literary and philosophical interest in existentialism with psychotherapy in a revolutionary new way.

Tom Greening actually preferred the work of Rollo May to that of Carl Rogers. He had more "craziness," was more artistic, and—particularly in drawing on European existentialism—was deeper and more philosophically grounded.[70]

• • •

Like Rogers, May had flown his Protestant Midwestern coop for the psychologized intellectual climate of New York City. But while Rogers's religiosity seemed almost detachable, May's spirituality was his connective tissue. In New York, he replaced his Methodism with the neo-orthodox theology of Paul Tillich and Reinhold Niebuhr, but ultimately abandoned both in favor of a soulful existentialism. His introduction to psychotherapy came first when he received training in pastoral counseling methods (as a counselor) at the YMCA, and later when he undertook psychoanalysis (as a patient) with Alfred Adler. His psychology would forever be absent the scientific lilt that defined both Maslow's and Rogers's approaches.[71]

As a practitioner, and not an academic, May had an entirely different agenda than either Maslow or Rogers. He hoped to reunite psychological concerns with their spiritual and philosophical bases. He endeavored to perform public ministry, offering a psychologized view of the human condition in the trade books he published. He also struggled to secure for psychologists the right to practice psychotherapy free from medical and scientific constraints.

Although he bent himself to the academic requirements of earning a doctorate at Teachers College, his humanistic inclinations were always evident. In studying anxiety for his doctoral thesis, he attempted to quantify fourteen individuals' experience of anxiety with techniques ranging from checklist questionnaires to Rorschach inkblot tests. Ultimately, though, he placed greater value on subjective reports and insights gained from interviews, and defaulted to philosophical interpretations. The greatest trigger of anxiety, he found, was itself subjective, a sense of being "trapped" with every choice threatening "vital value."[72]

May's dissertation didn't offer any earth-shattering insights about neurotic anxiety (though he did suggest that an individual's creative power was the key to overcoming it); it was more on the topic of normal anxiety that he made a contribution. Describing anxious states as part and parcel of human existence, he found the threat of sickness and the inevitability of death to be the constituents of an unavoidable, but potentially manageable, sense of human uneasiness.[73]

Needless to say, May's dissertation didn't earn him much academic esteem, but it did pave the way for his future theoretical and clinical pursuits. After publishing it in 1950 as *The Meaning of Anxiety*, he never again felt compelled to don the guise of empiricism. His next book, *Man's Search for Himself*, published in 1953, was written for a popular as well as professional audience, was entirely theoretical, and was his first *New York Times* bestseller.[74]

Man's Search for Himself reflected another of May's atypical interests: he was committed to the fusion of individual with cultural concerns. He considered himself a public minister, aiming to treat the spiritual, philosophical, and psychological condition of the culture as much as of the individual. In the opening of the book, he identified the reciprocal relationship between a culture gripped by anxiety (in the wake of two world wars, with the threat of a third, and with a fair amount of economic uncertainty) and individuals defined by symptoms of anxiety (loneliness, defensiveness, and neurotic fixations).[75] At the root of the self-perpetuating plague of anxiety, May argued, was a collapse of meaning and belief, the product of which was a stifling of our creative and constructive impulses.

The answer, for May, was an "ethics of inwardness," an elevation of the self above society, a retreat from cultural dependence. "This is what our society needs," he wrote, "not new ideas and inventions, important as these are, and not geniuses and supermen, but persons who can *be*, that is persons who have a center of strength within themselves."[76] Hardly stereotypical of the decade of conformity, and more in keeping with psychotherapy than academic psychology, May greeted the 1950s with a powerful call to the individual.

A summons for self-consciousness, self-love, creative engagement, a realization of potentialities, a full use of our powers. This is what May offered to America in 1953. This was the same year that Joseph McCarthy, whose witch hunt of government officials, teachers, and Hollywood icons had filled Americans with fear and suspicion, was called out publicly by Edward R. Murrow, and a year before he was censured by the Senate.[77] By taking a stand against McCarthy, Murrow urged Americans to let reason prevail over fear.[78]

As the first cracks of liberatory light permeated our national consciousness, May warned that conformity, perhaps as epitomized in McCarthy, was antithetical to selfhood, and to cultural health. He reminded Americans that while we are unavoidably interdependent, we need to assert our autonomous identities, to affirm our capacity for self-creation, to take responsibility for our own, and the world's, problems.[79]

This articulation of the inner locus of responsibility, and of creativity and power, paved the way for May's greatest, and most unique, contribution of the 1950s: a volume called *Existence*, which he published in 1958. The book joined the original essays of European philosophers and psychologists with summarative essays intended to clarify the nature of existential psychotherapy. In placing the individual at the center of her own misery, anxiety, and joy, it displayed a paradigm that had been nurtured in Western European dialogues, but had never before been transmitted to an American audience.

For many psychotherapists, *Existence* was their first introduction to the philosophy of existentialism. As May explained it, existentialism was most basically concerned with ontology, or the science of being, where being was understood as the point of balance that individuals negotiated between a deep fear of nonexistence and meaninglessness and a positive drive to explore existential freedom and possibility. Existential psychotherapy, as he proposed it, would focus on the concept of *Dasein*, or being, in which an individual is continually in the process of "being something," of actively choosing his own existence. The existential therapeutic approach was meant as a complement to more traditional psychoanalysis, where the emphasis was on one's past, and how that past shaped one's present orientation. Existential psychotherapy, as May proposed it, would acknowledge the past and its influence but would privilege the individual's choices and self-awareness in the present, and potential in the future, over the story of her past.[80]

Although May's collection represented a synthesis of European ideas, a reproduction of seminal writings that were widely popular in Europe, and a convergence of existentialist thought that had taken various forms in America, he recognized that American psychotherapists were likely to resist it.[81] May ascribed this resistance in part to the "still-Victorian" nature of the United States, but also to the narrowly scientistic approach of American psychology.[82] May argued that widespread commitment to behaviorism, combined with the "Lockean" or pragmatic tradition of American psychology, further inhibited the adoption of new paradigms that would step beyond technique.[83]

Existential psychology relied on a phenomenological method of inquiry that began with the intuitive experience of phenomena, as perceived with conscious awareness, and attempted to draw conclusions about the essential features of subjectivity in the hope of a fuller comprehension of being.[84] Anticipating criticism that this approach was unscientific, May argued that the existential-phenomenological movement in psychiatry and psychology had arisen "precisely out of a passion to be not less but more empirical."[85] Taking the phenomenological-existential psychologist Ludwig Binswanger—whom May featured in *Existence*—as an example, May argued that scholarship and practice that attempted to erect a bridge between psychiatry and phenomenology was "anything but anti-scientific."[86] Binswanger had advocated phenomenology for the fullness with which it treated data, the meaning of which had been previously obscured and hidden by narrow naturalistic methods.[87]

May intended existential psychotherapy to complement existing approaches rather than overthrow them. If one conceptualized human experience as multileveled, existentialism would come in at the foundation, analyzing the ground beneath human experience, with a particular emphasis on situations of human crisis.[88] May argued that a psychology that couldn't deal with such foundations, or have anything to say about the most profound crises, was scientific in only the narrowest senses. As an illustration of this, one of the essays in May's collection cited the work of Viktor Frankl, an Austrian-born psychiatrist whose theories had been forged in considerable part while he was imprisoned in the concentration camps of Auschwitz, Kaufering, and Türkheim.[89]

Frankl had been profoundly struck, while in the camps, by how some prisoners were able to continue to create meaning, and to hold on to some degree of optimism, even while watching their loved ones die and staring, plainly, at the likelihood of their own deaths. During and after his internment, Frankl focused on the memory of his wife and on the creation of his theory of logotherapy, which he was finally able to publish after his release. He concluded that the strength of the conscious ability to construct meaning was what differentiated individuals who survived inhuman obstacles more than anything else. Thus he proclaimed the "will to meaning" to be primary among successful human characteristics; instead of imagining that suffering could be avoided, Frankl focused on the catalyzing power of horrific pain to push individuals to transcendent levels of individual existence.[90] Quoting Nietzsche, Frankl asserted, "He who has a why to live can bear almost any how."[91]

Frankl went on to apply his existential theory to therapy through his practices of ontoanalysis (a form of existential therapy that focuses on uncovering hidden meaning in everyday actions and experiences) and logotherapy (a type of therapy focused on "will to meaning"). These practices aimed at uncovering meaning in even the most minute objects and events, enabling individuals—many of whom had been entirely stripped of existential freedom—to reanimate their existences. This constructive approach infused psychotherapy with a dialogue of meaning and values that had been absent in psychoanalysis.[92]

May's hope in publishing *Existence* was to cultivate in the field of psychotherapy a greater openness to the humanistically oriented work of theorists, like Frankl, Binswanger, and Erwin Straus, whose ideas pushed most therapists out of their comfort zones. Through the collection, May modeled a willingness to talk about meaning and values, and to reconnect psychology with the types of philosophy from which it had been so cleanly severed just decades before.

In laying his piece of the foundation of humanistic psychology, May posited not only the idea that our deepest problems were caused (and resolved) intrapsychically; he also complicated the optimism that Rogers and Maslow brought to their work by emphasizing the tragic dimension of human existence. If Maslow brought a view of the highest reaches that humans could achieve, and Rogers brought a psychotherapeutic technique to empower individuals to achieve them, May brought the counterweight—the idea that greatness was only possible through struggle and the awareness that struggle would never wholly remit.

4

Self, Being, and Growth People

"We must be courageous about exploring ourselves, write it out publicly, compare such personal theories with each other to see how general they are or how specific, & thus go toward a generalized phenomenology & general truth out of the varied personal truths."

ABRAHAM MASLOW[1]

Although they propelled their fields in exciting new directions, the founders of humanistic psychology hadn't planned to lead a movement. Rogers resisted the leadership role, rejected the ideas of control and authority attached to it, and feared being viewed as a guru. The leadership he did offer was gentle and unassuming—an extension of his therapeutic style. When he led a group, he was soft-spoken, deliberate, and patient. He deferred to the ideas of others, but carried his own convictions with grace.[2]

While May hoped to offer a new paradigm, to forge "a new dimension in psychiatry and psychology," he too was wary of leading a movement. He was preoccupied, in the 1950s, with a more basic struggle to maintain his professional existence, the

right of psychologists to practice psychotherapy rather than
ceding the realm to psychiatrists.[3] This battle was premised on
the goal of keeping the field open to multiple perspectives rather
than letting a single approach win out, as would have been required had he led a unified movement.

Maslow was more torn. His style, and his messianic aspirations, made him the most likely candidate to father humanistic psychology. By nature, he was more comfortable than the
average academic with being grandiose, and his interests were
better suited to a revolution than to the kind of incremental and
systematic change that professionals in the field had come to
expect and accept.[4] He didn't have much tolerance, however, for
the trappings of traditional leadership. "I have rejected all demands to be pope," he wrote in a journal entry, "or to accept
pure disciples (*students*, yes) & prick suckers who pledge total &
exclusive devotion."[5] He also didn't have much interest in the
kind of intellectual single-mindedness that tends to win the day
for ideas and schools of thought. His ideas, and his beliefs, were
constantly changing.

Maslow had in mind another type of leadership. "I am a
leader," wrote Maslow in the same journal entry, "in a *higher* &
better sense, which allows autonomy for the other, if he can take
it."[6] He hoped to lead by revealing the true nature of man's
potential, and by offering himself as an example. His goals were
utopian, revolutionary.

In a sense, Maslow felt leading an academic or professional movement in psychology was beneath him. It would require getting down into the muck rather than raising himself,
and others, up from it.

"If I can transcend the jungle," he wrote in his journal,
"by getting up above it and looking down calmly, then in prin-

ciple I can climb up above the human species itself as if I were nonhuman, a God, a Martian, or, better, a human being in his divine moments, in B-cognition, looking from above at himself below, as one does on the psychoanalytic couch. I can then look at human beings, pushing aside my identification, my interests, my stake in them."[7]

The result of Maslow's ambivalence was that he became, in most respects, the leader of the movement, but he often refused to lead. He sought out peers rather than followers, hoping to facilitate fruitful connections rather than effective organizations. He built networks, like the mailing list, to support and connect the people who shared his concerns, and frequently tried to enlist others in his own efforts. With Anthony Sutich, a private practitioner in California, he met perhaps his most significant success.

Sutich had, somewhat organically, developed a critique that paralleled Maslow's. Although he was no academic (because of a childhood baseball injury that led to lifelong physical immobilization, he had never even completed high school), he had been moved to write a few articles related to his specific frustration with the field of psychology.[8] The first, "Proposed Improvement in Terminology in Relation to Personal Psychological Problems," reflected his dismay over the objectification of patients and the pathologization of their concerns.[9] Another, "The Growth Experience and the Growth-Centered Attitude," proposed a positive agenda for psychologists, offering a growth-oriented perspective that would supplant the dominant adjustment orientation. In it, he outlined the optimal goal of therapy—"the development of the full-valued personality," characterized by "maximal democratic self-direction."[10]

Sutich had taken his inspiration from the humanistically leaning psychologists who had preceded him. From Karen Horney, he drew the idea that the goal of analysis was not a finished product. Instead, the end of therapy was signaled by the patient's ability to proceed on his own. Like Maslow, he took from Kurt Goldstein the concept of self-actualization. He also referred to Rogers's concept of individual "impulses to growth" and, more generally, to the growth-oriented work of Alfred Adler, Henri Bergson, and Erich Fromm.[11]

Interestingly, though, Sutich had developed his approach without being aware of Maslow. In fact, he was entirely unfamiliar with Maslow's work until the two were introduced by a mutual friend in 1949. The affinity of their interests was evident immediately, and Maslow made a strong impression. "He was the proverbial roaring lion," wrote Sutich years later. "He just paced back and forth, slashing right and left: he couldn't stand the adjustment people, he couldn't stand the behaviorists, and neither could I. Both of us realized we were isolated from the mainstream of psychology."[12]

They discussed, at length, the plight of humanistically oriented psychologists; funding was increasingly unavailable to them, and opportunities for publication pathetically few. Sutich later explained, "So overwhelming was the predominance of behaviorism that any publishable material outside its scope was typically met with scorn, ridicule, or even worse."[13]

Sutich himself had been affected by publication biases, and had been unsuccessful in getting a journal to accept "The Growth Experience and the Growth-Centered Attitude." Maslow, drawing on the academic capital he had acquired, arranged—just weeks after being apprised of the repeated rejections—for the paper to be published in the *Journal of Psychology*.[14] Sutich more than returned the favor.

In 1957, Sutich proposed to Maslow the idea of a journal that would formalize the channels of communication between humanistically oriented psychologists, give them the assurance of publication, and transmit their ideas more widely. Unsurprisingly, Maslow was enthusiastic, offering his wholehearted support for the idea. Also unsurprisingly, he delegated the organization of the journal to Sutich. The grander Maslow's vision became, the harder he found it to concern himself with the details.

"I guess one big factor underlying everything," Maslow wrote in his journal, "is the feeling that I have so much to give the world—the Great Message—and that this is the big thing. Anything else that cuts it or gets in the way is 'bad.' Before I die, I must say it all."[15] It was imperative, he concluded, to delegate administrative duties, as well as the empirical testing of his theory, to his colleagues and students.

For Maslow, the late fifties were a time of building generative alliances that would empower his goals. Another vital connection was his relationship with Clark Moustakas, which had begun with the publication of *The Self* in 1956. Moustakas was a man not unlike Carl Rogers, a quiet but expressive man, a "careful listener" with an intuitive preference for freedom over authority.[16] His unassuming nature, and his unwavering commitment to humanistic principles, were no doubt a complement to Maslow's wilder enthusiasms.

In 1957 and 1958, Maslow and Moustakas hosted two meetings through the Merrill-Palmer Institute in Detroit that sowed the seeds for a professional association to follow. The early meetings established a catalog of themes that would come to define the humanistic vision—these included self-actualization, health, creativity, human potential, intrinsic nature, individuality, being, and meaning.[17]

Meanwhile, the organization of the journal progressed despite several challenges. The first was in finding a good title. Maslow and Sutich had initially agreed on the *Journal of Orthopsychology* (from the Greek *orthos*, to straighten or correct), but when the Orthopsychiatric Association opposed the title, they discarded the idea. Maslow suggested other titles, like *Psychological Growth*, *Being and Becoming*, *Personality Development*, *Existence*, *Third Force*, and *Self-Psychology*, but nothing felt right. They eventually took the suggestion of Maslow's son-in-law, then a psychology student at Brandeis, and named it the *Journal of Humanistic Psychology* (JHP).[18]

Whether or not the title was "good" was a matter of debate within the soon-to-coalesce movement. It was evocative, but it also caused confusion. The use of the term "humanistic" was meant to be a selective one. It was intended to draw out the ideals related to "humanism"— specifically dignity, worth, responsibilities, and fulfillment—but to oppose the modern association with atheism. As Sutich explained, he and Maslow hoped to reclaim the term, banking on the idea that "in the long run the positive, affirming, explicit value commitments of psychologists with this orientation would restore 'humanistic' to its original positive emphasis."[19] But the title did tend to cause confusion about the journal's (and later the association's) purpose. Early in the journal's run, psychologist Gordon Allport worried that the label "humanistic psychology" implied "humanism without any scientific constraints," whereas the movement that Allport hoped for was one that "might be said to have the outlook of humanism, but the constraints of science." "Label not good," he wrote.[20] But it was too late. Humanistic psychologists were already sentenced to decades of explaining how they differed from humanists.[21]

Another impediment was the journal's lack of funding. This particular burden fell on Sutich's shoulders. The first meager infusion of money came from his personal savings and donations from his friends. Although the president of Brandeis, who had initially denied support of any kind, eventually agreed to sponsor the journal, he refused to fund it.[22]

In spite of these obstacles, the idea of the journal created a buzz. Even before the first issue was published in the spring of 1961, Sutich received numerous unsolicited manuscripts and expressions of interest. A host of psychological luminaries agreed to serve on the journal's board of directors, most notably Kurt Goldstein, Aldous Huxley, Lewis Mumford, David Riesman, Erich Fromm, and soon-to-be-central figures in the movement like Rollo May, Carl Rogers, and Charlotte Bühler.

Sutich initially relied on a core of contributors to provide repeat submissions. Maslow published an article in virtually every issue—eleven of the first fifteen. Charlotte Bühler's work was featured in seven of the first eighteen issues. Other frequent appearances were made by James Bugental, whose articles appeared in five of the first thirteen issues and whose column "Persons Behind Ideas" ran from the fourth through sixth volumes, and by Sidney Jourard, who made five contributions to the first nineteen issues of the journal.

Even from this fairly narrow base, however, the ideas being generated were expansive. The most common topics in the early years of the journal included the role of ideals and principles in the psychological conception of the self, individual striving for health and self-actualization, transcendence and peak experiences (spiritual or mystical experiences during which one is at one's best), and creativity. These first issues were also testing grounds for therapeutic concepts that would become popular later on. The idea of "sensitivity training," a form of group therapy involving open and direct communication, first appeared in the Spring 1963 issue of the journal in two separate articles.[23]

Early articles reflected the journal's novel commitment to viewing human psychology in a positive light. Not only did they seldom deal with psychopathology in any capacity, many charted an explicitly hopeful, generative approach to human experience. Sometimes this positive orientation manifested in explicitly utopian visions, as in the case of Maslow's article, "Eupsychia—The Good Society," or in visions of transcendence, as in his article "Health as Transcendence of Environment." More often, however, it was fairly down-to-earth. It didn't propose that healthy people would always be happy, or even satisfied. Instead, it argued that human struggle would always have meaning, that people would always be striving, that conflict could always be productive. Even while exploring neurotic resistance to therapy, one early contributor proposed a growth theory. And, in tackling the alienation of identity, another envisioned a path toward personality integration.[24]

By collecting research and theory on creativity, autonomous motivation, goals, and values, Sutich and Maslow hoped to amass a body of research and theory to reorient the psychological conception of the individual. The individual, they hoped, might begin to be seen—at least by psychologists—as productive and driven rather than rotely dysfunctional or pathological. An emphasis on human capacities and potentialities might come to replace, or at least complement, the predominant fascination with weakness and deficit.[25]

By 1961, after decades of behaviorism, and more than half a century of positivistic methods, these goals resonated with a substantial subgroup of psychologists. Submissions proliferated; interest bloomed; praise flowed freely from subscribers. It quickly became clear to Sutich that an organization was required to unite the growing ranks of humanistic psychology.[26] The American Association of Humanistic Psychology (AAHP) was established in 1962 at the first of a series of conferences sponsored by Sonoma State College.[27] At this founding meeting, James Bugental, a psychotherapist who had formerly held a tenured position at the University of California, Los Angeles, was named president.

The first official meeting of the association occurred in the summer of 1963, in Philadelphia, and attracted 75 participants (attendance would double the following year).[28] The meeting was professionally significant in establishing the new organization's themes, which were broadly oriented around ideas of personal growth and the infusion of values into the supposedly value-free realms of empirical psychology. But even more powerful was the meeting's personal significance to its participants, who, according to Sutich, felt they had created a new "belonging group" that would deliver them from professional and intellectual isolation and frustration.[29]

The new "belonging group" created by the formalization of humanistic psychology filled personal and cultural, as well as professional, needs. "My own work," wrote Maslow in a journal entry, "has been a personal search for a personal answer to personally felt problems which I was trying to solve for myself & for the world at the same time."[30] He'd concluded that the peaks of human experience, like his experience of the birth of his daughter, were so profound on their own terms that they provided justification for the humanistic approach. At the same time the troughs of human awfulness—for Maslow, the rise of fascism—highlighted the necessity of adopting it as counterbalance.

Anthony Sutich too found an avenue of inquiry that resonated with his personal experience. Having spent his entire adult life on a gurney, without even the use of his arms, Sutich had cobbled together a professional identity and a vital psychotherapy practice, proving, in much the way Kurt Goldstein's patients had, the innate human impulse toward growth and self-actualization. "He could tilt his head to the side, talk through clenched teeth, and move one of his hands," wrote one humanistic psychologist, but he found ways to read (using a hanging device), to counsel (using an overhead mirror), to attend the foundational meetings of humanistic psychology, and to surpass the doctors' predictions of his life expectancy by fifty years.[31]

Sutich was representative of humanistic psychologists who faced existential struggles beyond the average, and found ways (in the form of theories, values, belief systems) to conceive of them as meaningful. Real or imagined encounters with death were a particularly compelling motivation for becoming a humanistic psychologist; intensely focusing on personal meaning and values could serve as a generative way to reckon with a pressing sense of one's mortality. Maslow was another prime example: the possibility of his death was never far from his field of vision. His recurrent debilitating fatigue, heart problems, and generally poor health drove him to systematically evaluate what he hoped to accomplish before his inevitably premature end.[32]

Rollo May's existential confrontation was produced by a long bout of tuberculosis. During his "inner pitched battle between wanting to live and wanting to die," he came to identify will, faith, and personal responsibility as constitutive of psychological and physical health.[33] Confined to a sanatorium in upstate New York, stripped of his standard defenses—daily personal and professional distractions, sexual intimacy, and family responsibilities—he experienced firsthand the divisive nature of unmitigated anxiety.[34] He concluded that it could crush you, weaken you, and cause you to succumb to illness and death, or it could raise you up, expand your sense of purpose, and compel you to engage more fully with your own life.

James Bugental, the American Association of Humanistic Psychology's first president, sought a life-affirming theory in large part as a reaction to his own intense fear of death, which, though unrelated to any physical illness, could grow so acute at times that he would be nearly unable to breathe.[35]

As Harvard psychologist Gordon Allport wrote in 1960, "Suffering cleaves two ways: sometimes it seems to break, and sometimes to make, personality. Injury, disease, imprisonment, 'brain washing' often bring a permanent collapse and despair; but often, too, these same conditions bring firmness, richness and strength."[36]

Many humanistic psychologists, when dangling over the cliff, had glimpsed, and then followed, the path back to a stronger foothold. Their minds bore the imprint of both the terror and relief that the precipice embodied. And they forged their theories as maps that might take psychologists and patients from the pit of pathology to the perch of mental health. In some cases, the theories themselves served as anchors for other would-be humanistic psychologists, nourishing their own inclinations toward life-affirming theory (as in the case of Maslow, who studied with Goldstein and Max Wertheimer, or May, who drew inspiration from Kierkegaard and Ludwig Binswanger—both European existentialists whose work he showcased in *Existence*).

Of the European immigrants who influenced and participated in humanistic psychology, Viktor Frankl's trials were the most extreme. But the experience of political, intellectual, and cultural oppression under fascism shaped the views of many. Charlotte Bühler, for instance, lost first her funding, then her academic position, then her homeland due to the political instability in Vienna and her half-Jewish parentage. Bühler was an Austrian psychologist who, with her husband Karl Bühler, ran the world-renowned Vienna Psychological Institute and carried a ten-year grant from the Rockefeller Foundation. Shortly after Bühler was dismissed, her husband was arrested for his political beliefs and held in protective custody for six weeks; the two fled the country in 1938.[37]

Bühler's experience of political persecution intensified her humanistic leanings. In her early work, she had focused on intentional behavior, adaptation, creativity, and personal style from infancy to adolescence. Against common practice, she had performed naturalistic observation, and had used case studies and subjective report as data. With her grant, she and her students analyzed children and adolescents in a Viennese adoption center. In an attempt to form a unified theory of normal stages of childhood development, they gathered everything from minute-by-minute observations to diary entries and intelligence tests.[38]

"I once believed," she wrote, "that I had been carrying out behavior experiments like Watson, whose work I was studying just then. Only later did it become clear to me that—regardless of the design—what I observed were persons, and not reflexes. In fact, these early studies were, in a sense, precursory to humanistic psychology's interest in the personal-as-a-whole."[39]

Bühler's later work overtly displayed the mark of her own struggles to remain a whole person in a politically and culturally broken environment. She extended her research beyond childhood and adolescence to the entire life cycle, and replaced the concept of homeostasis that had influenced her earlier work with the ideas of self-realization and life goals.[40]

In the 1930s and 1940s, the theories of most thoughtful psychologists (and certainly most of the Jewish ones) were influenced by the rise of the Nazis. Abe Maslow, who had been born in the United States to immigrant parents, would come to believe that his entire shift in orientation, out of behaviorism toward something more encompassing, had been related to his experience as a Jew, and to the feeling that narrow behaviorist theories had little to say about evils as pernicious as anti-Semitism and racism. "I learned later in psychoanalysis," he wrote, "that much of my push and my change in direction came out of being the object of anti-Semitism (and also, therefore, of being especially horrified by anti-Negroism)."[41]

While the cultural circumstances of postwar America certainly weren't as dramatic as Frankl's experiences at Auschwitz, or those of Bühler and her colleagues in Vienna, they provided fertile enough ground for the positive assertions of humanistic psychologists. In 1962, the year of AAHP's founding, many

Americans were still deeply shaken by World War II and the scale of destruction it had involved. They were anxious as well about the possibility of nuclear annihilation. In 1962 alone, the US performed more nuclear tests than in any year before or since (nearly 100 separate tests in locations ranging from Nevada to the Johnston Atoll in the North Pacific and Eastern Kazakh, USSR).[42]

"If we talk in terms of probabilities," Maslow explained, "I'd say there is a real probability that we must take into account that the world may be blown up and we with it. This is clearly possible."[43]

The year brought a series of dramatic events that pitched Americans between optimistic and pessimistic extremes. The Cuban Missile Crisis, for example, evoked in many Americans a kind of opponent process, a contradictory emotional experience, in which Kennedy—in staring down Khrushchev—launched them to the height of their terror and the brink of nuclear war, before dramatically restoring them to a feeling of secure world dominance when the Soviets were reported to have balked and the immediate threat to have subsided.[44]

Civil rights activities in 1962 were similarly tumultuous, revealing both deep fear and hatred in American society and the desire to help and to heal. On September 30, when James Meredith, the first black student admitted to the University of Mississippi, tried to register for classes accompanied by four hundred federal marshals, a mob of more than two thousand people attacked them. The next day, three thousand federal troops quelled the riots, forcibly allowing Meredith to enroll.[45]

While these actions suggested that something was sick in American life, they also showed that organized cultural forces were rising to remedy the infection.[46]

Carl Rogers described the liberation effort as "a fresh current in our culture, a fresh breeze blowing through the world, that is showing itself in many ways and speaking through many voices." "As I endeavor to understand this vigorous new cultural trend," he said, "it seems to me to be the voice of subjective man speaking up loudly for himself. Man has long felt himself to be a puppet in life, molded by world forces, by economic forces. He has been enslaved by persons, by institutions, and, more recently, by aspects of modern science. But he is firmly setting forth a new declaration of independence. [. . .] He is choosing himself, endeavoring to become himself: not a puppet, not a slave, not a copy of some model, but his own unique individual self."[47]

Rogers's emphasis on the primacy of the self, and its potential for transcending societal obstacles, was a note that echoed through many levels of American society in the early 1960s. But it tended to sound the loudest when it came to civil rights.

Martin Luther King, Jr., in his address to Dartmouth College in 1962, framed the struggle for racial equality as a quest for "human dignity" and "freedom." But at the same time that he demanded the protection of an individual's selfhood, he also argued for the collective goal of elevating universal human worth. "The basic thing about a man," he stated, "is not his specificity but his fundamental; not the texture of his hair or the color of his skin, but his eternal dignity and worth." Because each man is intrinsically valuable, unique, and dignified, he argued, all men should have equal opportunities for fulfillment.[48] Social change, then, would aim at the collective, but would come about by placing a greater value on the individual.

The New Left (a collection of liberal, radical movements centered primarily around student activism in the sixties) seconded this sentiment, proclaiming its regard for the self-determining individual. In the Port Huron Statement, drafted in 1962, the leaders of Students for a Democratic Society (SDS) asserted: "The goal of man and society should be human independence: a concern not with the image of popularity but with finding a meaning in life that is personally authentic; a quality of mind not driven by a sense of powerlessness, nor one which unthinkingly adopts status values, nor one which represses all threats to its habits, but one which has full, spontaneous access to present and past experience, one which easily unites the fragmented parts of personal history, one which openly faces problems which are troubling and unresolved; one with an intuitive awareness of possibilities, an active sense of curiosity, an ability and willingness to learn."[49]

Humanistic psychologists fed on these kinds of proclamations. Maslow's journals, for example, are a testament to the inspiration he took from the social and intellectual movements of the 1960s. In a characteristically enthusiastic entry, he wrote, "The new *Zeitgeist* is value-full (value-directed, value-vectorial), human-need & metaneed centered (or based), moving toward basic-need gratification & metaneed metagratification—that is, toward full-humanness, Self-Actualization, psychological health, full-functioning human fulfillment, i.e., *toward* human perfection as the limit & as the direction."[50]

For an optimist like Maslow, all the talk of social revolution cast a bright glow on America. Previously unforeseeable social changes came into focus; previously limited individuals suddenly looked capable of so much more. These perceptions were reinforced almost daily by the parade of individuals who pronounced, in what sounded to Maslow like a distinctly Maslowian style, a new era of the self.

• • •

The convergence of the rhetoric of the liberation of the self—in psychology, civil rights, and the student movement—was new, as was the scale on which the language was adopted. But the themes were not. Such "humanistic" concerns were embedded in the history of America. They related to individual worth, human dignity, rights, responsibilities, and fulfillment. They pertained to the racial inequalities made manifest in the treatment of Native Americans and of African slaves; to debates about the role of government that originated in the discrepant views of political parties; and to questions about the role of science and religion in the modern world. Rather than converging spontaneously once the 1960s dawned, they had roots in the 1950s.

In 1955, Allport had identified the existence of a "healthy and contrary trend in America." In particular, he pointed to the liberalizing of philosophies of child rearing; to more holistic, humane treatment of workers in the industrial economy; and to the popularity of therapy as evidence of a growing belief that a "person must settle his own destiny" and that life presented an endless series of opportunities for the realization of growth.[51]

Allport saw humanistic psychology as an extension, and a culmination, of the kind of work he had been conducting for decades. Throughout the 1940s and 1950s, his theory and research were consistently oriented toward the uniqueness of the individual and her attempts at harmonious existence in the social sphere. Marrying cultural interests with psychological concerns, he probed questions of religious experience at a time when many Americans were either turning their backs on traditional religion or seeking a reconceptualization of religious experience. He also probed at racial tolerance at a time when tensions over civil rights were high.

In the early 1960s, Allport continued to pursue topics like racial prejudice, but with a newfound optimism. "The age-old disorder of prejudice is beginning to yield to diagnosis and treatment, much as other endemic diseases have yielded," he wrote in a collection of essays published in 1960. "We have, therefore, abundant reason to keep faith with all humane prophets of equimindedness in the past."[52] He saw gains in civil rights as related in large part to scientific progress. He noted that studies demonstrating the pathological nature of prejudice, and the environmental rather than genetic basis of many racial differences, had helped convince people to be more rational, compassionate, and understanding when it came to race.

Such progress for Allport stood against the backdrop of a broader reorientation of psychology toward the positive. As a pioneering "personality" psychologist—he had taught one of the first undergraduate personality seminars in the nation, titled Personality: Its Psychological and Social Aspects, as a lecturer at Harvard in 1924—Allport focused on establishing norms for the integrated, normal personality. In surveying scientific research in the field up to 1961, he found that a great deal of overlapping work could serve as a guide to determining the characteristics of a functional, real man, rather than an artificial ideal man or a symptomatic, pathological man. A mature individual, he concluded after sifting through theory and research, could be defined by his ever-extending sense of self, his warm relating to self and others, his emotional security, his realistic perceptions (free of prejudice or bigotry), his ability for self-objectification, and his unifying philosophy of life (religious or secular).[53]

Allport was one of a number of social scientists, mental health workers, and philosophers who had begun to focus on positive outcomes. He was also one of many who found in humanistic psychology a proper home for his interest in replacing the dominant abnormal paradigm with a health-focused psychology.

The founding of AAHP brought together a number of individual psychologists who had been struggling, in some cases for decades, to forge a definition of health that met the requirements of acceptable academic psychology. Above all, these concepts of health needed to be thoroughly scientific—both operationally valid and empirically based—to match, or preferably surpass, the conceptual weight of accepted categories of psychopathology.

Maslow doubted that most sympathetic psychologists fully grasped the extent of the transformation required to push psychology in this direction.[54] It required more than just empirical testing of new categories. Because the definitions of health put forward by humanistic psychologists stepped into the realm of values far more conspicuously than did those of their counterparts in pathology, the discipline of psychology would require a dramatic overhaul to accommodate them. It would require a broadening of psychologists' fundamental view of legitimate science. Maslow wrote, "Science has to be redefined & expanded to manage *all* human questions, including values = Taoistic, experiential, holistic science."[55]

This redefined science would take an approach to human values that the more theoretically inclined would have identified as hermeneutic. By putting forth ideas about human values that "seemed" true, humanistic psychologists hoped to then catalyze a dialogue that would encompass a series of theoretical revisions, propelling the definition of "true" values ever closer to validity.[56] Their scientific processes would mirror this cyclical, revisionary approach. Just as mainstream psychologists empirically tested concepts by repeated investigation into reliability and validity that incorporated only minor modifications, humanistic psychologists planned to fine-tune their theories by continually testing their assumptions against data (both subjective and experimental) gained from their investigations and discussions.

Both Maslow and Sidney Jourard had written explicitly about the dialogic process by which they hoped to arrive at a functional definition of the concept of health. In Jourard's 1958 book *Personal Adjustment: An Approach Through the Study of Healthy Personality*, he recognized the subjective territory into which he needed to travel in order to quantify health. He also argued, however, that such subjectivity was actually at the root, historically, of mainstream psychological methods. The steps humanistic psychologists would take to define the values of health, he contended, mirrored the process mainstream psychologists had used to arrive at ostensibly objective scientific categories and operational definitions of illness.[57]

Jourard's scale of health demonstrated the hermeneutic approach put into practice. The scale covered areas like family relationships, eating and drinking habits, and workplace dynamics, and enabled psychologists to evaluate individuals on a five-point scale of fulfillment for each component of health. In establishing the scope of the scale, Jourard claimed that "we needn't be that blind, because we already have some intelligent guesses about some of the determiners of optimum, ongoing, 'wellness-yielding' personality."[58] Heretically, Jourard argued that his own experience as a thinking, feeling, observing person had qualified him to make some preliminary guesses about what would constitute "true" health. His survey, designed to quantify "wellness," demonstrated these initial guesses: on a scale of marital health, for example, he included the following spectrum, ranging from unhealthy to healthy:

1. Feels a complete failure as a spouse. Gets no satisfactions out of being a spouse.
2. Can perform marital role with borderline adequacy, gets no enjoyment out of it.
3. Adequate as a spouse, gets more satisfactions than frustrations out of it.
4. Adequate as a spouse, gets positive satisfaction out of it.
5. Adequate as a spouse, the relationship is growing.[59]

Jourard's assessment of the "ideal" state of marriage portrayed what he believed to be the implicit condition of health: not a static state of achievement, but a dynamic state of continuous progress. This stood in sharp contrast to cultural illusions about happy marriages, which dictated that they be eternally romantic and consistently conflict-free.

Maslow had been consulted on Jourard's work, and in touting its value, he leveraged his own academic reputation to support the scientific risk Jourard was taking by moving into this realm.[60] While Maslow's 1950 study of self-actualizers had been risky, it had softened psychologists a bit on unconventional attempts to quantify health. The numerous psychological studies that followed up on Maslow's pilot study—many performed by researchers unknown to Maslow—supported his initial hypotheses.

They demonstrated substantial overlap in the identifiable qualities of self-actualized or healthy individuals, which suggested there was something valid and repeatable about these rather preliminary theories. Even Thomas Szasz, a reputable psychiatrist with a firm foundation in medical science, was ultimately convinced by the early 1960s that Maslow wasn't just arbitrarily creating notions of sickness and health as good and bad.[61]

While Jourard had forged his theories of healthy characteristics from his intuition, and Maslow had drawn on his observations of healthy friends and historical figures, Rogers garnered his impressions from his clinical work. In 1962, in a collection aimed at educational reform, Rogers described these observations, noting that the healthy individual seemed increasingly open to experience, and decreasingly defensive. He exemplified this point in an excerpt from a session in which his "client" began to find himself more open to his bodily experiences (of pain, exhaustion, and pleasure) as he got healthier. The healthy individual, he argued, had a fuller sense of being, an engagement with the *process* of existence, and an acceptance of life's fluid nature. A patient might experience this as a sense of forever becoming more himself, reorganizing and integrating himself even beyond the point at which therapy ends. Rogers also noticed that a healthy individual possessed a holistic self-trust; rather than confining decisions to the head, the heart, or specific data, the healthy individual would rely on his own experience, his total reaction, to dictate his direction. He likened this process to the method by which a computer instantaneously takes in all input, weighs it, and offers an approximation of the best way to meet its varied needs.[62]

The outlines of health offered by Rogers, Jourard, and Maslow differed somewhat in their specifics, but the substantial areas in which they overlapped constituted the very ground of humanistic psychology. These ideas were the basis of a super-structure of human potential. Taken as a whole, and interpreted beyond their descriptive detail, they suggested the possibilities of human existence, the goals for a good and meaningful life.

Humanistic psychologists' overarching view of human nature was simple in its form, but complex in its implications. To summarize it concisely, it was the romanticist belief that people are good. Most humanistic psychologists, Rollo May excepted, felt that humans were innately driven toward wholeness, and that their underlying nature was positive.[63] Rather than thinking that pathology, or even evil, naturally arose from individuals, they saw it as a product of an unhealthy environment. Their concept of human nature evoked Rousseau's notion that the natural state of man was characterized by a generative self-love (*amour de soi*), and uncorrupted by a socially imposed, competitive pride (*amour-propre*). Although they tended to subscribe to Freud's concept of the unconscious, they refused to define id impulses as "dark" and expanded these desires to include those for creation, inspiration, humor, and love.[64]

This positively oriented view of human nature served as the basis of a humanistic theory of individual motivation. Unimpeded, most humanistic psychologists believed, individuals would strive for self-actualization (according to Maslow, though, about 98 percent of us would be impeded). Evidence of this upward striving appeared repeatedly in psychotherapy, Rogers and others argued, where the creation of a healthy environment eroded obstacles to higher motivations, and helped to revise prior negative experiences that had blocked individuals' true natures from materializing.

In the early years of AAHP, the founding members wrangled over the specifics of the theory of human nature they embraced. For most, ideas of motivation were fairly nuanced, though they didn't depart too dramatically from the previous incarnations of human nature as laid out by psychoanalysts and behaviorists. Charlotte Bühler, for example, attempted to define explicitly these four "basic tendencies" of the individual:

1. Satisfying one's needs (for love, sex, ego, and recognition)
2. Making self-limiting adaptations (by fitting in, belonging, and remaining secure)
3. Moving toward creative expansion (through self-expression and creative accomplishments)
4. Upholding and restoring the inner order (by being true to one's conscience and values)[65]

Bühler's sketch was in line with a variety of theories that had preceded it. The first tendency fit with an id-driven theory of needs gratification as much as it did with Maslow's hierarchy of needs, or a behaviorist's idea of adaptive instincts. The second tendency also aligned with a psychoanalytic perspective, like the one outlined in Freud's *Civilization and Its Discontents*, in which the requirements of existing as an individual within a civilization entailed a fair amount of self-limiting adaptation, and it paralleled the behaviorist theory of environmental conditioning. The last tendency, to uphold and restore inner order, reflected Freud's concept of psychic homeostasis—the balanced tension of the tripartite psyche (id, ego, and superego)—as much as it did Maslow's being values or B-values, which were the highest values derived from peak experiences, including the appreciation of wholeness, beauty, truth, simplicity, and more.

Bühler's third proposition, though, displayed the departure of humanistic theory from the first and second forces of psychology. The idea that it was a basic human tendency to move toward creative expansion (essentially to grow) involved a reenvisioning of the individual in a bold, new light, and was difficult even for many within humanistic psychology to accept. This was partly because the proposition didn't resonate with everyone's experience. Where was the darkness, the cracks, the pathos? Hadn't we all met, in others or ourselves, evil, or at least extreme shittiness? It was also troubling, to many, because it seemed to lead away from an ethic of individual responsibility: if all negative behaviors were the consequence of the environment distorting the intrinsic goodness of the individual, then were people ever really at fault for the evil acts they did?

Rogers tended to see the matter most simplistically. For him, evil behaviors originated from cultural influences. "I see members of the human species," wrote Rogers in a correspondence with Rollo May, "as *essentially* constructive in their fundamental nature, but damaged by their experience."[66] This idea was appealing, in part because it made evil acts seem preventable, controllable. It offered an alternative, in the world that Hitler made, to the idea that the dark side of human nature knew no bounds. And it took the blame off individuals, allowing for a practice like psychotherapy to absolve them of their guilt.

When it came to human nature, Maslow also agreed that people were basically good, or could be made good. "Good social conditions," he wrote, "are necessary for personal growth, bad social conditions stunt human nature . . ."[67] But for Maslow, the equation was never as straightforward as it was for Rogers. He criticized Rogers, in fact, for being too simplistic. "Rogers doesn't have enough sin, evil, & psychopathology in his system," he wrote in his journal. "He speaks of the only drive as self-actualization, which is to imply there is only a tendency to health."[68] Maslow feared that Rogers was being Pollyannaish, and that it was irresponsible to disentangle negative actions from the conglomerated self. Health, after all, entailed an acceptance of our imperfection, rather than a sanding off (or denial) of our rough edges.

Rollo May was an even harsher critic. He saw Rogers's ideas as seductive, but dangerously naïve. Pathology, like health, he felt, was a product of the individual, and viewing destructive behavior solely as a product of culture didn't make sense. Cultures consisted of people, he argued, and to construct them as outside forces acting on individuals was illogical. More likely, he felt, culture reflected individuals themselves. It contained good and evil components, productive and destructive elements. "Yes, the culture admittedly has powerful effects on us," wrote May to Rogers. "But it could not have these effects were these tendencies not already present in us, for, I repeat, we constitute the culture."[69] May also suggested that positive change could only emerge from individual change, and did not exist as a disembodied cultural current that would sweep us all along.

Rogers's assumption that people were good was unreconcilable with much of May's theory, which rested on the idea of the productive value of negative emotion. May preferred to characterize the individual by the concept of the daimonic—"the urge in every being to affirm itself, assert itself, perpetuate and increase itself." "If the daimonic is integrated into personality," wrote May, "it results in creativity, is constructive." The unintegrated daimonic would result in destructive behavior.[70]

Although at odds, Rogers's and May's perspectives both effectively pointed to the potential cultural value of psychotherapy as a human practice, and to the potential value of focusing on the individual's capacity for health (rather than on her deficits). Rogers felt the psychotherapeutic relationship could heal by acting as a corrective to an individual's unhealthy relationship to the culture. Healthy conditions in therapy had the power to negate negative cultural influences, enabling people to realize their true potential and to thrive. At the same time, May held that psychotherapy could serve as an integrating force, channeling our daimonic energies toward positive ends. Essential to this integration, however, was a balanced view of the individual, an affirmation of his positive *and* negative emotions. A Rogerian therapist, May feared, might fail to validate an individual's angry and aggressive feelings. By being too nice and cheery, a therapist might also deprive an individual of an object against which to work out some of his negative emotions.[71]

The differences in Rogers's and May's perspectives on human nature were emblematic of fissures built into the movement. Although it was possible to make generalizations about humanistic psychology (it was positively oriented, health- and growth-focused, interested in innate strivings toward one's potential), in 1962 the specifics were up for grabs. Early meetings were directed toward a unifying vision, but there were times when the movement resembled little more than a pastiche of overlapping but ultimately dissimilar theories.

Recognizing the difficulty of unifying the fledgling movement in the direction of cohesive theory, Gordon Allport wrote, "all of us [. . .] sense significant pattern, maybe few central qualities."[72] The lack of a cohesive theory made it easy for adherents to pick and choose the elements that best justified their own designs. Just as many Americans had excerpted from psychoanalysis the elements that best aligned with their own interests (the importance of early childhood, the rational division of the mind, individual solutions to collective problems) while downplaying the most dissonant aspects (childhood sexuality, the death instinct), those interested in humanistic psychology would find in the 1960s the opportunity to interpret humanistic psychology in ways that validated even their baser interests (their self-absorption, their hedonism, even their denial of harsh social realities).[73]

5

Eupsychian Visions

"I've had only one idea in my life—a true idée fixe. To
put it as bluntly as possible—the idea of having my own
way. 'Control' expresses it. The control of human
behavior. In my early experimental days it was a
frenzied, selfish desire to dominate. I remember the rage
I used to feel when a prediction went awry. I could have
shouted at the subjects of my experiments, 'Behave,
damn you! Behave as you ought!'"

T. E. FRAZIER IN B. F. SKINNER'S *Walden Two*[1]

Most humanistic psychologists weren't shy about their idealism.
At the extreme they were starry-eyed, brimming with optimism, gushing about the possibility of remaking the world as
they knew it. More typically they were optimistic but methodical, interested in defining the upper limits of human potential,
and driven by the conviction that a positive focus to psychology
would restore balance to a field that had gone too far in the direction of pathology. Both average and extreme humanistic psychologists entered the 1960s as cultural nonentities, but they
did so with the confidence that their visions could compete in a
marketplace saturated with revolutionary visions.

Sociologist C. Wright Mills captured the tone of the new decade's revolutionary energy in his "Letter to the New Left," at the same time that he rejected the tendency to dismiss idealists as delusional and naïve. " 'Utopian' nowadays I think refers to any criticism or proposal that transcends the up-close milieu of a scatter of individuals: the milieu which men and women can understand directly and which they can reasonably hope directly to change," he wrote. "In this exact sense, our theoretical work is indeed utopian—in my own case, at least, deliberately so. What needs to be understood, and what needs to be changed, is not merely first this and then that detail of some institution or policy."[2] By aiming high, by taking on problems larger than themselves, activists and intellectuals like Mills hoped to achieve more than they would if they were to traffic in the smaller parcels of specific problems. The plan for the New Left movements was the plan for humanistic psychology: to have grander aspirations, keener vision, and a broader plan of action.

This kind of utopianism animated Maslow. He defended, on numerous occasions, the value of setting an ideal of optimal functioning to which individuals could aspire. He tried, in exhaustive lists and endless publications, to enumerate the qualities of self-actualization for which individuals should always be striving. He tried as well to develop a useful vision of utopia, which he termed "Eupsychia."

Eupsychia, as Maslow conceived it, was a society that would hypothetically come into existence when a thousand psychologically healthy families migrated to a desert island. Although Maslow didn't claim to know the specifics of what this would look like, he knew a couple of things. The society would be philosophically anarchistic, Taoistic but loving, governed by tolerance and free choice, and lacking in violence and control.

It would succeed mainly because, when given the ability to choose, healthy individuals would draw on their innate ability to make the right choices.[3]

How would Eupsychia be attained? With his answer, Maslow struck the same note for the society that Rogers struck for the individual: the promotion of growth-fostering conditions, unconditional positive regard, acceptance, understanding. "The implicit theory in Eupsychian ethics," he wrote, "is that if you trust people, give them freedom, affection, dignity, etc., then their higher nature will unfold & appear."[4]

Maslow believed that a Eupsychian society was possible and that American culture could move toward this prospect. It wouldn't be a perfect place. It would be full of self-actualizers who were themselves flawed. "They too are equipped with silly, wasteful, or thoughtless habits," he wrote. "They can be boring, stubborn, irritating. They are by no means free from a rather superficial vanity, pride, partiality to their own productions, family, friends, and children. Temper outbursts are not rare. [They] are occasionally capable of an extraordinary and unexpected ruthlessness." He also described them as, at times, possessing a surgical coldness, a lack of social graces, as well as absentmindedness, guilt, anxiety, and internal strife.[5]

This wasn't your ordinary utopia. It was less fantastical, more grounded.[6] Maslow didn't want to be an irresponsible idealist, and described his aversion to "perfectionists, the sick ones in the Freudian sense, destructivists, nihilists, the ones who could never conceivably be satisfied by anything actual because it can never live up to the perfect fantasies in their heads."[7] He was clear that his cultural ideal would be attained not when everyone achieved perfection, but when everyone was striving toward it.

Like other utopians, however, he failed to offer solutions to the obvious difficulties with creating such a society. How would health be attained in the first place, in order that it might promulgate more health? What would a healthy society look like on a day-to-day basis? And how could such abstract ideals take material shape in societal operations?

Maslow's Eupsychia was most useful as a thought experiment. As unattainable as it seemed, it served a practical purpose. It was an imagined society that could help concretize our collective ideals and serve as a measuring stick against which to assess our current culture. He explained that "the word Eupsychia can also be taken in other ways. It can mean 'moving toward psychological health' or 'healthward.' It can imply the actions taken to foster and encourage such a movement, whether by a psychotherapist or a teacher. It can refer to the mental or social conditions which make health more likely. Or it can be taken as an ideal limit; i.e., the far goals of therapy, education or work."[8]

In this sense, Eupsychia straddled the tension between the lofty and the practical, and it did so in a way that compelled the kinds of Americans who were notoriously pragmatic and idealistic at the same time. One Pacifica Radio interviewer exemplified the typical public interest in Maslow's theory. In his 1962 interview, he paid a disproportionate amount of attention to Maslow's ideas about good societies, at the expense of inquiries into his more systematic work.[9] This skewed fascination served as an impediment to the concretization of his more abstract insights and far-flung musings.

Liberal radio and its cultural equivalents were not ideal instruments for transcending Maslow's abstraction. Interestingly, Maslow found the corporate world a preferable environment in which to make his theory practicable. In the early 1960s, his warmest reception came from executives who were invested in making their employees happier and more productive. Business, much more than psychotherapy, seemed to be a realm in which he could really pin down what his ideas would look like implemented.

As humanistic psychologists worked, in the early years of the movement, to bring their lofty ideas down to earth, and to forge a unified vision out of many disparate views of health, human nature, motivation, and behavior, they were helped tremendously by having an adversary. B. F. Skinner, whose theories were enormously popular in the 1950s and 1960s, was the spokesman for a modern form of behaviorism. His "radical behaviorism" was a departure from Watson's methodological approach. It didn't abnegate consciousness, feelings, and mental states as Watson's theory had; rather, it relegated them to other forms of inquiry, and other schools of psychology.

Skinner's experimental analysis of behavior (EAB) tried neither to unravel the causes of behavior (which he considered a concoction of all prior conditioning, too complex to be distilled), nor to account for its products (perceptions and emotions, which others mistook to be the "causes" of behavior). Rather, it aimed to understand, and *change*, specific behavioral responses.[10]

It was in the potential for behavioral change that the charm (and the threat) of this form of behaviorism resided. Radical behaviorism's highly pragmatic and rational nature appealed uniquely to Americans; it reflected their modern interests in the advancement of automation and mass production.

"The new need for rote, repetitive responses on assembly lines," writes one psychologist, "promulgated support for a psychology that promised a technology of manipulation and control of such actions."[11] It also resonated with their residual progressivist commitments, symbolized as an inclination to optimize social betterment through objective findings.[12]

Radical behaviorism, like humanistic psychology, also responded meaningfully to Americans' feelings of postwar vulnerability. It offered a technology that was so rational it could reorder (and improve) our daily lives on its way to reordering the world.

The technologies of behaviorism were concrete in a way that other products of psychology couldn't hope to be. Skinner's concept of keeping a baby, throughout the day and night, in an "air crib," for example—a practice he described in *Ladies' Home Journal*—promised a happy, well-adjusted baby and at the same time offered to save young mothers time, effort, and stress. The crib looked something like a fish tank. It was temperature controlled (so the baby could always remain unclothed and unswaddled), had a rolling bottom sheet that could be cranked when soiled, and featured a large pane of safety glass (through which the child could be viewed and smiled at).[13]

Like the humanistic psychologists, Skinner was a utopian, and a human liberationist. He wanted the application of behavioral science to rank among the scientific achievements whose products had yielded "the design and construction of a world which has freed [man] from constraints and vastly extended his range."[14] His vision, which paralleled Maslow's thought experiment with Eupsychia, was transmitted to the public in his novel *Walden Two*.

The book, which eventually sold well over a million copies, describes a thousand-person technological utopia called Walden Two, in which efficiency, and the satisfaction it brings, have been literally engineered by a psychology professor named T. E. Frazier.[15] In this experimental community no one works more than four hours a day, all income is shared, and the burden of cooking and housework is dispersed among the members. People are happy, productive, and creative. They are even better looking.

"Here we are not so much at the mercy of commercial designers," explains Frazier, "and many of our women manage to appear quite beautiful simply because they are not required to dress within strict limits."[16]

Behavioral control, in Walden Two, originates with six Planners who can be neither elected nor impeached, and members are governed by a group of managers who are selected by the Planners. The social management techniques they employ affect the lives of members in every way, extending from the control of minute details (like the shape of teacups) to the management of reproductive choices (the community encourages rigorous population growth, with children in their teens encouraged to procreate).

The kind of engineering Skinner dramatized was, to judge from the book's sales, appealing to many readers. It was also profoundly threatening for several reasons. First, it didn't feel real, but rather contrived, inauthentic. Also, for Americans, who valued supremely their sense of uniqueness and capacity for self-determination, Walden Two seemed to strip them of their autonomy, reducing them to the status of rats in a maze. Skinner didn't necessarily understand this charge. "There is this

strange feeling," he mused, "that if you deny the individual freedom or deny an interpretation of the individual based upon
freedom and personal responsibility that somehow or other the
individual vanishes."[17] For Skinner, an individual could experience freedom at the same time that he was being controlled.
This happened all the time, he argued, to greater or lesser ex-
tents.

For many Americans, control existed on a spectrum that
ranged from relative autonomy to intensifying levels of intervention. While they were able to accept that their driving was
controlled by laws designed to ensure their safety, they preferred
to think their reproductive decisions, food choices, and career
choices were entirely self-determined. The exercise of overt control in these realms stank of totalitarianism. By disavowing a
democratic philosophy of human nature, many feared Skinner
was undermining democracy itself.[18]

Discussing the book in the sixties with Carl Rogers, Skinner recognized the public aversion to the extent of control he
described. "People object violently to the scene in *Walden Two*,"
he explained, "in which the children are to wear lollipops
around their necks but are not to touch them with their tongues
during the day." He defended, however, this way of educating
people in moral and ethical self-control. And he argued that,
despite what Americans chose to believe, bravery could be
taught: people could be conditioned to "take necessary painful
stimuli without flinching" and "not be disturbed by what would
otherwise be terribly emotional circumstances."[19] All societies,
Skinner argued, were behavioral experiments. What differed
was the consciousness with which they were planned. Greater
levels of intentionality, he felt, could reduce the potential misuse of behavioral technologies.

Maslow's Eupsychia, in contrast, allowed for a level of chaos that threatened its failure. If Rogers and others were right that, unhindered, humans would produce solely positive products (Maslow wasn't sure), Eupsychia might succeed. But if negative tendencies had any innate basis, and if even healthy individuals wrestled with, and on occasion fell victim to, their demons, such a loosely configured society couldn't possibly succeed. Rogers's ethic of growth-promoting characteristics might work in the psychotherapists' office, but could it succeed in the culture at large?

In 1962, radical behaviorism went toe-to-toe with humanistic psychology in a debate between Carl Rogers and B. F. Skinner titled "Education and the Control of Human Behavior."[20] In addition to providing an elucidation of two very different perspectives on psychological practice, the meeting represented a war of worldviews, a clash in visions of the future of society with implications that seemed to extend to the lives of every one of the five-hundred-plus people in attendance. The main points of contention centered on the concept of freedom, the value of subjective experience, and the requirements of treating individuals humanely.

Rogers started out on the offensive, constructing behaviorism as a grave threat to individual freedom and to subjectivity. "There seems to be no doubt," he said, "that the behavioral sciences will move steadily in the direction of making man an object to himself, a complex sequence of events no different in kind from the complex chain of equations by which various chemical substances interact to form new substances or to release energy." This self-objectification was to Rogers the death of the individual. It was also antagonistic to the form of psychotherapy he so highly valued, or really to any form of psychotherapy (Skinner had no interest in such insight-based talking cures).

Rogers attempted to convey to Skinner the goals of client-centered therapy, which he described as "a self-initiated process of learning to be free." "Clients move away," he explained, "from being driven by inner forces they do not understand, away from fear and distrust of these deep feelings and of themselves, and away from living by values they had taken from others." At the same time, they move toward introspection, self-acceptance, and self-worth. In the ideal situation, their new values will be based on their own inner experience, rather than prior environmental learning.[21]

Skinner, of course, refused to accept this picture of the unencumbered, internally motivated, insight-driven individual. He didn't see individual behavior as separable from learning. We are not, he felt, deprogrammable in that way. He also categorically denied the value of introspection in behavioral understanding and behavioral change, going so far as to discredit his own perceptions of his inner states. "I would put more faith," he told Rogers, "in someone else's proof that I had been angry toward you than I would in evidence from my own inner feelings."[22]

This perspective was, no doubt, shocking to his audience. How could we conceive of a world in which our own thoughts and perceptions (our reality!) were not to be trusted? One clear advantage that Rogers held over Skinner, in gaining popular acceptance, was that the subjective experience of insight just felt true. Adopting a blanket mistrust of our inner world, and leaving knowledge of our own minds to detached scientific experts, felt like an abdication of our power, our autonomy, our self-possession. In this respect, it was determinism to the nth degree.

Rogers argued, further, that behaviorism not only imperiled our sense of self and our belief in the veracity of our own perceptions, but also jeopardized our social principles. It was opposed, he argued, to the goals of liberal democracy—self-determination, equal access and participation, civil liberties, and human rights—and threatened instead a dehumanizing and dictatorial control. "To the extent that a behaviorist point of view in psychology is leading us toward a disregard of the person, toward treating persons primarily as manipulable objects, toward control of the person by shaping his behavior without his participant choice, or toward minimizing the significance of the subjective—to that extent I question it very deeply," argued Rogers.[23]

In his response, Skinner accused Rogers of naïveté and challenged his evasion of their shared assumptions about the current cultural predicament. We have already, he argued, created a world in which we are controlled, governed, employed, and hired, and the issue at stake is not *whether* or not we are controlled, but whether that control is punitive and surreptitious or health-promoting. Skinner's goal was social control based on a knowledge of human behavior and a sensitivity to the human condition.[24] He didn't refute Rogers's allegation that he was discarding a democratic philosophy of human nature. In fact, his argument implicitly opposed the idea that our society could be called democratic in the first place.

Skinner's undemocratic philosophy was hard for many to stomach. In spite of the clear distinctions he drew, its mechanisms were reminiscent of fascism, and its disavowal of the significance of the self-determining individual ran against the tide Rogers and others had identified as sweeping the culture in the early 1960s. Although behaviorism had dominated American psychology for more than fifty years, there were signs that it was injured, or even dying. Humanistic psychologists had moved in from one direction, employing a rhetoric that harmonized with modern cultural concerns and garnering more and more professional attention, while cognitivists had attacked from another angle.

The cognitive revolution marked the gradual displacement of the behaviorist paradigm by an interdisciplinary movement bridging psychology, anthropology, and linguistics (cognitive science). Cognitivists' main critique of behaviorism was that it unnecessarily excluded consideration of what was going on inside the mind. This exclusion had had practical consequences. During World War II, for instance, behaviorists had failed to provide practical assistance in training soldiers to use complex equipment, and in dealing with the attentional deficits that resulted from battle-related stress.[25] After the war, they had little to say about how to treat the debilitating anxiety that characterized many shell-shocked soldiers.

More significant, for cognitivists, was what they saw as the theoretical and empirical weakness of behaviorism's position. In his proclamatory statement, Watson had discarded all references to consciousness, perception, sensation, purpose, motivation, thinking, and emotion.[26] He'd argued that mental processes were scientifically unknowable and, moreover, that everything worth knowing could be deduced from observation of behavior. Beginning around 1956, cognitivists took on both propositions, arguing that it was not only possible but productive to make testable inferences about mental processes.[27]

George Miller was the first to gain recognition for espousing the new approach. His *Psychological Review* article "The Magical Number Seven, Plus or Minus Two," summarized several studies of the effective reorganization of mental processes, specifically related to the expansion of short-term memory.[28] In 1958 David Broadbent's *Perception and Communication* challenged behaviorist learning theory with an information-processing model.[29] And in 1959, in one of the most significant moments in academic history, Noam Chomsky published "A Review of B. F. Skinner's Verbal Behavior," which took apart the behaviorist idea of language as a learned habit and, in the process, essentially ended the reign of behaviorism.[30]

While the interests of cognitive psychologists differed from those of humanistic psychologists, they weren't antagonistic. Albert Ellis, an applied psychologist who forged a technique of cognitive therapy in the late 1950s, had a foot in both worlds. He was involved in AAHP's founding and considered himself a humanistic psychologist, though he also recognized that the meaning of that self-description varied widely.[31] In 1947 he had received, like Rogers and May, a doctorate from Teachers College, Columbia, where he had begun to develop a critique of behaviorist methods and psychoanalytic techniques. He had more cleanly broken from psychoanalysis in 1953, and began calling himself a "rational therapist."[32]

Like the founders of humanistic psychology, Ellis subscribed to the guiding concepts of self-actualization (he believed all humans possess an innate motivation for reaching their potential) and the idea that individuals could determine their emotional fate.[33] His applied techniques, however, differed markedly from the client-centered approach that came to dominate humanistic psychology. His work with patients was directive; he helped them to identify their self-defeating and irrational beliefs and behaviors, and to replace them systematically with more rational ideas through a form of self-talk. He began to teach this technique in the 1950s, formally proposed his theory in the latter part of the decade, and altered it somewhat in the 1960s in connection with Aaron Beck's cognitive-behavioral therapy. While his methods fit under the umbrella of humanistic psychology in the early 1960s, a time when the field of psychotherapy was still firmly dominated by psychoanalysis and all other approaches had to band together for recognition, cognitive therapy would become firmly established in the 1970s, and, by the 1980s, would be king.

Though cognitivism had begun to challenge behaviorism in the late 1950s, Skinner himself, when asked in 1987 what had happened to behaviorism, contended that the ascendance of humanistic psychology (specifically as incarnated in Rogers, Maslow, and others) had been the greatest factor in its demise.[34]

If Skinner was right that humanistic psychology was the agent of behaviorism's destruction, you wouldn't have known it from looking at the average psychology department in the early 1960s. While humanistic ideas began to leach out into the wider culture almost at the moment of the movement's founding, they met many obstacles to acceptance from American academic psychologists—a group that tended to be resistant to utopian thinking, slow to respond to intellectual paradigm shifts, and slower still to open up their definitions of science to revision.

Although Maslow and Rogers continued to publish at a fever pitch, and remained determined to reach intellectual audiences and generate acceptably rigorous scientific research, they experienced their academic positions as increasingly stultifying. Within their universities, they tended to feel unsupported, intellectually and financially. As early as 1959, Maslow wrote, "Very pleasant to be a big shot but doesn't do my Brandeis salary much good. Nor can I get my papers published. Nor do grad students do my work for me."[35]

Although Maslow would continue to publish in a way that more than fulfilled the expectations of a tenured professor, he grew increasingly impatient with performing the kind of science his peers seemed to expect. The frequency with which he proposed unconventional new theories without testing them was increasing. "It's just that I haven't got the time to do careful experiments myself," wrote Maslow. "They take too long, in view of the years that I have left and the extent of what I want to do. So I myself do only 'quick-and-dirty' little pilot explorations, mostly with a few subjects only, inadequate to publish but enough to convince myself that they are probably true and will be confirmed one day. Quick little commando raids, guerrilla attacks."[36]

Maslow did publish many of these pilot explorations, albeit with disclaimers about their methodological shortcomings and the necessity of further testing (by others).[37] "At present," wrote Maslow, "the only alternative is simply to refuse to work with the problem." He apologized, in his study of self-actualizers, to those who "insist on conventional reliability, validity, sampling, etc.[38] For the most part the apology wasn't accepted.

Maslow felt most appreciated outside of psychology departments. In 1961, he spent a sabbatical semester at a privately funded institute, the Western Behavioral Sciences Institute (WBSI) in La Jolla, California, where engineer-entrepreneur

Andrew Kay funded his fellowship.[39] The following year, he accepted another invitation from Kay to spend the summer consulting for his corporation, Non-Linear Systems, a plant at which workers assembled digital voltmeters (instruments for measuring the electric potential difference between two points in an electric circuit). Maslow was paid handsomely to visit the plant once a week, collecting his perceptions of management techniques and employee satisfaction and applying his theory of motivation in recommendations for increasing employee satisfaction.[40]

Rogers had been comparably dissatisfied with academia. Having accepted a research position at the University of Wisconsin in 1957, he spent the next several years in escalating conflict with his colleagues. In January of 1963 Rogers sent a memorandum to the faculty indicating his inclination to leave the university and describing his dissatisfaction with the department's "fixed policies and philosophy."[41]

The same year, Rogers received an offer from WBSI. Though he had turned down similar offers before, Rogers began to rethink his position. He wrote, "What was a university, at this stage in my career, offering me? I realized in my research it offered no particular help; in anything educational, I was forced to fit my beliefs into a totally alien mold; in stimulation, there was little from my colleagues because we were so far apart in thinking and in goals."[42]

Compelled by the absence of "bureaucratic entanglements," the "stimulation of a thoroughly congenial interdisciplinary group," and what he saw as the superiority of the group's educational model, Rogers accepted the offer from WBSI, leaving Wisconsin in 1964.[43] Among his new senior colleagues were Lawrence Solomon, a humanistic psychologist who insisted on the necessity of upholding the intellectual standards of humanistic psychology, and Sigmund Koch, a former behaviorist who had developed humanistic leanings while putting together a six-volume report, commissioned by the APA, on American psychology's first fifty years.[44]

In addition to offering exceptional peer support, WBSI provided a hospitable environment for innovation and creativity in research, and thus for the execution of truly humanistic science. In a letter to his friends in 1963, Rogers wrote of WBSI, "It offers the complete and untrammeled freedom for creative thought of which every scholar dreams. I will have no obligation except to be a creative contributor to a new, congenial, pioneering organization."[45] WBSI director Richard Farson wrote that the institute's "independence enabled it to avoid the limiting effects of the politics of knowledge that dominate establishment institutions, often closing down the investigation of unconventional thinking."[46] Independent research institutes also freed researchers from rigid expectations about consistent and measured contributions to their fields. Farson wrote that even beyond the impossibility of exercising "groundbreaking creativity" within universities, their sheer size was a major impediment to the production of novel theory, as "scale is the enemy of innovation."[47] Rogers agreed and explained to his friends that "this new emphasis in psychology—a humanistic, person-centered trend—has not had a chance to flower in University departments."[48]

In spite of the significant advantages of affiliation with independent research institutes like WBSI, however, the disadvantages were also numerous. The biggest problem was that they further estranged innovative thought from mainstream academia, thus reducing its ability to effect meaningful change in the field. The maintenance of university affiliation forced humanistic psychologists to try, at least occasionally, to change minds within the system, a dynamic that had been key to the influence of scholars like William James and Gordon Allport.[49]

Private institutes also gave researchers license to disregard even the most valid constraints of academic psychology. Without institutionally imposed standards for the content and methodology of scientific experimentation, many researchers took more liberties. Some went to extremes in this regard. Stanley Krippner, for example, was compelled by the powerful pull of the experiential, transcendental, and transpersonal. Krippner, who had earned his PhD from Northwestern University in 1961 and taught and directed a child-study center at Kent State for several years, transferred to the Maimonides Medical Center Dream Laboratory in 1964.[50] He soon located himself on the outskirts even of humanistic psychology, pursuing investigations of parapsychology and telepathy.[51]

Most humanistic psychologists, though, were rooted enough in their training, and committed enough to the idea of revising psychological science to be more inclusive of humanistic methods, to continue pursuing "reputable" science even at the new institutes. Abraham Maslow expressed his hope that what was then called "humanistic psychology" would one day just be called "psychology."[52]

6

Resacralizing Science

"So great good can come out of nutty precursors who dimly see a real truth but in a crapped-up form. Progress is partly in reworking the crap & rephrasing in a *more* scientific way the truths that were mixed up with chaff."

ABRAHAM MASLOW[1]

The questions of how to be scientific and how scientific to be loomed large for humanistic psychologists from the start. They knew that to speak to other academics, to influence professionals, to push the whole of American psychology in a positive new direction, they had to live in the real world, which meant they had to keep themselves from getting too far up in their heads, too theoretical, too ungroundedly idealistic. In addition to formalizing their scientific commitments and concretizing their approach, they needed to conduct scientific studies that built on the foundations of prior research. And they needed to publish them.

At the same time, however, humanistic psychologists

hoped to revise orthodox science. They proposed a "resacralized" vision of science, in which the "idiotic" pursuit of singular scientific truths had ceased, and in which personal value commitments openly guided research.[2] This practice would be more inclusive of human experience and human potential, and would be built on methods intended to capture the complexity of complete individuals rather than reduce them to their components. It would be directed at practical ends, bridging abstract theory and applications, always mindful that the usefulness of a theory was the supreme marker of its value.

Among the founders, Carl Rogers was the model of this new form of science, combining a carefulness in his methods with an honesty about his goals. He devised a scale to measure process change in psychotherapy; he created and tested a personal adjustment inventory; he performed several methodologically sound studies of psychotherapeutic outcomes with schizophrenics.[3] At the Western Behavioral Sciences Institute, he conducted extensive research on the efficacy of his client-centered approach and of group psychotherapy.[4] He broadcast his work far and wide, publishing six books between 1962 and 1972, as well as over fifty articles. Even Maslow, who could be fiercely critical of Rogers, was impressed by the rigor of his research, and grateful for the legitimacy it lent to the movement. "My respect for Rogers," wrote Maslow, "grows & grows because of his researches."[5]

Maslow's case was more complicated. He was undeniably prolific: over the course of the 1960s, he published three books (*Toward a Psychology of Being* in 1962, *Religions, Values, and Peak-Experiences* in 1964, and *Eupsychian Management* in 1965), and more than fifty articles. But by this point in his career he no longer performed scientific studies, and no longer wanted to.

In his journal, he tended to blame his students and his peers for not following up on his theory of human motivation with solid empirical testing.[6] Only in his darker moments did he blame himself.[7]

The ideological, if not the practical, priority early humanistic psychologists placed on science was displayed at their first invitational conference, an event they came to see as their "founding moment." The Old Saybrook Conference, which took place in the coastal town of Old Saybrook, Connecticut, and lasted from Friday, November 28, to Sunday, November 30, 1964, consisted of seven presentations and a panel discussion, all related to the science of humanistic psychology.

The conference was organized by Robert Knapp, a professor of psychology at Wesleyan University, and supported by the fundraising efforts of Victor Butterfield, the president of Wesleyan, who was also in attendance.[8] It was held at the Saybrook Inn, an elegant resort with abundant views of boats docked on coastal waters, several smoky bars, and plenty of quiet spaces in which to lay the intellectual foundations of humanistic psychology. Additional sessions were held on the Wesleyan campus, which was a thirty-minute drive from Old Saybrook.[9]

The meetings—like many such conferences of the time—consisted of a bunch of academic *guys*. The lynchpins of humanistic psychology were all present: Carl Rogers, Abe Maslow, Rollo May, Gordon Allport, Gardner Murphy, Henry Murray, James Bugental, Clark Moustakas, and Sidney Jourard, as well as soon-to-be-central figures like Miles Vich (future editor of the *Journal of Humanistic Psychology*). But nonpsychologists were represented, too. In addition to Butterfield, Jacques

Barzun—the dean of Columbia University—was present, as were a phenomenologist from Cornell, a cultural historian from Berkeley, and a biologist from Rockefeller University. Of the psychologists present, the majority identified as social and personality psychologists, though most performed clinical work as well.[10] Only two women participated: Charlotte Bühler, then a practicing psychologist in California, and Norma Rosenquist, the first organizational secretary for the American Association of Humanistic Psychology.

The tone of the conference was, predictably, intellectual and relatively subdued: it bore little resemblance to the radically experiential gatherings that would take place under the umbrella of humanistic psychology in the years to come.[11] It followed the standard format of an academic conference. However, the participants later described it as having a spark that was missing from most gatherings of its kind. The speakers were impassioned. At their best, they were provocative, incisive, and even inspiring.

Henry Murray, who was known for his piquant critiques of academic psychology, didn't disappoint. He opened the conference on Friday night with an unconventional keynote address/performance, titled "A Preliminary Sub-Symposium." In it, he divided his own persona into three alters who argued about the purpose and future of humanistic psychology.

The first, Si, represented the type of humanistic psychologist who thought that by developing a unified theory, the movement could singularly deliver the field of psychology from the "Land of Bondage" (academic departments of psychology). Si himself had attempted to sift through the "immense output" of his productive colleagues to find the common ground on which humanistic psychology could rest.

The second alter, Mo, symbolized the naïve belief that humanistic psychology would be readily accepted as a complement to other scientific disciplines (physics and chemistry) and psychological approaches (behaviorism) and that it would build on rather than negate prior insights. He was a general researcher who had never taken a psychology course nor been subjected to the "initiation rites and mutilations" of the discipline.

The third alter, Dy, synthesized the ideas of the others, arguing for the necessity of engaging in genuine dialogue in order to arrive at a functional conception of humanistic psychology. "We are accustomed in our business," he explained, "to polylogues, monologues, and long-winded monopologues such as Mo indulges in, but not to two-person confrontation, veritable dialogues."[12] Dy wisely argued for the necessity of not attaching intractably to one perspective and thereby reproducing the very habit that humanistic psychologists had criticized in others. He reminded his colleagues that they personally needed to cultivate the openness their own theory ascribed to healthy individuals.

Murray's talk introduced the basic challenges that faced humanistic psychology. It would have to depart from conventional academic methods without alienating academicians and students of psychology. At the same time that he displayed his vitriol for academic psychology, "a straight jacket to a man who is yearning for functional autonomy," he recognized the necessity of appealing, in particular, to graduate students. In his notes for the talk, he asked "whether we have anything in our heads that is comparable to the First Force: anything formulated that we can all subscribe to, anything that will appeal to the kind of all-A students that are nowadays selected for admission to our various graduate schools."[13]

Murray's concerns had been gnawing away at him for decades. In 1935, he published "Psychology and the University," a paper in which he offered an extensive critique of the failings of academic psychology. "If psychology is defined as the science which describes people and explains why they perceive, feel, think and act as they do," wrote Murray, "then, properly speaking, no science of the kind exists." He referred to psychologists as "encrusted specialists" from whose "web of activity consideration of man as a human being has somehow escaped." Attacking academic psychology specifically, he argued that researchers had contributed nothing more than "unusable truths."[14]

At Saybrook, Murray expressed his fear that humanistic psychologists, who represented diverse perspectives and approaches, would have trouble righting these wrongs. "How would they come together to form a cohesive vision, with a shared purpose and goals?" he wondered. He also worried that humanistic psychology wouldn't be able to live up to the challenge it had created in defining itself as a "third force." Its theory, its research—its firepower—would have to match that of both behaviorism and psychoanalysis. In his notes for his presentation he indicated his disdain for the term "third force," although he never spoke of the full extent of his condemnation (the lines were crossed out). "It has a militant ring to it," he wrote, "which makes me thing [*sic*] of deGaulle or a stock-pile of conceptual explosives. Isn't it a little premature? a little inflated? a challenge to Nemesis to punish us for intellectual hubris?"[15]

Rollo May saw the challenge differently. He was invigorated by the idea of rivaling the first and second forces. His Saturday morning talk, "Intentionality, The Heart of Human Will," suggested that his own contribution would be one of intellectual weight and substance. He would attempt to back up the grandiose claims of humanistic psychologists, and would try to inspire others to do the same.

May discussed the concept of intentionality, an idea meant to refer not to voluntary *intention*—the aims we are consciously aware of—but to a more holistic conception of both meaning and action that spans the conscious and unconscious. "Intentionality," he explained, "refers to a state of being, and involves to a greater or lesser degree the *totality* of the person's orientation to the world at that time." He argued for its relevance to psychotherapy, and its value in explaining all human action as motivated by a sense of meaning. And he indicted academic psychology for its omission of this concept, claiming that its absence impoverished our understanding of human experience and consciousness.[16]

In advocating for the inclusion of studies of intentionality in the realm of psychology, May argued, by extension, for the use of existential and phenomenological ideas, like those he explored in *Existence*. Such ideas would serve as whetstones against which humanistic psychologists could sharpen the insights they'd arrived at on their own, and they would add weight and depth in those areas where their theories were shallow. They would also, he believed, impart to the young science of humanistic psychology some of the prestige of European philosophy.

May's talk was significant for other reasons, as well. By offering a well-developed and specific model of the humanistic approach, he provided concrete ammunition for combating behaviorism. He urged a more nuanced conception of what academic psychology was lacking. And he presented a humanized conception of psychology that would appeal to Americans, who were invested in both science and subjectivity.

As May described it, phenomenology was noteworthy for

the fullness with which it treated data.[17] In contrast, the mainstream practice of psychology had evolved through a process of exclusion—of various objects of study, of overly subjective data—and a commitment to emulating the natural sciences. The unfortunate products had been a susceptibility to reductionism and a tendency toward logical positivism (manifested in the assumption that value-free singular truths were discernible). These consequences, humanistic psychologists felt, were disastrous for individuals. As psychologist Edward Shoben, who presented just after May, argued, "When a man treats himself as he treats heat, light, and electricity, he denudes himself of the very traits that make him distinctive in the universe, and his efforts at understanding are therefore sharply curtailed."[18]

Psychologists erred as well, Shoben argued, in treating the philosophy of logical positivism as a "*pre*scriptive set of procedural rules." Within these limits, the only problems psychologists were free to tackle were the ones that conformed to the methods they used.[19]

But Shoben wasn't arguing for the devaluation of quantitative methods. In fact, he saw humanistic psychology as promising precisely because of its intention to build on, rather than abandon, these empirical bases.

"Psychology's great opportunity," he said, "lies not in discarding its sturdily expanding methodological apparatus, but in informing it with the humanistic vision, the quest for an even fuller statement of the 'law for man' as against the law of thing. What this transformation most profoundly demands is a revised focus on the source of problems. Rather than coming from the structure of a science modeled on physics, problems could more fruitfully be derived from direct experience—of self, of interpersonal relations, of society, of education and art, of science and religion, etc."[20]

In a similar way, other Saybrook presenters argued for a humanistic psychology that would expand on, rather than discredit, the work that had preceded theirs. This meant, most importantly, that they would build on psychoanalytic and behavioristic theory and research.

Despite the popular misconception that humanistic psychologists intended to discard the insights of previous movements, Maslow aimed for humanistic psychology to be "epi-Freudian," "epi-behavioristic," and "epi-positivistic." By "epi-Freudian," he meant, "building *upon* Freud. Not repudiating, not fighting, not either-or, no loyalties or counter-loyalties. Just taking for granted his clinical discoveries, psychodynamics, etc. insofar as they are true. *Using* them, building upon them the superstructure which they lack. This does *not* involve swallowing any of his mistakes." Comparably, by speaking of "epi-behaviorism" and "epi-positivism," Maslow was asserting that humanistic psychologists should begin with the traditions and insights of academic psychology, and then refine, adopt, reject, replace, or expand upon them according to what they learned through the application of their new methods and theories.[21]

In Carl Rogers's Saturday afternoon speech, he praised the scientific virtues of behaviorism. "I value the concepts which are near and dear to the heart of the behavioral sciences," he said. "The concern with observable behavior, the casting of all variables in operational terms, the adequate testing of hypotheses, the use of increasingly sophisticated design and statistics, all have meaning to me."[22] Rogers described himself as a true scientist—passionate about testing hypotheses, awed by the precision and elegance of empiricism.

His ideal, then, was to balance hard experimental science with complex subjective experience. For him, humanistic psychology existed between the polar extremes of psychoanalysis and behaviorism. It possessed qualities of both, but wasn't a fanaticist's religion. It was moderate, and thus more flexible. It was in dialogue with both sides but rejected the closed systems of the extremes.

Mainstream psychological science, and behaviorism in particular, were, for the founders of humanistic psychology, manifestations of a trend toward reduction, control, and mechanization that they saw as endemic to American culture as a whole. This inclination, many argued, was motivated by 1950s fears related to the degradation of traditional values and the more concrete threat of nuclear annihilation. Behavioral control promised a kind of orderliness that felt safe, but that, in reality, threatened the very nature of human existence. "It appears to me," stated Rogers, "that many of the modern trends would indicate that we are moving inexorably toward a world in which men will be no more than conditioned ants in a gigantic anthill."[23]

Biologist René Dubos, who presented later on Saturday evening, recognized, for good or ill, the tremendous powers that technological advances had granted us, including the ability to alter our lives, manipulate our environment, even change our physiology. He argued that the grave danger of science lay not in the acquisition of these new powers, but in failing to establish positive values to guide them. Without identifying our ideals and taking a stand, he warned, "we shall find ourselves drifting aimlessly toward a state incompatible with the maintenance of the humanistic values from which we derive our uniqueness."[24]

Dubos's presence at Old Saybrook testified to the significance of humanistic psychology to the pressing issues of the time. Dubos, who had begun his career as a soil microbiologist, had earned fame from his contributions to the development of the first antibiotics in the 1940s. In the years that followed he had turned from a "bench" science focused on experimental results to a humanistic science focused on human values.[25] His main interest in the 1960s was in trying to create a science of human nature, one that was sensitive to an individual's environment and sought to define health as creative adaptation.[26]

Although it's unclear how Dubos found his way to the conference, his intellectual and personal affinity for Maslow, Rogers, and others is quite apparent. While his peers in biology sought absolute truths and flew to reductionistic extremes, Dubos kept an eye on the complexity of phenomena, and deemed the assumed rationality and orderliness of the scientific method to be an illusion.[27] His concern for the social context of all science reflected the kinds of concerns Maslow and others prioritized. He urged scientists to identify their personal and social goals, and make "courageous choices" based on subjective judgments and ethical standards before embarking on research.[28]

In a way atypical of a biologist, Dubos viewed good science as contextualized inquiry informed by subjective evaluation. "Indeed, it is commonly stated," he explained at Old Saybrook, "that biology has lost contact with the humanities because it has become too 'scientific' and as a consequence no longer deals with the problems peculiar to the humaneness of man. There is no doubt, of course, about the loss of contact, but the explanation of the difficulty, in my judgment, is that biology is not scientific enough."[29]

The isolation of biology, like the isolation of psychology, indicated to humanistic psychologists a larger cultural trend—one of compartmentalization, dehumanization, reduction. In his Sunday morning presentation, "Humanistic Science and Transcendent Experiences," Maslow described this trend as our present *Weltanschauung*, or worldview. He warned against the dangers of indulging our desire for control, of clinging to a false sense of order and security, of channeling our fears into suspicion and obsession.[30]

Speaking in the generalizations that were becoming more and more characteristic of him, he indicted conventional science, and standard scientific training, for its cowardice and aversion to risk. Normal scientists, he argued, clung too tightly to illusions of objectivity; they were overly cautious, fearful, small, unworthy, stubborn, and obsessive. They were "coral-reef makers rather than eagles."[31] They were a local manifestation of a cultural response to global threats (of nuclear annihilation, racial strife, the dissolution of traditional values) characterized by extreme caution and obsessive fear. They were small men who cowered in bomb shelters rather than trying to remake the world that had caused their fear in the first place.

In contrast, researchers willing to discard orthodox science in favor of a more humanized conception were tall men, able to grasp and generate big ideas.[32] They were "worthy" of great thought. They were models of full human development.

Maslow's comments were self-congratulatory. They were also an expression of uncertainty. He knew he had been bold, and had gone out on a limb with his theory, and he was energized by the risks he had taken.[33] At the same time, though, he suffered from recurrent self-doubt and anxiety. He was wary of the extent to which he subjected himself to scrutiny and laid bare his own insecurities, and knew he couldn't survive long without approval from his peers.[34]

Their pursuit of intuitive convictions put humanistic psychologists in a vulnerable place. And they felt that vulnerability. They also believed, however, that there was a certain honesty in their own admission of subjectivity that was absent in the perspectives of more conventional scientists. After all, they argued, all science rests on subjectivity. By relying on induction and intuition, they weren't doing anything differently from any other scientist. More traditional scientists invoked their own values daily when they decided what to study, how to study it, and how to interpret the results.

"I have come to realize," Rogers stated at Saybrook, "that all science is based on a recognition—usually prelogical, intuitive, involving all the capacities of the organism—of a dimly sensed gestalt, a hidden reality." He saw the intuitive leaps being made by humanistic psychologists as categorically similar to the leaps made by all scientists, when accepting all truths, no matter how "objectively" they were deduced. "All knowledge," claimed Rogers, "including all scientific knowledge, is a vast inverted pyramid resting on [a] tiny, personal subjective base."[35]

These were the kinds of inductive leaps Maslow had called "pre-science." He had argued that all science began on shaky ground, born from common-sense assumptions and the intuitions and values of researchers. As long as researchers were human, we would never be able to distill scientific pursuits to purely objective bases. And it was better, Maslow and Rogers agreed, to honestly identify one's values and potential biases than to allow them to inform research covertly.[36]

The final presenter, a clinical psychologist from Ohio State named George Kelly, again took up the argument for the necessity of the kind of pre-science Maslow was talking about.[37] Scientists needed to be open-minded and flexible, he argued, rather than guided by rigid expectations. He warned against "the notion that we ought always to be right before we commit ourselves," and advocated instead for the creation of an academic climate that would allow researchers to concede mistakes and revise their constructions.[38] The scientific method itself depended on a hypothetical leap, but too many researchers stuck to safe hypotheses that were readily verifiable.

He warned that the entire stimulus-response paradigm, on which psychologists relied so heavily, was overly narrow and would lead to interpretational errors. By relying solely on observable behavior and making the assumption that intentions could be objectively deduced from actions, stimulus-response theorists, he found, often got it totally wrong. In the case of aggressive behavior, for example, an observer would ascribe aggressive intent to the actor, and would blind herself to cases in which the aggressive behavior was intended to elicit positive change. Aggression could be initiative, argued Kelly. The aggressive person could be doing something wrong to set something right. From his perspective, subjectivity was key, and accurate assessment could only be gained by also looking at personal evaluations.[39]

Although Kelly was a humanistic psychologist, he was also a cognitivist. He was best known for his Personal Construct Theory, which suggested that individual perspectives were formed and reinforced through expectations and experience.[40] His presence at the conference, like the presence of others with distinct perspectives, suggested humanistic psychology was a broadly encompassing orientation that was more about a philosophy of science than any one specific theory. This generalism was a source of strength, but it was also an impediment. The varied perspectives humanistic psychology embodied were hard to unify, and hard to pin down in practical terms.

The founders themselves were conflicted (amongst themselves and within themselves) about what they wanted humanistic psychology to be. They hoped to translate their philosophy of science into a concrete school of psychology that could rival the interests that had oppressed them. But they tended to fall down in conducting the foundational research that would build the scientific superstructure of humanistic psychology, and in their own professional lives the tendency was to move away from the kinds of affiliations and alliances that might actually bring an influential school of psychology into being. Rogers's research was valuable, but it was inadequate, in itself, to concretize and operationalize a humanistic psychology movement. Murray maintained an often tense appointment at Harvard, where his interests were at odds with those of the larger department of psychology and of the university. And Maslow had ceased to perform his own research.

In order to produce research output on a scale that would rival behaviorism, humanistic psychology needed greater numbers. But while the numbers in the movement would grow dramatically in the coming years, they wouldn't be the right kind of numbers. The ranks would fill with psychologists who were drawn to the irreverence of the theory, or to what was perceived as its defiance of traditional academic practice. Others would seek the thrill of the derivative experiential techniques. Far fewer would join the movement in order to perform meticulous, systematic research.

A few participants came away from the Saybrook with presentiments of these problems. They feared that humanistic psychologists' resources were inadequate to achieve the grand goals they had proposed. And they worried that the collection of humanistic theories the movement embodied didn't hang together. Despite his respect for figures like Maslow, May, and Rogers, Murray concluded that the "third force" was "at once strident and confused."[41] He doubted its ability to effect meaningful change within mainstream psychology.[42] He also questioned his own ability to contribute meaningfully to the movement and declared the guiding vision and dimensions of humanistic psychology difficult to articulate. He was the only participant unwilling to publish his contributions to the conference, deeming them unworthy.[43]

Murray was in the minority, however. Most of the presenters, and participants, at Old Saybrook left the conference enthusiastic, inspired by the insights shared, renewed by their connection to like-minded scholars, and ready to chart a new course for the field. In his journal, Maslow described his satisfaction with the meeting, focusing in particular on the sense of kinship he was beginning to feel in his efforts to remake psychology.[44] Gordon Allport described the "overwhelming enthusiasm" of fellow participants, identifying humanistic psychology not as "a school, or a person, or a theory of Personality, but a ground swell."[45]

7

Spreading the News

"The way to change a society must necessarily be to change it simultaneously on all fronts, in all its institutions, ideally even, in all its single individuals within the society . . ."

ABRAHAM MASLOW[1]

Maslow and Allport's belief that America was on the verge of greatness seemed to be confirmed at all levels of society. With the early displays of the student movement (the birth of the Berkeley Free Speech Movement, for example), and the dawn of American youth culture (signified by the frenzy of the Beatles' 1964 tour), younger Americans already inclined toward optimism seemed poised to help bring about a new and better age. In 1964, Martin Luther King, Jr., was awarded the Nobel Peace Prize, and Lyndon B. Johnson signed the Civil Rights Act into law and created the Equal Employment Opportunity Commission to enforce it. These gains suggested that the dedicated effort to improve race relations now had support at the highest levels. These new measures applied to women, as well, who were (at least in theory) also protected by the Equal Pay Act.[2]

Also in 1964, President Johnson described an ideal for America that sounded strikingly like Eupsychia. The "Great Society," he proclaimed, "is a place where the city of man serves not only the needs of the body and the demands of commerce but the desire for beauty and the hunger for community. . . . It is a place where men are more concerned with the quality of their goals than the quantity of their goods. . . . But most of all, the 'Great Society' is not a safe harbor, a resting place, a final objective, a finished work. It is a challenge constantly renewed, beckoning us toward a destiny where the meaning of our lives matches the marvelous products of our labor."[3]

As Americans paused between the death of John F. Kennedy and the intense and deeply disturbing escalation of the Vietnam War, they were buoyed by such rhetoric. It spoke to what one psychiatrist writing for the *New York Times* termed their "hypomanic" orientation—bounding energy, optimism, and lust for freedom. He described Americans as possessing a commitment to autonomy and individual freedom that was unparalleled not only in all the world, but in the entire history of mankind.[4]

Within psychology and psychotherapy, this liberatory optimism didn't manifest as a consensus in which all scholars and practitioners agreed they had found a universal theory or methodological approach that would reign supreme. Instead, it manifested as a dissolution of consensus. Pluralism in perspectives was now the rule. Psychology departments expanded their course offerings dramatically in the decades following World War II. Texas A&M, for example, added classes on human motivation; learning; personality adjustment; and comparative, abnormal, child, differential, physiological, and industrial psychology in the 1950s and 1960s.[5] California State University's 1964–65 catalog reflected the diversity of perspectives being taught to the ever-increasing ranks of psychology majors: the school offered courses with developmental, analytical, behaviorist, experimental, social, personality, clinical, and industrial emphases.[6]

Psychotherapeutic practice saw a comparable proliferation of new approaches in the mid-1960s. In addition to the growth of cognitive-behavioral and client-centered techniques, the decade saw the emergence of techniques like transactional analysis, which aimed at offering a paradigm for group psychotherapy that framed interpersonal interactions in terms of the "games" and roles people play, and reality therapy, which focused on ameliorating symptoms directly rather than on attempting to treat core pathology.[7] Other approaches that emerged or crystallized in the 1960s included family systems therapy, which approached problems in the context of relationships rather than in isolation; brief therapy, a short-term intervention aimed at problem solving rather than insight; and body psychotherapy, which combined insight-oriented approaches with touch, movement, and breathing techniques.[8]

Humanistic psychology had a lot in common with some of these theories. Reality therapy, for example, shared the present orientation and the ethic of self-determination that characterized humanistic psychology. It viewed human problems as endemic to human existence, rather than as products of mental illness. And it held that most problems could be mitigated by constructively addressing the areas in which a client's basic needs were not being met.[9] Echoed in its principles was Maslow's motivational theory, as well as Rogers's theory of growth.

The hospitality of the academic discipline of psychology to humanistic ideas, though, was just part of what was exciting about the psychological revolution of the 1960s. American culture itself seemed to have arrived in a place where it was open to the kinds of ideas humanistic psychology had to offer. For the first time, as a result of this openness, humanistic psychology began to change the lives of Americans who had little direct contact with psychology.

By mid-decade, it was reaching teachers and students. It reached managers and employees. It reached people dissatisfied with religion or looking for new forms of religious experience. It reached individuals seeking personal liberation, deeper connection, and sometimes just fun.

Although Carl Rogers had published scattered articles prior to the mid-1960s that extended his insights to educational theory, he began a more concentrated effort to reform the education system around 1965.[10] He published in journals like *Educational Leadership*, and in edited books like *Five Fields and Teacher Education*, *Contemporary Theories of Instruction*, and *Teacher Education and Mental Health*.[11]

The basic message Rogers had for teachers regarding learning was the same one he had offered psychologists regarding psychotherapy. Learning is growth. The drive toward it springs from a "natural potentiality" that needs to be nurtured rather than controlled. For Rogers, self-discovered learning was the only effective means of learning. Likewise, the only acceptable role for a teacher was as a facilitator. Facilitators needed to serve as flexible resources, providing clarity and organization but not direction. They also needed to accept their own limitations, and to act as participant learners, offering their own motivation as a model.[12]

In the 1960s, when the progressive ideas of John Dewey were already being radicalized by reformers like Paul Goodman and George Dennison who advocated a thoroughly student-centered approach, Carl Rogers's educational theory found a particularly eager audience.[13] Like Goodman and Dennison, who advocated smaller student bodies and ungraded schools, and argued that learning was facilitated by *relationships* rather than *instruction*, Rogers boldly suggested that we do away with teaching altogether. His aversion to hierarchical, conclusion-based learning led him to conjecture that grades, examinations, and degrees had no place in the learning process.[14]

According to Rogers, an effective teacher/facilitator would look a lot like an effective psychotherapist. For one, he would be *real*. Unlike a conventional teacher who stands stiffly at the front of the classroom as "a faceless embodiment of a curricular requirement or a sterile tube through which knowledge is passed from one generation to the next," a good teacher wouldn't hide behind a façade. He would enter into an authentic relationship with the learner, and would show his true feelings (whether they be excitement, boredom, anger, or sadness). He would also *accept* his students, prizing them not as trophies, but as imperfect people with great potential. Finally, he would display sensitive *empathy*, validating his students in a way that met their basic needs and freed them up for true growth and learning.[15]

Teachers couldn't be expected to display these qualities if their own educational experiences were "cut from a different cloth." For this reason, Rogers focused his energies on reforming teacher training, banking on the hope that the gains would trickle down. He taught classes for teachers in training, lectured on the topic, and published detailed suggestions for teacher training programs.[16]

His recommendations included taking an unstructured approach to teacher training. Rather than giving them structured assignments, book lists, and study guides, he advocated giving them the freedom to follow their own desires in learning. He also recommended doing group work—in the style of groups variously known as training groups (T-groups), encounter groups, and sensitivity training groups that were used commonly in industry—that would encourage future teachers, through experiential learning, to better understand their own internal dynamics, as well as their impact on others.[17]

In addition to informing teacher training theory, Rogers's ideas helped spawn a whole field called humanistic education, which centered on the premise that students should have a sense of choice and control in learning, that the curriculum should incorporate the interests of the whole person, that evaluation should be self-directed, and that teachers should be more supportive than critical.[18] In the 1960s, the humanistic education movement helped to revive the Montessori model, as well as to expand Waldorf schools.[19] It also helped public school educators to look critically at their classroom practices.

Although Maslow, too, valued humanistic education, he found himself, almost by accident, serving as the movement's ambassador to industrial management.

Describing the evolution of his priorities, he wrote, "I gave up long ago on the possibility of improving the world or the whole human species via individual psychotherapy. This is impracticable. As a matter of fact it is impossible quantitatively. . . . Then I turned for my utopian purposes (eupsychian) to education as a way of reaching the whole species. I then thought of the lessons from individual psychotherapy as essentially research data, the most important usefulness of which was application to the eupsychian improvement of educational institutions so that they could make people better en masse. Only recently has it dawned on me that as important as education, perhaps even more important, is the work life of the individual, since everybody works."[20]

Maslow's willingness to enter the realm of business was a product of his holistic theory of social change. Operating under the assumption that every unit of society is related to every other unit, he felt that inciting a humanistic revolution would require a simultaneous attack on all fronts. When he first applied his theories of human motivation, Eupsychia, growth, and self-actualization to management, though, he almost certainly didn't anticipate how much of his time and energy that realm would end up absorbing. He did recognize from the beginning, however, that in America industry was indisputably the most powerful institution.[21]

Unlike other realms, where humanistic psychologists actively pushed their insights, the corporate world came to Maslow, entreating him to offer any business-related ideas he could muster. In 1962, when Andrew Kay offered Maslow a handsomely paid summer fellowship at Non-Linear Systems, he requested only that Maslow dictate into a tape recorder off-the-cuff possibilities for motivating employees and encouraging them to self-actualize.[22] Maslow, frustrated by his middling academic salary, and by the sense that he was underappreciated both at Brandeis and within the broader field of psychology, had been unable to refuse.

That summer, Maslow's attention was occupied by the vital activities of the plant, and by the utopian experiment Kay was trying to implement. Relying on the theory put forth in Maslow's *Motivation and Personality*, on the ideas of WBSI's president Richard Farson, and on other motivational texts, Kay had already undertaken a radical participatory management experiment. He had dismantled assembly lines, abandoned scheduled breaks and time cards, removed penalties for lateness and sickness, and placed the reins of management in the hands of production teams. The teams managed their own finances, decorated their own workroom, and saw products through from inception to completion.[23]

Maslow was enlivened by the results: high employee morale; low turnover; high customer satisfaction, sales, and productivity. The scientist in him was elated that his theories were being put to the test in the real world. At the same time, though, he was concerned that his rather provisional theory had been the inspiration for such sweeping changes. He feared his ideas were "being taken as gospel truth" without sufficient inquiry into their scientific validity or reliability. "The carry-over from clinic to industry is really a huge and shaky step," he wrote, "but they're going ahead enthusiastically and optimistically, like Andy Kay, as if all the facts were in and it was proven scientifically."[24]

Unlike academics, whose interest in psychological health or illness tended to be intellectual, business leaders like Kay were highly motivated to adopt Maslow's principles. Humanistic management promised advantages beyond increased worker satisfaction. If successful, it could yield greater productivity, profit, and innovation. It also might have a liberatory effect on managers, freeing them from non-trusting, antagonistic relationships with workers and promoting a more gratifying daily existence.

Kay's enthusiasm for Maslow proved to be evidence of more than just a personal affinity. Almost everywhere Maslow went in the world of California business and management theory, he encountered enthusiasm. At UCLA's Graduate School of Business Administration, for instance, he forged a connection with Fred Massarik, who was trained as a psychologist, and James V. Clark, a management theorist who'd helped bring T-group methods for training managers to the West Coast. At the Western Training Labs (WTL), a West Coast version of Bethel, Maine's National Training Laboratories (NTL), Maslow met Bob Tannenbaum (who was also on the faculty at UCLA). Tannenbaum and Massarik had coauthored a book, *Leadership and Organization*, that advocated the use of group processes to promote self-awareness and self-development in workers—thereby generating human capital that would in turn serve as a corporate asset.

Tannenbaum, Massarik, and Clark helped persuade Maslow that, in spite of the potential for businesses to misuse humanistic principles in the ruthless pursuit of profit, industrial applications of his theory were a piece of his Eupsychian vision. By propelling man's economic life in an "enlightened direction," they could broaden the scale of humanistic psychology's impact, far exceeding the potential of individual psychotherapy to effect change. "Psychotherapy tends to focus too exclusively on the development of the individual, the self, the identity, and so forth," Maslow wrote. "I have thought of creative education and now also of creative management as not only doing this for the individual but also developing him via the community, the team, the group, the organization—which is just as legitimate a path of personal growth as the autonomous paths."[25]

Seeing this intuition play out in an actual American corporation in the summer of 1962 fed Maslow's optimism; it persuaded him that democratic values were winning over imperialistic or aristocratic ones, that American business was progressive, that American workers were more satisfied and accomplished than workers anywhere else. The centrality of his own theory to enlightened management approaches gave him a further boost. He came to see himself as something of an abolitionist, extending democratic principles to the workplace; emancipating workers who had been downtrodden, angry, and only passively resistant; and giving them an avenue for creative expression.[26] It comforted him to know that, while academic psychologists had failed to extend his work, there were realms in which people were willing and eager to press forward on his behalf.

At the same time that Maslow was extending his insights to business, he was finding ways to apply them to religious seekers. In 1964, in the spirit of William James's *Varieties of Religious Experience*, Maslow published *Religions, Values, and Peak-Experiences*, in which his purpose was to extend spirituality beyond organized religion. "I want to demonstrate that spiritual values have naturalistic meaning, that they are not the exclusive possession of organized churches, that they do not need supernatural concepts to validate them, that they are well within the jurisdiction of a suitably enlarged science, and that, therefore, they are the general responsibility of *all* of mankind."[27]

The fundamental unit of all religions, he argued, was actually a psychological state. He saw peak experiences as the building block of all religions, but also as the basis for personal forms of spirituality that didn't depend on organized churches. Peaks were natural, not supernatural, and could be investigated and discussed using a naturalistic approach.[28]

Peak experiences were not, he argued, the sole property of the pious or devout, or even always available to them. They belonged most reliably, instead, to the psychologically healthy. Someone too rational would inevitably be a "non-peaker," as would someone who was afraid of losing control or going insane. Although he was careful not to set religion and science in opposition, he warned that "ultra-scientific" people would not be open to the flood of emotion characteristic of religious or peak experiences.[29]

In the mid-1960s, when people seemed eager for ecstatic experience, and anxious to be free of institutional constraints, humanistic psychology introduced new avenues of spiritual experience. One California Episcopal chaplain, Reverend James J. Baar, was quoted in the *New York Times* identifying this trend: "What everybody wants to do is to be turned on. . . . People feel boxed up, they don't know why. They feel frightened by challenges instead of lusting for them."[30] Baar saw the practices of humanistic psychology as providing a better answer than the church for improving people's daily lives. In fact, he left the church with the express intention of facilitating workshops designed to extend humanistic principles to individuals.

Rogers had done the same thing decades earlier. Rejecting what he perceived to be the doctrinaire Union Theological Seminary, he found solace in the intellectual freedoms of Teachers College.[31] Too much structure had always offended him: he saw it as hindering rather than fostering learning and growth. But while Rogers may have been done with organized religion, it wasn't done with him.

In the 1950s and 1960s, pastoral counselors took to Rogers's theory like fish to water. His core concepts of empathy, congruence, and unconditional positive regard seemed to channel for them the ideal of gentle guidance that characterized many Protestant churches. His positive view was in tune with the way many American Protestant denominations had long since evolved away from the harsher views of human nature and potential that had been characteristic of the early American church. His ethic of acceptance echoed the idea of God's forgiveness. By offering pastoral counselors an alternative to the reigning psychoanalytic theory, with its emphasis on a kind of secularized version of original sin, he also freed counselors from a structure that didn't mesh well with their preference for focusing on the potential good rather than evil in man.[32]

As the field of pastoral counseling gained steam in the early 1960s, Rogers's ideas found analogues in professional theory. Carroll Wise, for example, proposed the idea of "noncoercive counseling," and Paul Johnson developed a theory of "responsive counseling," both in application to the pastoral counseling situation.[33] The infusion of new theory aided in the growth of the field. "Clergy have been in the business of healing broken hearts, minds and souls for years," explained one reverend.[34] "The pastoral counselor has taken his gift for that area of ministry and expanded on it."

In 1963, the American Association of Pastoral Counselors was founded on the theoretical orientation of Carl Rogers and the principles of humanistic psychology. Its practical purpose was to accredit pastoral counseling training programs, but its larger mission was to join psychological insight and nondirective practice with religious tradition and spiritual commitment, in the hopes of yielding a holistic approach to human experience.[35]

• • •

In the early 1960s, growth centers and communes provided another channel for exploring personal spirituality and therapeutic growth in the spirit of humanistic psychology. Around the country, growth centers drew visitors for weekend or weeklong retreats in which group leaders employed a variety of techniques ranging from encounter groups to workshops on yoga and meditation. In brief or extended interventions, the aim was the same: people were looking for self-actualization.

Communal living experiments proliferated in the 1960s, as well, and offered an immersion experience in therapeutic thinking about human growth. One of the most interesting examples was Synanon, which began in 1958 in Santa Monica, California, as a drug rehabilitation program, but evolved in the 1960s into a collection of alternative communities aimed at self-realization through authentic living. One of Synanon's key features was its mandatory "truth-telling" group, which came to be known as the "Synanon Game." The groups were led by former addicts who modeled honesty and openness. They typically lasted two to three hours, occurred three times a week, and consisted of ten to fifteen people. Participants, and leaders, were expected to tell their personal stories and then to face the brutal criticisms of fellow group members.[36]

In demanding utter directness with regard to the self and others, the groups possessed a rawness that seemed to go deeper than ordinary interactions. Charles Dederich, Synanon's founder, felt these groups to be uniquely appealing to addicts, who he believed had often been unconsciously seeking peak experiences in their consumption of drugs and alcohol. They had the right idea, he argued, but had been going about it in the wrong way.[37]

Maslow recognized in Synanon a value that transcended drug and alcohol rehabilitation. "(1) First of all," he wrote, "it raises for me the question of the 'dark night of the soul,' of symbolic death before rebirth. These people have hit the bottom of the barrel. Is this a necessary prerequisite to rebirth, to real honesty & bluntness? . . . (2) My guess from what I've read is that real, blunt, tough candor is *the* leading thing in Synanon, & maybe that's what we can learn from it. Also that people can take it under the right conditions. (3) Part of 'the right conditions' is experiential-knowledge of the cures. [The leaders have] gone thru the same mill & the patients know it."[38]

When Maslow learned that Synanon had begun to admit nonaddicts, he was pleased. In their stripping of defenses, the groups possessed an innocence and naïveté he found therapeutic. He also approved of the general toughness of the groups, and of how the participants were "not afraid to hurt" themselves or one another in their quests to take responsibility for their actions. Maslow identified in places like Synanon the potential for raising people's self-awareness without depending on psychotherapy.[39]

By the late 1960s, almost fifteen hundred people were living in Synanon centers nationwide, and as many as six thousand nonaddicts regularly attended the truth-telling sessions.[40] Maslow saw this as a success for humanistic psychology, and for society. In 1966, he addressed members of Synanon, priding the center as a family, an educational system, a culture, a world.[41]

8

From the Ivory Tower to the Golden Coast

"Whatever colors you have in your mind, I'll show them to you, and you'll see them shine."

BOB DYLAN[1]

When Maslow came to California in the summer of 1962, he hadn't yet theorized communes as mini-Eupsychias, or imagined the ways that growth centers would serve as boot camps for self-actualization. More importantly, he hadn't been to Esalen, an idyllic growth center tucked within the cliffs of Big Sur, whose existence and cultural significance were for Maslow a most unexpected surprise.

One night that summer, though, Maslow found himself on Esalen's doorstep. He and his wife, Bertha, had been following the California coastline, tracing the serpentine roads of Big Sur.[2] The particular stretch of highway they were driving, as one journalist described it, was "hung halfway between water and sky, on perilous cliffs, spanning gigantic gorges, rushing through sudden strands of sweet-smelling eucalyptus and towering redwoods."[3] Just beneath them, the ocean pounded madly against the cliffs.

Of this dramatic beauty, though, Abe and Bertha could see nothing. In fact, they could see almost nothing at all, save the abrupt and dramatic curves in the road. The night was exceptionally dark, the roads were sparsely lit, and the intermittent establishments that lined it—set back from the highway and tucked beneath forests—were difficult, if not impossible, to find. They were looking for a place to stay.

By a stroke of luck, Abe and Bertha found themselves at the check-in counter of the Esalen Institute, then called Big Sur Hot Springs. Whether because of poor English or astonishment, the desk attendant, a gruff Chinese man named Al Huang, had trouble catching Maslow's name. He instructed Maslow to write it down. Upon seeing Maslow's signature, his abrasive demeanor changed drastically. "*The* Abraham Maslow?" he asked excitedly. Then he repeated "Maslow! Maslow! Maslow!" as he ran to find other members of the institute.[4]

Richard Price, cofounder of Esalen, came rushing in to greet Maslow. He explained that *Toward a Psychology of Being* was required reading for the staff at Esalen, and that the mission of the fledgling growth center was to host workshops led by writers and therapists interested in humanistic psychology.[5]

Maslow was, predictably, flattered by the adulation, and gratified to find another real-world laboratory dedicated to ideas like his own. At Esalen, he found kindred souls, people who really listened to his thoughts (unlike his peers at Brandeis).

The visit marked the beginning of a significant and complicated relationship between one of the nation's premier growth institutes and one of its heroes. And although Michael Murphy, cofounder and intellectual lynchpin of Esalen, had been away the night Maslow dropped in, the two soon began to correspond, quickly striking up an intimate friendship.[6]

In contrast to the disdain Maslow had for most of his East Coast peers, Maslow came to prize his relationship with Murphy. It was defined by "self-exposure," "feedback of intimacies," and directness.[7] A unique character even within the emerging humanistic psychology movement, the tall, athletic, and rather handsome Murphy was "far-out but still really open, curious, not tied to a system."[8] Maslow also considered Murphy a true scientist, and had nothing but respect for the project he had undertaken in the creation of Esalen.[9]

Esalen became, over the course of the 1960s, a cultural beacon of humanistic psychology, and in this sense served, for many Americans, as a proxy for any direct orientation with the founders or their theory. Here, the ideas Maslow and others generated for understanding human psychology were grafted onto lived experience, where they mingled with other approaches and morphed into novel practices. This more personal outgrowth of humanistic psychology would be known as the human potential movement. In 1962, its goals (as manifested at Esalen) and those of humanistic psychology (as embodied by the founders) were harmonious.

Like Non-Linear Systems, Esalen began as a well-reasoned experiment. Murphy conceived of the institute as a vessel for the exploration of his spiritual and philosophical interests. Meanwhile, cofounder Richard Price hoped the institute would serve as an alternative to punitive mental health interventions, relying instead on the person-centered application of the principles of humanistic psychology.[10]

The two came from divergent backgrounds. Price was an extroverted Stanford graduate, a recovering mental patient, and the son of wealthy Midwesterners whose oppressive religious interests he rejected. Michael Murphy was an introverted Stanford graduate, an aspiring "mystic," and the son of wealthy Californians (who actually owned the Hot Springs property). Their paths intersected when they were Stanford classmates, and again in San Francisco when they lived at the Cultural Integration Fellowship meditation center. There they found that, in addition to their common educational backgrounds and affluent families, they shared interests in Eastern philosophy and meditation, having both studied under teachers Alan Watts (for whom a building at Esalen was named in 1968), Frederic Spiegelberg (whose Stanford class first aroused Murphy's interest in Indian philosopher and yogi Sri Aurobindo), and Haridas Chaudhuri (the founder of the Cultural Integration Fellowship).[11]

Both Price and Murphy had rejected their parents' rigid expectations and developed their own personal philosophies in protest. Murphy had fled to India in search of mystical experience, while Price had landed in treatment at the Institute of Living in Hartford, Connecticut, where he received a battery of gruesome shock treatments. Murphy's hopes for Esalen included a desire to extend his mystical and intellectual curiosity to others. Price hoped, with Esalen, to help develop an alternative to the mainstream psychiatric establishments where he'd received such inhumane treatment.[12]

While Murphy's aims for Esalen overlapped with Price's in their common emphasis on creating an environment most hospitable to individual development and exploration, Murphy's intellectual and spiritual leanings dictated that he form a more personally and physically distant relationship to the institute. He tended to avoid its experiential activities, focusing instead on the more intellectual seminars.[13]

Despite his preference, however, Murphy was also significantly involved in shaping the institute's spiritual emphases. He infused Esalen with the wisdom he had gained from a sixteen-month retreat to Aurobindo's ashram in Pondicherry, India. There he had engaged in a "hermeneutic mysticism" with Aurobindo's ideas.[14] Aurobindo, one of the first Indian mystics to develop a significant corpus of writings in English, had synthesized Eastern and Western philosophy, yoga, religion, literature, and psychology to propose a vision of man's divine possibilities that resonated with the idea of human potentialities. "Everyone has in him something divine," he wrote, "something his own, a chance of perfection and strength in however small a sphere which God offers him to take or refuse. The task is to find it, develop it and use it. The chief aim of education should be to help the growing soul to draw out that in itself which is best and make it perfect for a noble use."[15]

Aurobindo's idea of perfectibility through personal discipline was particularly compelling to Murphy, who meditated eight hours a day.[16] The aim of such practice, though, was not limited to personal transformation; instead, it was the grander goal of the liberation and transformation of mankind. Devoted yogic practices, Aurobindo had claimed, could "bring down a divine nature and a divine life into the mental, vital and physical nature and life of humanity."[17]

Aurobindo's inspiration was evident in Murphy's choice of seminarians, who used yoga and tantra and represented Eastern influences. These seminars were vastly popular, and their themes pervaded Esalen so thoroughly that scholars like Jeffrey

Kripal, author of *Esalen: America and the Religion of No Religion*, later interpreted Esalen as one of the great modern religious centers of twentieth-century America.[18]

Although Murphy's interests were deeply personal, he preferred spiritual exploration at Esalen to be private, dialogic, and intellectual. In fact, most of the Esalen seminars in the early 1960s were fairly academic. Many incorporated lists of requisite reading that spanned philosophy, Eastern and Western religion, evolutionary theory, and, of course, psychology. Esalen's first public offering came just after Maslow's serendipitous visit, in the form of a lecture series titled "The Human Potentiality," which aptly represented the diverse and complementary interests of the founders.[19] The program ran as follows:

SEPTEMBER 22-23:	"The Expanding Vision," led by Stanford engineering professor Willis Harman[20]
OCTOBER 6-7:	"Individual and Cultural Definitions of Rationality," led by clinical psychologist Joe K. Adams and ethnologist Gregory Bateson[21]
OCTOBER 26:	"Art and Religion," Special Lecture by college administrator, writer, and visionary Gerald Heard[22]
NOVEMBER 3-4:	"Drug-Induced Mysticism," led by psychologist Paul Kurtz and Russian-born inventor and industrialist Myron Stolaroff[23]
DECEMBER 1-2:	Panel Discussion (on human potential) by Joe Adams, Willis W. Harman, Paul S. Kurtz, and Myron J. Stolaroff[24]

Like early AAHP meetings, the Esalen 1962 seminars were largely cerebral. They were thrilling for the participants because of their intellectual daring, but were conducted in the traditions of academic discussion. In the first seminar, participants sat in wooden chairs listening to a Stanford professor lecture on new possibilities for human experience. Adams and Bateson offered a seminar that was comparably buttoned-up and intellectual, but more revolutionarily suggestive, particularly when they argued for the subjectivity of social belief systems and the relativity of defined reality.[25]

The topic of the second-to-last seminar of the year, "Drug-Induced Mysticism," suggested the impending Dionysian turn of Esalen. Delivered about a year before LSD experimentation fully hit America, the seminar considered the possibilities for psychedelic expansion of consciousness. Kurtz and Stolaroff piqued participants' interest and nudged them toward their own experimentation.[26]

In the early 1960s, most humanistic psychologists were receptive to the potential value of psychedelic experimentation. Many saw a consonance between their own goals—of self-actualization, expanded self- and transpersonal awareness, and intensified experience—and the qualities of psychedelic experience, which produced in users everything from a feeling of temporary transcendence to the (at least temporary) experience of a complete reorganization of perception and meaning.[27]

Reports of psychedelic experience evoked, in particular, Maslow's notion of peak experiences. "What I experienced was essentially, and with few exceptions, the usual content of experience but that, of everything, there was MORE," said one

LSD-user, a thirty-six-year-old assistant professor of English whose account of a trip was published, in 1966, in *The Varieties of Psychedelic Experience.*

Writing under the influence of the drug, he noted that he was able to sense, think, and feel *more*. Of objects, he saw *more* color, detail, and form. Of his own emotions, he felt more intensity, more depth, more comprehensiveness. He felt that his mind was able to contain more. "Awareness has MORE levels, is many-dimensioned." He also felt a sense of more time, more unity with people and things, more self-knowledge, and more alternatives.[28]

Maslow noted a similar sense of amplification when describing peaks. During a peak experience, he wrote, individuals feel more integrated: "unified, whole, all-of a piece." They are "more able to fuse with the world." For example, "the appreciater *becomes* the music (and it becomes *him*) or the painting, or the dance." Peakers, he wrote, feel themselves to be at the height of their powers; they experience a sense of "effortlessness and ease of functioning"; they feel free of blocks and inhibitions; they feel more spontaneous and expressive, more "freely flowering outward"; and they feel "more of a pure psyche and less a thing-of-the-world living under the laws of the world." Peakers also feel more creative, connected to the present, unique, and grateful.[29]

Although Maslow had never imagined peak experiences to be replicable in a laboratory, LSD experiences suggested new possibilities. As an exceptionally liberal place that tended to attract experientially curious individuals, Esalen proved a good place to start a dialogue about this kind of experimentation.

• • •

The parallel between Maslow's descriptions of peaking and the personal accounts of psychedelic users helps explain the natural affinity that humanistic psychologists and psychedelic users felt for one another. And, indeed, the early pioneers of LSD experimentation were similar in many respects to the founders of humanistic psychology. They were academics and research scientists. They tended to be intellectual adventurers rather than rebels. And they were serious in their hopes for the drug. By the time the two cultures converged at the nexus of the human potential movement in the 1960s at places like Esalen, however, the time when they might have achieved some kind of genuine intellectual synchrony had passed. The psychedelic movement had already abandoned most of its scientific commitments and had given itself over to the more chaotic elements of uncontrolled experimentation.

The modern era of psychedelics had begun in Switzerland in 1943 when chemist Albert Hofmann unwittingly discovered the hallucinogenic effects of a compound he had synthesized five years earlier. Upon accidentally ingesting lysergic acid diethylamide (LSD) in the lab, he quickly became restless and dizzy and left for home. "At home," he wrote, "I lay down and sank into a not unpleasant intoxicated-like condition, characterized by an extremely stimulated imagination. In a dreamlike state, with eyes closed (I found the daylight to be glaring), I perceived an uninterrupted stream of fantastic pictures, extraordinary shapes with intense, kaleidoscopic play of colors. After some two hours this condition faded away."[30]

Although he'd been searching for a circulatory and respiratory stimulant, Hofmann had unintentionally propelled himself into the realm of alternative consciousness. Enraptured by the experience and unclear on how he had absorbed the substance (he had only touched it), he replicated the experiment three days later. Although his second trip began with the characteristic dizziness and disorientation of the first, he soon went into crisis. His grotesque and threatening furniture spun around; his neighbor became a "malevolent, insidious witch with a colored mask." He felt possessed by a demon; he jumped and screamed and flailed; he felt certain he was going insane or dying. Then, "the horror softened," and he returned to a reality in which the colors were more vivid, and the acoustics more resonant.[31]

Hofmann approached the whole experience with the intellectual curiosity of a scientist; he was not deterred by fear, and continued to study the compound. His experimentation soon took him beyond the Swiss laboratories of Sandoz Pharmaceuticals; he sought hallucinatory plants and mushrooms in Mexico in the 1950s and 1960s. Compelled by the adventure and enthusiastic about its therapeutic potential as "medicine for the soul," Hofmann brought the hallucinogens back to his laboratory, where he continued to experiment extensively (mostly on himself), documenting the effects of various compounds and attempting to replicate their chemical structures.[32]

In America, firsthand information about psychedelic experiences came primarily from nonscientists who traveled to locations in southern Mexico, where psychedelic mushrooms were used in tribal rituals.[33] R. Gordon Wasson, for example, was a New York banker who traveled to Mexico in 1955 to sample psilocybin mushrooms with the Mixtec Indians. He published an account of his experience in *Life* magazine in June 1957, describing his own hallucinogenic experience. His first trip began, he wrote, just after midnight in an unlit thatched cabin on the side of a mountain. His "visions," as he described them, "were in vivid color, always harmonious. They began with art motifs, angular such as might decorate carpets or textiles or wallpaper or the drawing board of an architect. Then they evolved into palaces with courts, arcades, gardens— resplendent palaces all laid over with semiprecious stones. Then I saw a mythological beast drawing a regal chariot. Later it was as though the walls of our house had dissolved, and my spirit had flown forth, and I was suspended in mid-air viewing land-scapes of mountains, with camel caravans advancing slowly across the slopes, the mountains rising tier above tier to the very heavens."[34]

Articles like Wasson's began to stir popular interest in psychedelics. They also began to chip away at the negative repu-tation that earlier accounts of LSD inebriation had perpetu-ated.[35] Sidney Katz's 1953 *Maclean's* article "My Twelve Hours as a Madman," for example, had stoked anxiety about the drug by conflating hallucinogenic experience with madness. Describ-ing his participation in an LSD research experiment conducted by the Saskatchewan Schizophrenia Research Group, in which he turned into a "raving schizophrenic," Katz recalled the terror of the experience: "I saw the faces of familiar friends turn into fleshless skulls and the heads of menacing witches, pigs and weasels," he wrote. "The gaily patterned carpet at my feet was transformed into a fabulous heaving mass of living matter, part vegetable, part animal. An ordinary sketch of a woman's head and shoulders suddenly sprang to life. She moved her head from side to side, eyeing me critically, changing back and forth from woman into man. Her hair and her neckpiece became the nest of a thousand famished serpents who leaped out to devour me. The texture of my skin changed several times. After handling a painted card I could feel my body suffocating for want of air because my skin had turned to enamel."[36]

In spite of the fear he was able to evoke with this vivid description, even Katz refused to reduce LSD experience to its purely negative elements, instead offering a more complex picture that fed public fascination. At the same time that he detailed his most gruesome visions, he also highlighted glimpses of "dazzling beauty" more comparable to those witnessed by Wasson. In these moments, he wrote, "I lived in a paradise where the sky was a mass of jewels set in a background of shimmering aquamarine blue; where the clouds were apricot-colored; where the air was filled with liquid golden arrows, glittering fountains of iridescent bubbles, filigree lace of pearl and silver, sheaths of rainbow light—all constantly changing in color, design, texture and dimension so that each scene was more lovely than the one that preceded it."[37]

The sublime, terrifying, and beautiful experiences of LSD compelled readers, in part, because they were unlikely products of the kind of laboratory conditions that produced them. Katz's trip, for example, occurred in the lounge of Saskatchewan Hospital in Weburn, Canada, where he was flanked by the clinical directors of the hospital, as well as a staff psychologist and a sociologist. After ingesting the drug, he was interviewed incessantly by the directors and photographed extensively by a photographer from *Maclean's*.[38]

The study in which Katz participated was typical of the decade's psychological and sociological research into psychedelic experience. The medical research community, in particular, took psychedelics seriously, exploring a range of potential medical and psychological benefits. Even with his new interests, Hofmann's position at Sandoz was secure; he became the director of the natural substances department. In this new capacity, he and his fellow researchers studied a range of possible applications of LSD, exploring its potential as a serotonin blocker, a treatment for migraines, and an anti-inflammatory.[39]

The earliest psychiatric research on LSD, performed in Europe and the United Sstates, used the compound to facilitate mental relaxation in the recovery of repressed memories and to achieve a better understanding of psychosis.[40] Other experimental uses included the treatment of schizophrenia and alcoholism.[41] Significant research on the treatment of alcoholics occurred between 1954 and 1960, when Humphry Osmond and Abram Hoffer treated approximately two thousand alcoholics under carefully controlled conditions, reporting that forty to forty-five percent of the alcoholics who were treated with LSD had not returned to drinking after a year.[42]

It was under the aegis of scientific experimentation, too, that Harvard psychology department lecturer Timothy Leary first traveled to Mexico to experience psychedelic mushroom inebriation. Of the experience, Leary later wrote, "I was first drugged out of my mind in Cuernavaca, August 1960. I ate seven of the Sacred Mushrooms of Mexico and discovered that beauty, revelation, sensuality, the cellular history of the past, God, the Devil—all lie inside my body, outside my mind."[43]

Leary was one of a number of psychologists who were studying that summer in Cuernavaca. Just down the road was psychoanalyst Erich Fromm, who was performing a sociopsychological study of the village, and Harvard professor David McClelland, who hoped to offer psychological techniques to improve the economic standards of underdeveloped countries. Although he didn't name names, Leary wrote, suggestively, "Many of the scientists who were working and vacationing there that season had their lives dramatically changed, and none of them will ever completely escape from the mysterious power, the challenge, the paradox of what started to unfold."[44]

In the fall of 1960, Leary founded the first psilocybin laboratory in the United States, with the support and participation of psychologist Henry Murray and assistant professor of education and psychology Richard Alpert. The explicit goal of the laboratory was to explore the potential psychological benefits of psychedelics, particularly in the realms of emotional and creative expression, and to pursue the effects of psychedelic inebriation.[45]

The early results of Leary's research were promising. In his first study, in which 175 participants from all walks of life ingested psilocybin, Leary reported that more than half had reached new heights of self-understanding; an equally high percentage felt the experience had permanently improved their lives; and 90 percent wanted to repeat the experience.[46] Subsequently, Leary conducted the Concord Prison Experiment, in which psilocybin therapy was administered to prisoners. Improvements in the mental health and morale of participants were so marked that Leary was invited to Washington to explore the possibility of a national psilocybin program that would extend throughout the penal system.[47]

The kind of well-reasoned and cautious experimentation that Leary initially practiced attracted many of humanistic psychology's leaders. Some participated directly in psychedelic experimentation. Stanley Krippner, for example, who was then an assistant professor of clinical psychology at Kent State and later a president of the American Association of Humanistic Psychology, was enthusiastic about the possibilities of LSD and eager to try it himself.[48] Accepting an invitation from Leary to participate in LSD experimentation at Harvard in April 1962, Krippner traveled to Cambridge for the experience. He was so motivated to take the drug that he appeared for the session despite the fact that he had been violently ill from food poisoning the night before and had to be physically assisted to Leary's lab by a friend.[49] His nausea abated the moment the drug took effect.

Krippner was not disappointed by the trip. Describing his kaleidoscopic visions, he wrote, "A spiral of numbers, letters, and words blew away in a cyclone, stripping me of the verbal and numerical symbols by which I had constructed my world. [. . .] The recordings of Beethoven and Mussorgsky had never sounded better, and I seemed to be surrounded by chords and tones. The clock on the mantel seemed to be a work from a Cellini studio. I visualized delicate Persian miniatures and arabesques. I was in the court of Kublai Khan; inside a Buckminster Fuller geodesic dome; at Versailles with Benjamin Franklin; and danced flamenco with gypsies in Spain, one of whom threw roses into the air which exploded like firecrackers. I was with Thomas Jefferson at Monticello; I watched Edgar Allan Poe write poetry in Baltimore."[50]

Feeling that he had encountered the "ground of being," Krippner described the experience as both religious and transpersonal, concluding that LSD had a useful function in giving individuals a "road map" to expanded consciousness and self-exploration.[51]

Although Krippner's experience was compelling, most humanistic psychologists offered only intellectual or ideological support to psychedelic experimentation. In December 1961,

Maslow wrote in his journal of the potential of psychedelic trips to yield "stable, permanent & nonvanishing, nonundoable" truths.[52]

"It has become quite clear," wrote Maslow, "that certain drugs called 'psychedelic,' especially LSD and psilocybin, give us some possibility of control in this realm of peak-experiences. It looks as if these drugs often produce peak-experiences in the right people under the right circumstances, so that perhaps we needn't wait for them to occur by good fortune. Perhaps we can actually produce a private personal peak-experience under observation and whenever we wish under religious or nonreligious circumstances. We may then be able to study in its moment of birth the experience of illumination or revelation. Even more important, it may be that these drugs, and perhaps also hypnosis, could be used to produce a peak-experience, with core-religious revelation, in non-peakers, thus bridging the chasm between these two separated halves of mankind."[53]

In November 1962, Maslow collaborated directly with Leary, serving on a panel on drug peaks at the annual Massachusetts Association of Psychology meeting. And, as late as December 7, 1968, Maslow participated in an LSD study group conference at MIT, where he spoke on peak and plateau.[54]

Rollo May conveyed his approval of psychedelic research by lending his intellectual support to colleagues studying LSD. On September 18, 1965, he congratulated colleague Charles Dahlberg for getting a grant to study LSD with psychotherapy patients. May wrote, "I am interested, beyond the clinical phenomena as such, in the underlying meaning of the changes of consciousness that take place. I would like very much to observe what light LSD throws on the nature and function of consciousness."[55]

Even if they chose not to experiment, Maslow, May, and others were drawn to the topic of psychedelics out of scholarly *and* personal interests. It bridged the areas of their deepest interest: human capabilities, awareness and insight, religious and mystical experience. Good psychedelic research also embodied their scientific ideals, combining the precision of laboratory experimentation with the descriptive value of subjective report. In incorporating an otherwise elusive experience (of expanded consciousness) into the realm of valid research, psychedelic studies had the potential to push back against the narrow definitions of psychological science that humanistic psychologists so vehemently opposed.

Leary's 1962 "Good Friday Study" was a prime example of the attempt to meld scientific and personal interests. In the study, he tested the hypothesis that ingesting a psychedelic drug in a "supportive and religiously meaningful" environment would produce a mystical experience in students who were "spiritually inclined."[56] The experiential reports were powerful. Mike Young, then a twenty-three-year-old divinity student at Andover Newton Theological School, felt that he saw death that day. Describing the experience thirty-two years later, Young recounted his visions. He saw a "radial design like a mandala, with the colors in the center leading out to the sides, each one a different color and pattern." Frozen in the center, Young viewed each band as "a different life experience. A different path to take. And I was in the center where they all started. I could choose any path I wanted. It was incredible freedom . . . but I had to choose one. To stay in the center was to die. I couldn't choose. I just . . . couldn't . . . pick one." Suspended in agony and indecision, he hung there, until he "died," only to return momentarily to more pleasant images. Young later attributed to the drug the solidification of his career in the ministry and the obliteration of his fear of death.[57]

Leary's scientific interpretation of the reports lacked the power of the personal accounts. He claimed in 1963 that of the ten divinity school participants who ingested the drug (ten others received a placebo), 40 to 90 percent (a significant margin) had experienced a full-on religious experience. Regardless, he brashly argued that the results of such studies "systematically" and conclusively demonstrated that psychedelics could produce a "changed man and a changed life."[58]

In attempting to combine scholarly investigation with transcendental experience, Leary's work was ideally suited to the emerging human potential movement, and to Esalen specifically. Although early Esalen seminars were genuinely committed to an intellectual analysis of the value of psychedelics, group leaders steered participants toward experimentation. At first, this encouragement was only by implication. In discussing the mystical value of drug use, for example, the first psychedelic seminar leaders, cofounders of the International Foundation for Advanced Study, a laboratory for the investigation of the effects of LSD, were enthusiastic about the potential of the drug but were careful to discuss it only in the context of controlled experimentation in a research laboratory.[59] With each psychedelic seminar that followed, the assumption that participants would experiment or had experimented on their own became more explicit.

In early 1963, another version of Stolaroff and Kurtz's seminar, now titled "Religion and Drug-Induced Mysticism," was held. And that summer, Paul Kurtz led a "post-psychedelic seminar" for those who had experimented with LSD and wanted to discuss their experiences. Leary himself led a seminar in late 1963 with his former Harvard colleague Richard Alpert. The seminar, held first as a weekend retreat from October 30 to November 1 and then as a five-day seminar from November 1 to 6, was titled "The Ecstatic Experience," and was the basis of their 1966 book *Psychedelic Experience*.[60]

Unsurprisingly, the enthusiasm for taking LSD soon eclipsed the interest in having intellectually serious discussions about it. As visitors to Esalen became more and more actively engaged in seeking personal transformation (through encounter groups and bodywork), they grew dissatisfied with abstract discussions that treated transformation as an intellectual object.[61] Personal use became more common, in many cases informing self-improvement programs.

The increasing interest in recreational experimentation was reinforced by the growing visibility, and self-awareness, of the counterculture. Authors like Aldous Huxley, for example, romanticized LSD use, constructing it as a tool for consciousness-expansion, pleasure, and religious awakening.[62] In 1962, Huxley published an account of what he perceived to be the transcendent elements of psychedelic experience in his novel *Island*. He wrote, "Even if it doesn't refer to anything outside itself, it's still the most important thing that ever happened to you. Like music, only incomparably more so. And if you give the experience a chance, if you're prepared to go along with it, the results are incomparably more therapeutic and transforming. So maybe the whole thing does happen inside one's skull. Maybe it is private and there's no unitive knowledge of anything but one's own physiology. Who cares? The fact remains that the experience can open one's eyes and make one blessed and transform one's whole life."[63] In the final chapter of the book, he challenged the idea that cautious psychological experimentation was the best approach to psychedelics, suggesting instead that the fearless pursuit of religious ecstasy might be a more worthy goal.

Just as Huxley's concept of human potentiality had served as an inspiration for the human potential movement that took root at Esalen, his belief in the enormous potential of psychedelics aligned well with the interests of Esalen participants. For many, his 1956 book *The Doors of Perception* had become a kind of bible.[64] Describing a single mescaline trip, the book helped to identify psychedelic use as a means of increasing an individual's sensitivity to the world, allowing him to admit all kinds of perceptions that his brain usually filtered out. By this logic, LSD could serve as a useful tool in the pursuit of self-actualization and increased awareness. Many Esalen participants embraced this idea and began to use the drug liberally, finding the peacefulness and permissiveness of the institute ideally suited to their experimentation.

Liberal drug use invited a chaotic element to Esalen that was more than the founders had bargained for. Although Murphy and Price attempted to prevent uncontrolled experimentation on-site, residents and visitors largely disregarded their opposition.[65] The most they were able to accomplish in terms of control was the elimination of drug use from meetings and the limitation of experimentation to the rented rooms of participants (a domain protected under state law).[66] "We put a bulletin up on the board that anybody found dealing drugs or having drug trips was going to be evicted instantly since it was against the law," said Murphy. "But, we knew, of course, that these people with that particular look on their face, some of whom couldn't walk very well, were under the influence of something other than beer or wine."[67]

The rampant drug use at Esalen was unsettling to figures like Maslow, who, though supportive of controlled experimentation, questioned the wisdom of rampant LSD inebriation. Several of his journal entries in the mid-1960s conveyed his growing ambivalence. In 1965, he wrote about the risks of LSD abuse, suggesting that extensive use was more likely to result in intellectual "atrophy," aimlessness, and disconnection than in self-actualization.[68]

At the same time that Maslow expressed his disapproval of trends in psychedelic experimentation at Esalen and elsewhere, he began to lose faith in Leary's research. Although the two had worked closely in 1962, their interests seemed to have diverged rather abruptly. Leary's data collection had become sporadic at best, and his scientific integrity seemed to be declining. Critics reported that by 1963, Leary's laboratory, which had once attempted to perform valid scientific experiments, had become the supplier of a "semipermanent cocktail party" full of entranced intellectuals who thought they had discovered the panacea for a sick society.[69]

Leary seemed to be spouting grandiose claims about LSD at every opportunity. In addition to arguing for the power of LSD to forever change one's life, he maintained that the mass distribution of LSD would improve society, in part by bringing about global peace. As the media paid more attention to his sensational statements, his fellow researchers, like Humphry Osmond and Albert Hofmann, feared that his simplistic vision and exaggerated reports would compromise the future of LSD research.[70]

In 1963, Harvard closed Leary's laboratory and dismissed him from his post. This decision came just months after the

FDA's pronouncement that LSD had become too powerful and its results too chaotic, and that the agency would begin to regulate noncontrolled uses.[71] At this point the FDA didn't want to end scientific experimentation, but wanted to prevent abuse.[72] The same was true of Harvard, which continued to support controlled experimentation with LSD. As late as 1966, research came out of Harvard supporting the idea that mystical experiences from LSD could be therapeutically useful in treating personality and behavioral disorders.[73]

Maslow continued to defend, in principle, Leary's unorthodox experimental methods, but he criticized what he deemed "the Leary technique.[74] "The "Leary technique," Maslow wrote in his journal in 1964, "is a denial of the very principle itself of stages of knowledge for which appropriate stages of personality development are necessary."[75] In eliciting peaks at will, Leary bypassed important steps. It was as if he propelled himself, in one fell swoop, from the ignorance of infancy to the wisdom of old age, without having had an adolescence or adulthood. Where were the formative learning experiences? The bold achievements and awkward failures? The rallying that follows humiliation and defeat? The pride and confidence that develops from hard-won personality integration? Drugs seemed to allow users to skip all this.

Maslow's primary reservation about Leary's vision of psychedelic use was theoretical. He quickly came to believe that peak experiences achieved exclusively through psychedelic use were less meaningful than those that occurred spontaneously, but not arbitrarily, after an individual had done the long, hard work of self-exploration. He formulated his critique of psychedelic peaks in much the same way that Dietrich Bonhoeffer, the German Lutheran theologian, described the idea of "cheap grace"—it was unearned and undeserved. "Cheap grace," wrote Bonhoeffer, "means grace sold on the market like cheapjacks' wares. [. . .] Cheap grace is the grace we bestow on ourselves."[76] Psychedelic experiences could, of course, be literally purchased. And, unlike the peaks achieved from the arduous activities that Maslow describes (childbirth, for instance), drug-induced peaks were not the product of striving, process, or work of any kind.[77]

In an unpublished paper titled "Drugs—Critique," Maslow described the ideal peak experience as akin to "costly grace," one that, because it was earned, would promote self-confidence, pride in one's powers, and a sense of achievement. He drew a parallel to the way that earning money would be "health-fostering," whereas receiving unearned money would be "sickness-fostering."[78]

"Even if the drugs were not harmful psychologically," Maslow wrote, "I think they can be harmful spiritually, characterologically, etc. I think it's clearly better to work for your blessings, instead of to buy them. I think an unearned Paradise becomes worthless."[79] Maslow's strongest objections to the LSD culture stemmed from "essentially moral reasons—something like should we build an escalator to the top of Mt. Everest or should we put more automobile roads through the wilderness or should we make life easier in general . . ."[80] There was something utterly capitalistic about the consumptive ritual of LSD use. Leary wanted to have, and to transmit, more good feeling, with more intensity and more immediacy. And he didn't want to have to earn it.

Beat generation author William S. Burroughs concurred with this critique of Leary, recognizing that while LSD could "open the doors of perception . . . only deliberate cultivation of new habits of consciousness could endow such visions with enduring significance."[81] In this respect, there really were no shortcuts to self-actualization, no drug-induced insights that would last.

Even avid users of LSD expressed doubts about the enduring value of psychedelic trips. The day after a trip, writer Arthur Koestler told Leary, "This is wonderful, no doubt. . . . But it is fake, ersatz. Instant mysticism . . . there's no wisdom there. I solved the secret of the universe last night, but this morning I forgot what it was."[82] LSD use generated a series of epiphanies in which each devalued the last, and in which the cycle devalued the entire project. It was true that psychedelic users experienced moments of sensing that they had found the meaning of existence, but they didn't seem able to take the insight with them when the trip ended. They needed to do more drugs to access the awareness they had already achieved, and doing more drugs seemed to make it harder for them to function sober.

The cautious criticisms of humanistic psychologists and other thoughtful experimenters were thrown to the wind by outside critics. In many cases, LSD use mimicked the patterns of other already-demonized drugs like heroin, cocaine, or alcohol. Use moved to abuse, and threatened a level of disconnection and impairment in functioning that was threatening to the social structure.

Almost from the beginning, the media's portrayals of LSD use dramatized this destructive side of LSD. Reports tended to be sensational and to play to the fear that drug use corrupted youth and undermined American establishments.[83] One typical article, published in the *New York Times* in 1964, described psychedelic drug use with barely veiled contempt and anxiety. Journalist Graham Blaine wrote: "Students feel that these drugs increase their perceptiveness and sensitivity, bring out latent talents and inspire a feeling of extraordinary togetherness among the group which is enjoying the 'drug experience.' Of course, the drug generally provides only the briefest of delusional respites. But some of it leads to hopeless addiction or months of insanity."[84]

After his dismissal from Harvard, Leary's own actions and statements provided additional fodder for reporters. In 1966, he founded his own religion, the League for Spiritual Discovery, which was oriented around the sacramental use of LSD, peyote, and marijuana. In one of many public appearances (at a press conference in the New York Advertising Club), Leary announced, "We have a blueprint and we're going to change society in the next ten years."[85] Leary planned to test in the courts the constitutional rights of members of the new religion to use the drugs at home, in their "shrines." He grandly asserted that, "Like every great religion of the past [. . .] we seek to find the divinity within and to express this revelation in a life of glorification and worship of God. These ancient goals we define in the metaphor of the present—turn on, tune in and drop out."[86]

Leary's nonconformist rhetoric aligned, superficially, with Maslow's understanding of the place in society of self-actualized individuals, who display a "resistance to acculturation" and a "certain inner detachment from the culture" coupled with an extreme sense of autonomy.[87] In Maslow's studies of self-actualizers in the early 1950s, he had observed among them a general lack of conformity to cultural norms.[88] Rather than suggesting emotional immaturity, nonconformity, he found, could signal superior social functioning.[89] Not all rebellion was without a cause. In mature individuals, in fact, balanced critiques of cultural norms, choices about living that diverged from the status quo, and well-reasoned rejections of oppressive standards were a sign of higher, not lower, functioning.

Maslow drew a sharp distinction, however, between non-conformist self-actualizers and most other kinds of nonconformists. He described self-actualizers as able to function effectively *within* the wider culture, notwithstanding their criticisms of it. He found that they have generally "settled down to . . . an accepting, calm, good-humored, everyday effort to improve the culture, usually from within, rather than to reject it and fight it from without."[90]

In stark contrast was Leary's notion of "dropping out." In 1965, in *The Politics of Ecstasy*, Leary wrote: "Quit school. Quit your job. Don't vote. . . . Do not waste conscious thinking on TV-studio games. Political choices are meaningless." In addition to encouraging frequent use of psychedelics, he suggested that dropouts should form their own "cults."[91]

Even after his departure from academics, Leary's irreverent attitude toward American institutions generated interest from the media, which often focused on the questionable legality of his activities, portraying him as threatening to the moral order of the nation.[92] Of the Dutchess County trial of Leary in 1966, a *New York Times* reporter wrote, "The jurors are trying to determine whether the Foundation [Leary's communal living experiment] has been promoting LSD experimentation through the country, impairing the morality of children and running a disorderly house."[93] Critics sensed but couldn't always articulate the threat that Leary posed, and often pathologized even the slightest aberrations from "normal" behavior. Media depictions latched onto the metaphor, and the actuality, of filth as a way to convey the moral disorder and taint that drug users embodied. *Look* magazine described the archetypal hippie pad as "a filthy litter strewn swarming dope fortress that was a great deal less savory and sanitary than a sewer."[94]

Media attention to LSD only escalated as the decade wore on. Historian Jay Stevens writes, "Scarcely a week went by that this curious creature [LSD] wasn't in the news columns, either raping or murdering or committing suicide in stories that were usually anonymous, uncheckable, and bizarre."[95] Local papers transmitted the mistaken idea that so many people were driven psychotic from LSD that local emergency rooms were being overwhelmed. The media descriptions grossly distorted reality; LSD-related narcotic arrests actually represented a very small percentage of national narcotics arrests in the 1960s, and LSD-related accidents were far rarer than accidents related to the abuse of other narcotics (alcohol in particular).[96]

By mid-1966, governors were competing to enact anti-LSD legislation, and Congress soon passed federal legislation banning the drug. In October, possession was deemed illegal in every state. With the enactment of such laws, open-ended research came to an end, and researchers encountered obstacles to completing even the funded projects that were underway. Sandoz Pharmaceuticals recalled all the LSD it had distributed.[97]

In 1967, popular magazines fixated on the potential damage LSD could cause. An article in *Science News* warned of broken chromosomes, one in *Time* of cell damage, and the journal *Science* alarmed readers with reports of chromosomal abnormalities resulting from using the drug.[98] *Newsweek*, *Time*, and *McCall's* published stories about dangers to unborn babies.[99] In most articles, the message was the same: LSD use needed to be curbed, and American society needed to be saved from the "rising problem" it posed.[100]

The black market that resulted from the change in legal status, however, ensured a steady supply of LSD, and the now illegal status of the drug, combined with its continued use and availability, resulted in an even greater public anxiety about the danger its use posed to American institutions.[101] Political figures construed drug use as an act of political rebellion that undermined the protective structures of government. President Lyndon Johnson, in his 1968 State of the Union address, highlighted his concern over the advancing cultural interest in drug use, promising to put measures in place to stop it.[102] In July 1969, President Nixon asked Congress for more money for enforcement, heavier penalties for violations involving LSD, and the federal authority to break into residences unannounced to seize drug evidence quickly. Nixon also reported that juvenile arrests involving use of drugs rose almost 800 percent between 1960 and 1967.[103]

Meanwhile, a passion for LSD bloomed in the counterculture. Psychedelic imagery suffused beat poetry. In several poems, including "Lysergic Acid" and "Mescaline," Allen Ginsberg extolled the drug's virtues and romanticized his trips. His poem "Graffiti 12th Cubicle Men's Room Syracuse Airport" contained the following lines:

Man, I'm really stoned out of my skull really O-Zoned— good old LSD the colors in here are so nice really fine colors and the floor tile is really outasight if you haven't tried it you ought to since it is the only way to really get your head together by first getting it apart LSD Forever.[104]

In the late 1960s, Leary left the puritanical northeast for California. Here, he ensconced himself in the epicenter of the nation's countercultural fringe. Estranged from his academic origins, Leary embarked on a series of adventures that included ingesting massive amounts of LSD, challenging Ronald Reagan in the 1969 gubernatorial race, spending some time in state prison for marijuana possession, laying out plans for space colonization, and attempting to be frozen in cryogenic suspension. Characters like Leary fed on California's far-out energy as much as they fueled it.

By the late 1960s, California had become a national site of experimentation and a safe haven for progressive thought. According to *Look* magazine editor George Leonard, "If the United States was a laboratory of social and cultural change, California was that part of the lab where the most advanced experimentation was taking place."[105] *Look* had launched a California issue on September 25, 1962, and *Life* had followed with its own California issue a month later. The cover of *Look*'s California issue proclaimed that "Tomorrow's Hopes and Tomorrow's Headaches Are Here Today in Our Soon-to-Be Largest State." Articles referred to California as a "Promised Land for Millions of Migrating Americans" and the harbinger of "The Way-Out Way of Life." According to one historian, California was the answer to Americans' new surplus of leisure time, uniquely attuned to individual quests for sensation and stimulation. "Everything was bigger, newer, better, faster, shinier in California; it was the jewel in the technocracy's crown," he wrote.[106]

California also embodied productive tensions, a simultaneous threat and a promise, that fueled an ethos of energy and change. Many Americans, still true to their sense of pioneerism and to their traditional Puritan roots, found the rapid change and cultural flux of California simultaneously exciting and frightening—"a window to the future, good and bad."[107] Those who witnessed student protests in Berkeley, race riots in Watts, or drug culture in Haight-Ashbury would certainly attest that California did not consist solely of starry-eyed youth with flowers in their hair. The Haight, for example was often a site more of dissolution and confusion than of harmony and goodwill. One historian wrote that the "madness of the place, the shouts, the chasing, the gunning bikes, the chaotic, occasional screams of girls running has convinced people that the Haight is a rare species of insane organization."[108] Joan Didion, in her 1967 essay "Slouching Towards Bethlehem," described San Francisco as a site of "social hemorrhaging."[109]

In the broader cultural perception of California, however, the promise did tend to outweigh the threat. Idealistic, self-seeking Americans followed a path to California that the federal government itself had charted. In 1962 alone, the U.S. government channeled forty-two percent of all government funds for research and development into the state.[110] California seemed to possess a surplus of great minds capable of leading America toward great things. In contrast to the intellectuals of the Northeast, California's thinkers seemed more receptive to experimental ideas—more flexible, open, and experientially daring.

Unsurprisingly, many humanistic psychologists also felt the pull of California's promise. In 1967, Maslow wrote, "It dawned on me again that I feel closer to so many of the California people than to my friends & acquaintances here (in the Northeast). I'd always thought this was the accident of nearness & distance. But now it occurs to me that these are all T-group people, & it makes a difference. They're more direct, honest, candid, undefended, open, feedbacky, etc. And so I actually *do* justly & correctly feel more intimate with them than I do with non-T-group people here.[111]

By using the term "T-group people," Maslow was referring to those who participated in sensitivity training groups, a form of group therapy in which people learned about themselves through their interactions with others. T-groups most often took place in the growth centers that drew personal growth seekers to weekend and weeklong programs. Like Esalen, these growth centers employed a variety of techniques ranging from encounter groups (or T-groups) to workshops on yoga and meditation.[112]

Growth centers, too, had a reciprocal relationship to the California environs. They drew the seekers, the emotionally and intellectually curious, the experimenters. And their success was heightened by their idyllic surroundings and the state's vibe of possibility. Many centers were located on the coast, in view of dramatic cliffs and the alternating peaceful and forceful Pacific Ocean. Those in Northern California were often ensconced in tall trees, like the redwoods that surrounded Esalen. At the same time that the surroundings suggested the revolutionary possibility of social and self-transcendence, they also harked back to the traditions of early American pioneers and transcendentalists like Thoreau. "While one may need as-yet-undiscovered drugs to imagine how Thoreau would have reacted to the hugging, shouting and acid-dropping at Big Sur," wrote one journalist, "his quest at Walden Pond is certainly one fountainhead of the Esalen Hot Springs experiment."[113]

Seminal AAHP members, including Carl Rogers, Rollo May, George Leonard, Jackie Doyle, and Abe Maslow, were lured from around the country to this mecca of experimentation and progressive thought. Rogers moved to California in 1964, Maslow in 1969, and May in 1975. Eight of AAHP's first twenty-five conferences took place in California, and the *Journal of Humanistic Psychology*, though originally sponsored by Brandeis, was published in California.[114] The majority of early adherents to humanistic psychology, too, were Californians. This fact was reflected both in the numbers of AAHP members who resided in the state and in the decision to open AAHP's first office in San Francisco in 1965.[115]

The West Coast localization represented a literal break from the Northeastern and Midwestern universities at which the ideals of humanistic psychology were first conceptualized. Figuratively, the move to California suggested a new zeitgeist for humanistic psychology, a stronger connection to the rebellious energy of the 1960s, and a cultural fructification of what had begun as an academically and professionally based movement.[116]

9

The Sledgehammer Approach to Human Growth

"Esalen can be Hell as much as Paradise. The air is rarefied, the energy from the mountains, the canyon, the ocean, is powerful and prone to dramatic shifts. It is a climate only for those who are both vigorous and capable of total defeat. For here your nightmares must come true in order to fulfill your dreams. Here you are forced to fall flat on your face before you can drink the cool, sweet waters of joy. Many do not enjoy too long a stay, for here the mirror is ruthlessly turned round to face inward: the demons, flushed to the surface, are no longer 'out there.' The pace of karma quickens and comes home."

RICK TARNAS[1]

In the summer of 1967, the summer of love, John Heider and his wife, Anne, drove their BMW motorcycle from New York to California, by way of Mexico City. John remembers the summer fondly: "Flower children had not yet become bitter. Heroin and speed and beggars were just beginning. The revolution of love based on community, drugs, and mysticism appeared translucent . . ."

A friend took them to Esalen in late July. "The baths in the evening light brought tears to my eyes," wrote Heider. "Esalen was surely the Promised Land." Enraptured, they stayed for four years.

Heider was on the verge of earning his doctoral degree in psychology. He'd spent his life in academics, growing up on the Smith College campus in Northampton, Massachusetts, as the son of a well-known Gestalt psychologist. He'd been to Harvard and Duke, been steeped in academic theory and scientific practice, and emerged from his studies a "grown-up scientist." But along the way, he noted, "I lost my feeling of adventure in exploring the psychological world. I had traded excitement for professionalism and felt that sadness that comes when adult responsibility drives out the child's sense of play."[2]

At Esalen, Heider discovered a kind of science that reanimated him. It was "unsystematic" and "vaguely immoral." It embodied Maslow's concept of pre-science to the maximum. It challenged Heider's ingrained belief that "no discovery, however fascinating or unusual, was *real* unless it had been adequately researched and presented to the scientific community by publication in a journal."[3]

" 'Research' at Esalen, I learned, was quite a simple matter," wrote Heider. "If you have an idea, do it."[4]

While Heider was at Esalen his fellow seekers experimented with alternating heat and cold while hyperventilating, heat and cold while fasting, trance states, extended silence, rebirth rituals, death rituals, nursing bottles for adults, inhaling

CO_2, confessional games, induced emotional outbursts, adults playing doctor, social nudity, fantasy trips, dream work, wrestling, and dancing.

The most common practice at Esalen, however, the one for which it became famous, was encounter.

Although Heider had participated in encounter as early as 1963, the groups he found at Esalen were a different animal. In the early groups, participants had assembled around a table "like executives," with sharpened pencils and paper in hand.[5] They were considerate, polite, accommodating. At Esalen, participants were shouting, touching, shoving, and curling up on the ground.

Esalen groups were defined by the principle of "letting it all hang out." Openness and directness were the currency. As Heider described it, "I will tell you what I think and feel and want. I may want to hit you or to fuck you or your wife. I hate you, I envy you, I love you, I wish to exclude you, I don't like your smell, my cock is bigger than yours, you are a bitch, you bore me, I am great. All this is being up front about what I am thinking anyway."[6]

Encounter group participants were also likely to manifest their thoughts, feelings, and wants physically, and to direct their desires or aversions toward other group members. Displaying affection in the form of hugging, kissing, or groping was customary; expressing distaste by slapping and hitting and punching was rarer, but not infrequent. Sexual liaisons were often initiated in groups, though they were carried out in the cabins or dark recesses of Esalen's grounds. For Heider, as for others, these unconstrained opportunities for self-expression were wildly liberating.

George Leonard, who with his wife had participated in an early group led by psychologist Will Schutz, noted the extraordinary desire for emotional intensity that defined the groups.

The group he attended began with each participant screaming and pounding the floor. The participants, all couples in this case, were then asked to tell three secrets to their spouses that would threaten their relationships. Leonard recalls that a war bride from England confessed she had never wanted to get married and had hated every minute of it. A husband confessed he had been sleeping with his wife's best friend; she responded by hitting him violently and repeatedly, then crying and claiming that he was a "shit" but she loved him anyway. Other tactics Schutz employed to encourage the experience of strong emotion included making faces, Indian hand wrestling, and growling. According to Leonard, the emotional catharsis attached to these activities served as a "quick fix" that wore off soon after the retreat ended. The woman who had hit her husband, for example, felt intensely connected to him by the end of the weekend, but divorced him six months later. Although he admitted the groups could be destructive, and the insights gained were likely to be unsustainable, he also thought they were wonderful.[7]

Esalen's encounter groups had historical roots in the more conservative realms of academia and corporate training (T-groups). Aimed more at improving interpersonal dynamics than at personal transformation, the groups required a comparable level of interpersonal confrontation and often resulted in a comparable increase in self-awareness, but differed substantially in the amount of excitement they provided.

Heider credited Will Schutz singularly with the transformation of the staid T-groups of the 1950s and early 1960s into the extravagant and exciting groups of the mid-1960s. Schutz had been trained at UCLA as a social psychologist, found a niche in academics studying group processes, and held a hard-won assistant professorship at the Albert Einstein School of Medicine in New York. He abruptly abandoned this position, however, when he received an unusual offer from Michael Murphy in 1967.[8] "[Murphy] said he could not pay me," explained Schutz, "but I could offer three workshops, and if anyone came I would make some money. He could not provide a place to live; there was a garage where I could put a sleeping bag. But he could give me a title, any title I chose. I found this offer irresistible, and so I became the Emperor of Esalen (in my own mind). . . . I resigned from Einstein, got divorced, put my belongings in a Volkswagen, and headed west to Big Sur."[9]

Schutz had developed his interest in encounter as a group leader at National Training Laboratories (NTL) in Bethel, Maine, where training groups (T-groups) had first emerged.[10] NTL's T-groups required participants to work together over extended periods of time (usually ten to forty hours total and sometimes throughout a two-week residential program), analyzing and discussing their experiences, feelings, perceptions, and behaviors with an open agenda.[11]

Although the groups were explicitly concerned with individual experience and striving, NTL had been guided by an interest in corporate leadership, a desire to effect personal change to improve business functioning. Corporations, for example, paid to send executives to NTL in the hopes of improving their productivity and increasing the company's profits. Whatever augmented sense of fulfillment or ambition the participants gained, then, was most often merely instrumental in maximizing the company's performance.

While many of NTL's programs were excellent, participants became increasingly critical of their organizational objectives as the 1960s wore on. Whether or not they were sent by employers, many participants felt the business component was at odds with the personal component. Maslow, who spent some time in Bethel, wrote that NTL "mostly focuses on organization, group dynamics, watching form and process. [. . .] But this is in direct contradiction to the fact that most people are interested in it as a therapeutic and a growth experience on the personal side."[12]

Humanistic psychologists like Carl Rogers extracted the principles of group work in the service of individual psychotherapy from places like the Western Behavioral Sciences Institute. Rogers geared much of his research at WBSI to the study of individual outcomes in the context of encounter groups.[13] His experimentation ranged from making modifications to traditional group practices (replacing the facilitator with a tape recorder, for example) to conducting groups for schizophrenics.

Encounter groups provided Rogers with an opportunity to apply the principles of client-centered therapy in a broader way. A healthy group dynamic multiplied the number of potential growth-fostering contacts, surpassing the singular power of the therapist to give and receive empathy, and to engage in authentic communication.

For Rogers, an effective group facilitator was an entirely nondirective one. He approached his groups exactly as he approached individual psychotherapy, acting as a facilitator without imposing his own goals, biases, or analyses on the participants. In enumerating what he considered "nonfacilitative behavior," he included pushing or manipulating a group, making rules for it, judging the success or failure of the group by its dramatics, attacking group members, and either imposing or withholding one's own interests.[14]

Although Schutz's approach was more directive, he too saw groups as more of a tool for self-analysis and awareness than a method for group change. When he imported NTL's T-groups to Esalen in 1965, he constructed them mainly in terms of this personal side.[15] His concern was with "making it real," lending an experiential primacy to what had been an analytical abstraction.[16]

In this new incarnation of T-groups, he not only urged people to access their emotions and to express them, but he got participants to feel *more*, to be realer than real. Both the content and the structure of the groups operated to push people to their limits. Schutz was more confrontational than he had been at NTL, and he was more forthright in expressing his own perceptions and criticisms. He also conducted the groups as marathon weekend-long events in which sleep deprivation eroded inhibitions. After twenty-four hours without sleep, open and honest expression, as well as actual tears, seemed to flow more easily.

"Encounter sessions, particularly of the Schutz variety, were often wild events," wrote Tom Wolfe in an influential essay. "Such aggression! such sobs! moans, hysteria, vile recriminations, shocking revelations, such explosions of hostility between husbands and wives, such mudballs of profanity from previously mousy mommies and workadaddies, such red-mad attacks."[17]

Schutz's methods diverged from the T-group model in more than just their personal emphasis. The countercultural interests of participants—in alternative sexual practices, nudity (the hot-spring-fed tubs on the grounds quickly became both coed and nude), and drug experimentation—gave group leaders license to be more experimental and radical than they could have been at a place like NTL. Maslow noted that Schutz's move to Esalen was good for Esalen intellectually, but was perhaps bad for Schutz, who quickly adopted more eccentric practices.[18]

Media attention probably egged Schutz on. Journalists consistently highlighted the more extreme elements of Esalen, focusing in particular on the breaking of social taboos and the transformative power of encounter groups. Leo Litwak's 1968 article for the *New York Times Sunday Magazine* was representative of the kind of attention Esalen received at the time. The article began with Litwak as a skeptic, armed with "all kinds of tricks for avoiding encounter," reluctantly attending one of Schutz's groups.[19] In the early group activities, he was uncomfortable with the indiscriminate touching of strangers and the awkward expressions of private emotions. His defenses eroded slowly then quickly, ultimately dissolving in a revelatory arm-wrestling match with a sullen teenager to whom he'd taken an immediate dislike. Litwak found himself, in this heated moment, tapping into new depths of his own emotions at the same time that he was propelled to new heights of empathy. By the end of the weekend, his perspective on encounter was completely transformed: "Our group gathered in a tight circle, hugging and kissing, and I found myself hugging everyone, behaving like the idiots I had noticed on first arriving at Esalen." He attributed this change, in no small part, to Schutz's confrontational style and unorthodox practices.[20]

More and more, Esalen became identified with its characters. Overpowering personalities like Schutz's affected not only the experience of specific encounter groups, and the cultural perceptions that surrounded the institute, but the tone and direction of the institute itself. Esalen proved uniquely susceptible to such influences, despite the fact that early in its development, Murphy and Price had laid down ground rules to prevent it. One rule stated that "No one captures the flag," meaning that no individual, however charismatic, would be allowed to dominate the culture. Another rule was that "We hold our dogmas lightly," meaning that all religious dogma would be treated as essentially psychological and never taken literally.[21] Ironically, the antihierarchical power structure prevented enforcement of these imperatives.

Fritz Perls was another eccentric and extravagant figure, who, through the force of his personality, became a dominant figure at Esalen.[22] When Heider arrived, Perls was 75, and "a distinguished, if controversial therapist."[23] Trained as a psychiatrist and psychoanalyst, Perls had actually led his first encounter groups at Esalen in February 1964, billing them as a form of "Gestalt Therapy," and describing their goals as expanding the "scope of awareness," connecting the individual to the environment, and "ending the subject object split."[24]

In contrast to traditional encounter groups that relied on the self-direction of group members, Perls held the reins in his groups. He utilized the concept of a "hot seat," a position in which the seated individual received his full attention. Another empty chair was set beside the seated individual and served as an object of projection (it became the victim's mother, father, spouse, etc. as needed). Perls then proceeded, in the words of one Esalen historian, to "take the person apart by noticing and commenting on every defense mechanism, every body posture, every quiver of the voice or eyes." Instead of allowing group members to interact with the hot-seated individual, Perls assumed full control while the group watched on in silence and, often, awe. After a brutal dissection of his subject, Perls measured his success in tears. He then attempted to reintegrate the "fractured" person in order to create an all-new gestalt, or whole person.

"When I first met Fritz," wrote Heider, "I was afraid of him. I was afraid he would waste me with a glance or a word. He does this to importunate strangers, especially stuffed shirts and I incline in that direction."[25] But for many, Perls's drama, humiliation, and attention were irresistible. They were inspired to come to Esalen just to work with him.

Perls quickly ascended as Esalen's "star," earning a guru status the founders had never intended for their group leaders. He embraced the role with zeal. Described by his wife, Laura, as "a mixture of a prophet and a bum," he often wore long white robes or flowing multicolored shirts and sandals.[26]

Aside from his dramatic appeal, the themes Perls espoused were particularly resonant with the emerging counterculture. He wrote and spoke about the centrality of emotion, the search for meaning, the importance of interpersonal relationship and self-expression, and the value of erotic passion.[27]

At the same time that he met the needs of many participants, he also offended and angered his peers at the institute and subverted the founders' influence. Some of Perls's favorite sayings directly opposed Murphy's vision of Esalen. Perls was proudly anti-intellectual and claimed to hate philosophical discourse, calling it "mind-fucking" or "elephant shit," "for its size and importance."[28] According to humanistic psychologist Maureen O'Hara, Perls felt that if it was intellectual, it was shit, hence his other mantra, "Lose your mind and come to your senses."[29]

Perls also ridiculed Murphy's commitment to meditation, deeming it "neither shitting nor getting off the pot." He opposed the presence of "mystics and occultists" at Esalen, dismissing their brand of enlightenment as frivolous. But Perls himself often experienced a quasi-mystical sense of illumination, both through his groups and through his experimentation with psychedelics.[30] He so strongly advocated the use of LSD, in fact, that he sometimes rejected students who had never taken the drug.[31]

Perls justified his techniques as a product of Gestalt psychology, a perspective he described in *Gestalt Therapy* in 1951, *Gestalt Therapy Verbatim* in 1969, and *The Gestalt Approach and Eye Witness to Therapy*, which was published posthumously in 1973.[32] His introduction to *The Gestalt Approach* captures the vision of Gestalt psychology he advocated. Attempting to shrug off "professional jargon" and psychological complexity, Perls explained, "The basic premise of Gestalt psychology is that human nature is organized into patterns or wholes, that it is experienced by the individual in these terms, and that it can only be understood as a function of the patterns or wholes of which it is made."[33] Although he located the foundations of his practice in German Gestalt psychology, he drew from it selectively, omitting some of its most central elements.[34]

As Perls's six-year stay wore on, he became a problem for those trying to run Esalen. With a massive sense of entitlement and a guru complex, Perls acted as "an institution within the institute."[35] His programs were listed separately, and he lived in a private residence on Esalen's grounds, an odd round house with a grass-covered roof that he had extracted from Murphy by promising to pay for it (a promise he didn't keep).[36] In the vein of what many of his colleagues at Esalen identified as one of the most toxic themes of American culture, Fritz seemed to care only about himself and urged others to do the same. This attitude was evident in his Gestalt "prayer":

> *I do my thing and you do your thing.*
> *I am not in this world to live up to your expectations,*
> *And you are not in this world to live up to mine.*
> *You are you, and I am I, and if by chance we find*
>   *each other, it's beautiful.*
> *If not, it can't be helped.*[37]

Perls was also infamous for his seduction of female participants and his proselytization of sexual promiscuity. One of his female patients recalled: "He told me I should fuck around. It was really a crazy thing to tell me. He created problems I didn't really want. I'm 'supposed' to fuck around because my therapist tells me that."[38]

Group leaders like Perls often did worse than exacerbating the problems of group participants. In several cases, they did real damage—stripping individuals of their familiar defenses and sending them home emotionally fragile and psychologically vulnerable.[39] The more extreme results ranged from divorces to physical violence. Although Price had intended Esalen as a "proving ground" for applying the insights of humanistic psychology to diagnosably mentally ill and severely struggling individuals, the institute had proved far more efficacious for those with average problems.[40] Several suicides at Esalen in 1968 and 1969 served as painful indications of the Esalen staff's inability to provide comprehensive services to the severely disturbed.[41]

The "here and now" philosophy espoused by Perls and others often prevented encounter group leaders from seeing the

bigger picture, which included the inevitable personal and social consequences of individual action. In his notes on this type
of encounter, Maslow wrote that there is more to learn than "to
give honest feedback and expect honest feedback, to be authentic and candid and the like. With the wrong sort of people, this
automatically leads to getting clobbered or to getting defeated
rather than achieving anything."[42] Perls thought Maslow, in
turn, was a "a sugar-coated Nazi . . . [who] pandered to a happy
world of optimism that did not in fact exist."[43]

Though Maslow's criticism posed a challenge to him,
Perls was relatively insulated from it. Maslow was rarely at Esalen, and the two occupied different realms—one academic
and one cultural. Perls was more threatened instead by the permanent presence and radical practices of Will Schutz. When
Schutz came to Esalen in 1965, he inherited from Virginia Satir
the supervision of Esalen's nine-month residential program—a
group that John Heider joined in September 1967. Schutz intended for the program to train encounter group leaders and
shape them in his image.

The intensity of Perls's groups was, if anything, surpassed
by Schutz's activities. Schutz encouraged his groups to do all
kinds of things that "the culture would not approve of," which
typically involved getting nude as quickly as possible.[44] Perls
derisively referred to Schutz's team of encounter group leaders
as his "circus," while Schutz trivialized Perls's workshops by
calling them "the Flying Circus."[45]

According to George Leonard, who was the vice president
of Esalen in the late 1960s and throughout the 1970s, while
Perls was a physically deteriorating man in his seventies, Schutz
was "the great conquistador," a physically dominating presence.
With an ego comparable to that of Perls, he would challenge

others to "break him"—expose his vulnerability and bring him to tears. As far as Leonard knew, this was never accomplished. His model for encounter was the "more openness, the better," and his success was judged by his ability to reduce his residents to a sense of despair that would ultimately yield to a feeling of transcendence.[46]

Schutz's method of compelling catharsis provided an appealing form of instant gratification and release, and his groups became nationally acclaimed. His book *Joy* went through five printings, and his unorthodox techniques, his frankness with talk show hosts, and his encouragement of the audience to emulate his candor earned him many television appearances.[47] In 1968 alone, he went on the air with Johnny Carson, Phil Donahue, David Susskind, Dick Cavett, and Merv Griffin.[48]

Despite their rivalry, Schutz and Perls ran groups that were more alike than they were different. They both depended, perhaps too heavily, on the concept of catharsis. As a group leader, Heider grew increasingly conscious of the limits, and potential dangers, of this reliance. Like Maslow, he harbored concerns about "unearned" peaks. "I believe that it is preferable," he wrote, "to allow the participant to confront the anxiety over a period of time than to perform a cesarean and take the infant from the womb."[49] The line between the drama that the groups required and a superfluous, sensationalistic drama was a fine one, and one often stumbled across by the sometimes reckless, and certainly self-righteous, Schutz and Perls.

The founders were aware of these oversteps. "Many of our programs," explained Michael Murphy, "were kind of the sledgehammer approach to human growth. [. . .] There were encounter groups there where the darkest and the dirtiest things you could dig up from your own psyche or accuse someone else of was being tossed around. People were saying things to one another that thirty years later they haven't forgiven one another for."[50] Whether or not such emotional violence was therapeutic was a matter of contention. Therapy, for decades, had been acknowledged as a process that tended to amp up discomfort on the way to reducing it. But it was one thing to deconstruct yourself in the service of self-improvement, and another to tear down someone else, indulging, as one might, in a certain amount of sadistic pleasure.

Destructive or not, emotional release was one of the main goals of thousands of Americans who turned toward therapy in the 1960s. While hordes flocked to Esalen for encounter group therapy in the mid to late 1960s, still more sought individual psychotherapy.

One popular article described this mass interest as evidence of a revolution "that threatens in the long run to have a greater effect on our society than all the political turmoil that the headlines chronicle." Lives, the author argued, would never be the same; man's basic concept of himself was "about to undergo a most convulsive change."[51] It seemed, to some, the last nail in the coffin of organized religion and, to others, the death knell for traditional structures of living, including defined gender roles and generational hierarchies. What would it look like if we were all living examined lives? Or worse, if we were all capable of examining the lives of others?

While psychology had expanded greatly in the postwar years, it took on a new life in the 1960s. It seduced even fairly non-neurotic people into therapy and expanded cultural interest in all things psychological. In contrast to the near monopoly that the psychoanalytic orientation had had over therapy since the 1920s, a plethora of diverse psychological theories, services, and techniques were now emerging. As a result, Americans were confronted with an "imponderable dilemma of choice."[52] In the 1960s, Americans were introduced to transactional analysis, reality therapy, family therapy, behavioral therapy, cognitive-behavioral therapy, nude marathon therapy, and of course encounter group therapy.

The variety of interventions under the umbrella of "humanism" alone were innumerable. According to cognitive behaviorist Albert Ellis, a subgroup of members at the first meeting of the Association of Humanistic Psychology arrived at a minimum of twenty radically different concepts of humanism applied to psychology, many of which were contradictory.[53] Ellis's self-identification as a humanistic psychologist itself was a bit surprising, since many viewed his rational-emotive therapy (RET) as contradictory to AAHP's goals. People tended to view it as antihumanistic, wrote Ellis, because it is "exceptionally hard-headed, persuasive, educational, and active-directive. [. . .]"[54] But he defended his form of therapy as "the most humanistic means of personality change that have yet been invented." Focused on creativity, beliefs, attitudes, values, and maximizing human potential, its goals, if not its techniques, aligned perfectly with those of other humanistic psychologists.

The disparity between Ellis's approach and other forms of humanistic psychotherapy was highlighted in a 1965 film titled *Three Approaches to Psychotherapy*. In the film, thirty-year-old Gloria undergoes three sessions with separate therapists: Ellis, Rogers, and Perls.

Gloria is relieved, in the first session, to encounter Carl Rogers's gentle demeanor; his soft voice assuages her nervousness. As she presents her concerns about integrating her new identity as a sexually adventuresome divorcée (her devilish side) with her more "wholesome" role as a mother, he is unconditionally accepting, nondirective, earnest. He leans forward, nods frequently, and smiles. When Gloria explains her uncertainty about whether or not to be honest with her daughter about her sexual promiscuity, he empathizes, affirms what she's saying, and lends more clarity to the issues she's confronting.

Gloria, however, grows frustrated and makes plain her desire for Rogers to weigh in as a psychological expert. She wants to know whether her daughter will be more damaged by knowing that her mother's sleeping around or by being lied to. "I'm going to ask you," says Gloria, "and I want you to give me a direct answer."

Rogers won't give her an answer. "I guess I'd like to say," he delicately explains, "no, I don't want to let you stew in your own feelings, but this is the kind of private thing I couldn't possibly answer for you . . . but I'd like to help you get to an answer." His unconditional acceptance spurs Gloria to the climax of the session, when she remarks, "Gee, I'd like you for my father." Rogers follows by saying, "You look to me like a pretty nice daughter."

By earning her emotional trust, respect, and admiration, Rogers ultimately convinces Gloria that she does, in fact, know how she wants to proceed. But the session leaves the viewer with the sense that she wanted something harsher: to be punished or vindicated, rather than accepted.

Fritz Perls gave her what she wanted in this regard. Though Gloria repeatedly claimed to be scared of him, there was a subtext of flirtation to their banter even while the overt tone of the session was, at times, antagonistic. The session was formless; they didn't discuss Gloria's problems, her life, her history. Instead, they existed in the "here and now," which meant Perls picked at her statements, focused on her orientation toward him, and drew attention to her every movement. She smiled throughout, chain-smoked, and wiggled like a little girl. At the same time, she grew incensed when he played games, and when he accused her of being phony.

Gloria's repeated remarks to Perls suggested the antihumanistic strain that ran through his version of Gestalt therapy. "I want you to be more human," she pleaded. "I don't feel close to you at all, Mr. Perls," she claimed. "You seem so detached. I feel like you're not recognizing me at all."

As Perls explained it, his form of therapy was aimed at humanistic goals, because it forced the patient to recover her lost potential and stand on her own feet. His relentless attempts to manipulate and frustrate Gloria were intentional efforts to make her confront herself.

Ellis's session was comparably antagonistic, though neither as playful nor as hostile as that of Perls. With his didacticism, abrasive New York accent, and unemotional style, he engendered neither feelings of warmth nor anger. He went immediately to the problem Gloria said she wanted to solve: she attracted men whom she didn't respect or find interesting, while she repelled or withdrew from the men she desired.

Ellis focused on the cognitive components of her conflict—her catastrophizing, her negative self-concept, and her fear of coming across as "dumb." He explained to her, in depth, the irrational beliefs she was imposing on various interactions, and the ways that she was overgeneralizing singular rejections as blanket rejections. He ended the session by giving her a "homework assignment," a simple prescription to try being herself with the men she found desirable.

Gloria left the session feeling that the three distinct forms of humanistic psychotherapy had more contradictions than commonalities. Each approach had played to a different side of her. She referred specifically to Perls bringing out her "fighting" side, and Ellis engaging her "thinking" side. And she implied that Rogers elicited her self-acceptance, even if he left little room for her self-contempt.[55]

The viewer was left with a comparable sense of dislocation. How could three such dramatically different approaches, premised on three thoroughly distinct sets of values, serve the same goals? As humanistic psychologists had been arguing, they couldn't. The outcome of therapy was going to look really different depending on the orientation of the therapist you encountered, particularly if the goal of therapy wasn't simply the remission of pathological symptoms but evolution toward a better, more expansive self. A protégé of Perls might end up living a rough-hewn life characterized by off-putting interpersonal directness and experiential intensity, while a successful patient of Ellis might be defined by her utter practically, rationality, and Vulcan-like lack of emotion. Meanwhile, a well-therapized patient of Rogers might adopt an overwhelmingly optimistic attitude, a powerful sense of ambition, or, as Gloria feared, a tendency toward a blob-like softness. In any case, it was becoming clear that popular magazines had it wrong when they talked about psychotherapy as a concrete process in which diverse individuals sought uniform treatment for their problems and obediently swallowed the answers the "experts" provided. Thanks in large part to humanistic psychologists, and their efforts to bring new perspectives to the treatment of individuals, psychotherapy in the mid-1960s was a many-colored thing.

10

Such Beauty and Such Ugliness

"Like a bird on a wire, like a drunk in a midnight choir,
I have tried in my way to be free."

LEONARD COHEN[1]

After their taped psychotherapy session, Gloria reached out to shake hands with Perls. He extended his cigarette and ashed on her palm. Gloria was humiliated.[2] Still, when she was confronted with the choice of which psychotherapist to work with on a regular basis, she chose Perls.

The choice seemed to be between the therapist who would gently teach her to accept and trust herself, the therapist who would pragmatically guide her toward constructive behavioral change, and the therapist who would brutally tear down her defenses, leaving her exposed, vulnerable, and scrambling to regain her dignity.

Gloria's decision, while somewhat unexpected, was the choice of thousands of Americans in the mid to late 1960s who flocked to encounter groups, to Esalen, and to many of the other, more intensity-seeking pockets of the counterculture.

Perls's groups, like his individual therapy sessions, were modeled on his devotion to the ideal of utter self-reliance, individualism, and freedom. He denigrated dependence and vulnerability in all their forms, dismissing these qualities as immature and linked to interpersonal manipulation.[3] Rather than offering a supportive model of empowerment, though, Perls offered a hostile approach that bordered on sadism.

"If I get myself in a corner," Gloria told Perls during the session, "you're going to just let me drown." He seemed to enjoy her struggle, repeatedly mocking her and calling her a phony. Indeed, the only emotion he seemed to accept from her was anger. Gloria justifiably accused him of acknowledging as genuine only her brave, independent statements, and of dismissing as phony her earnest expressions of fear and anxiety.

Perls's tough love seemed to spur Gloria to action, flooding her with adrenaline, and making her more proactive than she would have been in a less charged interaction. But his contempt bias—against the qualities that make people existentially fragile, interpersonally accountable, complicatedly human—was dehumanizing, as well. This element, characteristic both of Perls's sessions and of other encounter groups, was what made certain manifestations of the encounter group craze in the late 1960s particularly toxic.

Over the course of the 1960s, Schutz and Perls threw down in a pound-for-pound contest of escalating extremes designed to evoke catharsis. John Heider likened the process to an addiction in which leaders sought "ever more potent blowouts," with the illusion that they would yield ever more dramatic highs.[4] A more common outcome, however, was an increase in the depressions that followed. Peaks were often followed by exaggerations of the original discomforts. For this reason, both leaders and participants became like junkies chasing a high.

Many were literal junkies, as well. In the summer of 1967, in particular, hundreds of LSD heads, and as many stoners, gathered at Esalen.

Heider described this time at Esalen as wonderful and awful, compelling and repulsive. The flip side of the extravagant beauty of Esalen, the utter sense of freedom, the promise of illumination and awakening, was pain and darkness that ran deep.

"I have never seen such beauty and such ugliness before," he wrote. "I have never seen the human spirit so exalted or so degraded. The baths: an eternal flow of hot water, sited on the cliff face, sea, sky, mountains, families bathing together, lovers, meditation and massage in the sun. The baths: dreadful grime, old cinder blocks, body lice and staph, heroin and death from 'unknown causes.'"[5]

Some lived in filth, in tents and trucks on the grounds of Esalen, which Heider described as a "refugee camp."[6] While some attended encounter groups, others were basically there to score a kind of contact high, neither attending workshops nor supporting the institute monetarily. Without an invitation to do so, they forced a connection between their own goals and those of the already mythologized retreat.

Although armed with aphorisms of peace and love, these squatters compromised the atmosphere of Esalen and damaged its standing in the community. One local restaurant owner refused to serve "hippies" and "beatniks."[7] Neighbors perceived Esalen to be an escalating threat to their safety and security. According to Murphy, they infused the air with a "drunken mysticism that undermined every discipline we set for the place."[8]

The chaotic intrusion of counterculturalists, who tended to lack commitment to the goals of human potential and who sought little more than a safe haven where they could "drop out" of American culture, deeply troubled Esalen leaders, who found themselves trapped by their own antihierarchical and democratic philosophies.[9] In 1968, George Leonard and Michael Murphy experienced a profound dismay with some outgrowths of human potential, even expressing urges to disown the whole movement. As Leonard later professed, "We quickly learned that just as it was much easier to change the world than to change it the way we planned, it was much easier to name a movement than to unname it."[10]

The problems at Esalen were emblematic of what was happening at other growth centers across the country. In the late 1960s, an often destructive permissiveness seemed to be the rule at many of these retreats. Maslow saw several parallels between the practices of growth centers and of rebellious youth. They both tended to scrap reason and rationality in favor of emotion, and were too singularly "Dionysian"; they perceived education, science, and other forms of logical thought as akin to imprisonment; and they mistook impulsiveness for healthy spontaneity. In distrusting all authority, they expressed a blind allegiance to absolute freedom that rested on the assumption that human nature was fundamentally good, and that evil was solely a product of social inhibitions and restraints. They also didn't seem to understand the ways in which law and order facilitated freedom. "They think of power as evil," he wrote, "not realizing that they must temper, restrain, and control the forces of inhumanity and chaos within the human soul."[11]

Maslow's criticism of growth centers stemmed, in part, from the distance between his personal experience and the experiences of the rebellious human potentialists. Maslow—like Rogers—was, above all, an academic psychologist and a staid husband and father: his interest in experiential rebellion was largely intellectual.[12]

His ambivalence about countercultural activities, like drug use, was intellectual as well. Because he believed that psychedelics offered a valuable experimental opportunity to study higher realms of human consciousness, as well as an experiential opportunity to glimpse self-actualization, he agonized over their destructive potential.[13] On January 18, 1968, armed with anecdotal data from the events at Esalen and from Leary's exploits, Maslow wrote decisively, "I think LSD is clearly dangerous now, so no conflict there—dangerous, that is, for self-administration."[14]

The cautious line that Maslow and others had advocated, between open exploration and thoughtful moderation, proved too difficult for many Esalen participants to tread. The thrill of drug-induced stimulation had seduced many visitors into the singular pursuits of these ends. As a direct effect of the rampant drug use, Esalen suffered a series of misfortunes. In 1968, Lois Delattre, a graduate of Esalen's first residential program and an administrative employee of the San Francisco office, experimented with MDA, a psychedelic drug of the amphetamine group. She died within hours.[15] Delattre's death was devastating to the Esalen staff, who had known her well. Many blamed Esalen for her misfortune.[16]

This event eroded Esalen's air of security and utopian invulnerability. Closely following Delattre's accidental death were the suicides of Marcia Price and Judith Gold (a shooting and a drowning in the baths, respectively). The deaths further shook the Esalen community, causing them to seriously question what Esalen had become.[17]

Meanwhile, the founders of humanistic psychology, like the founders of Esalen, expressed a mounting sense of frustration with the excesses of the encounter group movement. Maslow's Esalen critique file grew "fatter & fatter."[18] In 1969, he wrote, "Too many shits at Esalen, too many selfish, narcissistic, noncaring types. I think I'll be detaching myself from it more & more."[19] May expressed a similar dissatisfaction, describing, in 1971, his avoidance of encounter groups and his temporary resignation from the Association of Humanistic Psychology as protest.[20]

Not every humanistic psychologist grew as disillusioned as Maslow and May. "You had to be present at the time to understand the tremendous energy of the movement," explained former AAHP director John Levy, who saw the association move in many of the same kinds of experiential directions as Esalen had. Levy, who was later nostalgic for the excitement of the times, didn't regret the strongly experiential turn in the least. "It was what people wanted."[21]

Esalen leaders like Murphy, Leonard, and Price were at least as excited by the dramatic turns Esalen took as they were dismayed. Murphy, for instance, eventually conceded that Esalen's divergence from his vision was natural and inevitable.[22] Just as painful experiences, tragedy, and loss were often the price of growth and increased awareness, he felt that Esalen's adolescent phase was a necessary step toward the maturation of the institute. He refused to engage in a reductionistic dialogue that artificially dichotomized Esalen's founding years and the more chaotic events of the late 1960s. Both were of a cloth, and both were valuable in distinct ways.

The cultural energy that blew through Esalen fueled humanistic psychology as much as it derived fuel from it. And the encounter groups, whose excesses were a source of dismay, earned at least as much esteem as disapproval. In fact, the enthusiasm they generated inspired many to widen their application and use them in the service of other interests.

Psychedelic enthusiast Paul Kurtz supported encounter to aid in self-transcendence. California politician John Vasconcellos advocated a form of encounter for self-esteem building. And *Look* magazine editor George Leonard touted the groups as a potential solution for racial inequality in America.

While Leonard's goals seemed grandiose, he found encounter to cut to the heart of racial struggles. What was needed to achieve interracial harmony, he felt, was brutal honesty, a willingness to reckon with our own deep-seated prejudices, and a solid attempt to achieve understanding across races.[23]

Leonard was perhaps more attuned to racial problems than most. Born in Atlanta in 1923, he had had firsthand exposure to the racism of the Deep South. He had seen the horrors of black tenant farming during his summers in Monroe, Georgia, and considered the practice to be "probably worse than slavery."[24] His discomfort with the elusive and apologetic presence of blacks in the small town incited in him a commitment to racial reform that shaped his career. By 1953, when he moved to California, Leonard was an anomaly: he was Southern, white, and an integrationist.[25] As a senior editor for a major national magazine, he created special issues on civil rights, reporting the confrontation over integration at the University of Mississippi himself.[26]

Although Leonard had no background in psychology, he had been drawn into the orbit of humanistic psychology through his introduction to Michael Murphy on February 2, 1965. The two instantly connected, partially on the basis of their concern for the systematic denial of the ability of oppressed Americans to reach their highest potential. Two weeks later, they spent three nights at Leonard's house brainstorming ways to extend civil rights and to aid individuals from diverse backgrounds in achieving self-realization.[27]

Leonard immediately began to envision ways to get blacks to Esalen, where they could experience the personal transformation he felt they so deeply needed. This transformation, he hoped, would be a crucial step in the eradication of racial inequality in America. Murphy and cofounder Dick Price agreed that greater racial diversity and the consequent inclusion of varied perspectives would enrich the experience of all participants. The consistent lack of diversity at seminars had perplexed and sometimes disturbed them. Still, neither had taken action to target seminars and workshops specifically to blacks.[28]

In 1967, Leonard enlisted the help of friend and neighbor Price Cobbs in the cause. He proposed that together they create a series of black-white encounter groups, which would operate like traditional groups, but with mixed-race participants and pointed honesty about concerns, emotions, and beliefs related to race. Cobbs, a black psychiatrist whom Leonard had first met during an interview for a *Look* piece on Cobbs's experience of moving into an all-white San Francisco neighborhood, was reluctant to join in Leonard's lofty attempts to achieve interracial harmony and secretly feared that Leonard's interest was driven by textbook white liberal guilt.[29] Cobbs was also reluctant to get involved specifically with Esalen.[30] Unlike many blacks, Cobbs had heard of Esalen, but had "identified it as a playground of middle-class white dilettantes."[31]

He was compelled, however, by what he perceived as Leonard's genuine commitment to racial issues.[32] As anyone who has spoken to him even briefly knows, Leonard was persuasive, and his enthusiasm infectious. He argued that the traditional ways weren't working. Explaining his motivation for bringing interracial encounter to Esalen, he later wrote, "Black-power militants screamed their hurt, anger, and hatred. By revealing themselves and voicing the truth, they begged for encounter. White leaders responded with conventional language, cautious words. How could there be understanding without self-revelation? Didn't the whites feel outrage, fear, repressed prejudice? The measured, judicious response seemed a lie."[33] Leonard was determined to make racial change mean something more than superficial policy-based actions; he wanted to cut to the emotional center of interracial attitudes and experiences.

Cobbs "shared this sentiment" and agreed to work with Leonard. He had sensed in his own practice a deepening divide between the races rather than the healing one would expect in the era of civil rights. He was concerned that by pushing racial issues to the forefront, the nation had unintentionally opened a floodgate to a deep fount of poisonous rage. He was as desperate as Leonard to find a solution, but he was also ambivalent. Even after committing to run the group, he considered canceling it in favor of attending a black power workshop on the East Coast. His wife convinced him to honor his commitment.[34]

The first black-white encounter group was titled "Racial Confrontation as a Transcendental Experience." It was structured in the traditional Esalen manner, as a full weekend marathon event with neither the participants nor the leaders allowed to sleep, and was advertised in the Esalen brochure with the following description:

> Racial segregation exists among people with divided selves. A person who is alien to some part of himself is invariably separated from anyone who represents that alien part. The historic effort to integrate black man and white has involved us all in a vast working out of our divided human nature.
>
> Racial confrontation can be an example for all kinds of human encounter. When it goes deep enough—past superficial niceties and role-playing—it can be a vehicle for transcendental experience. Price Cobbs, a Negro psychiatrist from San Francisco, and George Leonard, a white journalist and author born and raised in Georgia, will conduct a marathon group encounter between races. The group will try to get past the roles and attitudes that divide its participants, so that they may encounter at a level beyond race.[35]

The participants arrived on the evening on Friday, July 21, 1967, in casual attire, eyeing one another suspiciously. While the group was large (thirty-five participants) and racially mixed, it replicated the class composition of previous groups, largely drawing from the upper-middle class. It was also unbalanced in its ratio of whites to blacks and of black men to black women (more whites and black *men*). Cobbs later wrote, "In terms of how they looked, my fears were immediately dispelled. They all appeared to be the kind of people who attended seminars and lectures and were interested in something called 'race relations.'"[36] The only anomalous participant was a young black man who worked for the highway department and had been repairing roads at Esalen. The man had noticed a flyer posted about the workshop and was struck by its inclusion of race and by the novelty of this as compared to the many flyers he'd seen posted that had never mentioned race.[37]

Like traditional Esalen encounter groups, the weekend began with physical stretching exercises led by a "Chinese guru." The participants then moved to a larger seminar room where they made themselves comfortable in chairs or on oversized pillows on the floor. At the urging of Cobbs and Leonard, they began to introduce themselves and explain why they were there. The exceptionally charged nature of the group immediately began to manifest itself. A white schoolteacher from Los Angeles explained, a little too emphatically, "I'm here to find out what blacks really want." A black man expressed his assumption that his white peers were college graduates who played tennis and chess. A white man explained his interest in racial encounter with a description of his liberalism.[38]

Cobbs, in an effort to prevent more division among participants than what already existed, opted out of conducting the small group work that was typical of encounter. He kept the larger group intact, and made sure all members were engaged. Since encounter groups differed from group psychotherapy in that the leaders were also active participants, Cobbs and Leonard attempted to model their own interracial friendship to the group. Even in this united context, however, the group was deeply divided. The civilized demeanor that governed the daily lives of the participants quickly devolved into angry accusations, infused with a growing sense of bitterness and desolation.

The black participants engaged in what Cobbs referred to as a game of "one-upsmanship," before directing their hostility against white participants. There was a lot of name-calling and accusations that certain blacks were either not black enough or not appropriately black. One light-skinned black woman called a darker-skinned black man "a dirty little nigger" when he described his interest in sleeping with a white woman in the group.[39] Even within the races, or perhaps more so within the races, suspicion and hostility ran deep.

By the second night, the group devolved into an "angry pissing match." "What do you know about having your kids called 'nigger' and there's nothing you can do about it?" shouted the group's one black woman to a white woman. "When's your kid ever been spit on because he was black?"[40] It seemed impossible that a member of the ruling class could ever really understand the experience of the oppressed, and it seemed offensive for her to try.

Black participants zeroed in on what they saw as the problem of the "white good-guy liberal," a person who defined himself as against racism but replicated the subtle dynamics of racial prejudice with his ignorance of black reality.[41] The category, of course, applied to white women as well. When a white woman asked a black participant for his friendship, he responded with intolerance. "Fuck you!" he shouted. "And fuck your condescension. Fuck your pity!" Other participants threatened violence.[42]

The rage was so free-flowing and unabating that both Leonard and Cobbs began to give up hope. "Everything, it seemed, had failed," wrote Esalen chronicler Walter Anderson.

"The weekend was a failure, the people themselves were failures, and the prospects for tearing down the barriers between races were nil."[43]

On Sunday morning, however, some time after the sun rose, a transformation occurred. Emotionally overwrought, a white woman began to cry, claiming that she only dated black men because she had given up on white men. She was laid bare, exhausted from the weekend's strife, no longer willing to defend her views or her actions. She was at a breaking point. Fortunately, it was a collective breaking point. Her desperation struck a deeply human chord; it existed not because of logic or strategy or defensiveness. It was involuntary, authentic, uncontrollable, and it was powerful enough to evoke the sympathy of both the white and black participants. The episode ended in tearful hugging and emotional reconciliation.[44]

To Leonard, the moment of tearful recognition testified that the group had worked its magic, unleashing an emotional catharsis that represented a new level of understanding between individual participants and suggesting the possibilities for broader interracial understanding in the culture. He was euphoric; the group had been saved. Cobbs also left the group optimistic, but without dreams of reconciliation or even resolution. Cobbs later wrote in his 2006 memoir, "The participants at this first black/white confrontation group learned so much about one another that weekend that few, if any, of them, went home unaffected. Many friendships were formed. Some of the participants came away offended and upset. A few seemed shell-shocked."[45]

Cobbs's primary impression was of the unveiling of a common black experience of anger and frustration and a common white experience of prejudice and ignorance. Encouraging others to see "the truth of black rage" soon became his primary interest. For this reason, he heightened his commitment to encounter groups, deciding to venture to Big Sur on weekends for modified versions of the same experience.[46]

In the flush of preliminary success, Leonard saw the black-white encounter group as a model for how broad social change would occur.[47] To heal a culture that harbored deep racial tensions, it was necessary first to recognize and then to exorcise them through mutual understanding. But like Murphy, who was always skeptical of encounter, Cobbs had practical concerns about the ability of the groups to elicit enduring and pervasive change in cultural attitudes. He doubted as well the ability of humanistic psychotherapy to effectively address the needs of blacks.

Without a thorough knowledge of the "Black Norm," Cobbs argued, even the most sensitive humanistic therapist would fail to offer effective treatment. "To find the amount of sickness a black man has," Cobbs suggested, "one must first total all that appears to represent illness and then subtract the Black Norm. What remains is illness and a proper subject for therapeutic endeavor. To regard the Black Norm as pathological and attempt to remove such traits by treatment would be akin to analyzing away a hunter's cunning or a banker's prudence. This is a body of characteristics essential to life for black men in America and woe unto that therapist who does not recognize it."[48] The components of the "Black Norm" included both a cultural depression that Cobbs explained as a realistic sadness acquired from actual injuries suffered and a cultural antisocialism that he described as a general lack of respect for laws that hadn't been created in the interests of blacks.[49] Cobbs felt that the ignorance of psychotherapists with regard to the Black

Norm, and their subsequent tendency to pathologize black characteristics, was responsible, in part, for the distaste many blacks felt for the entire institution of psychology.

If humanistic psychologists were going to effectively prioritize black Americans, they were also going to have to overcome black resistance to psychotherapy, and to arouse broader black interest. Unfortunately, the historically tortured relationship between blacks and psychology was a major impediment to black acceptance of any given set of psychological theories or techniques. While humanistic psychology diverged dramatically from psychological schools that had relied on medical and scientific power to control and manipulate individuals, it also possessed similarities to the movements that preceded it. For one, it was a largely white movement, led by scholars who had very little knowledge of black experience. Also, it was largely inaccessible. Seeking therapy from humanistic psychologists required money and knowledge about where to seek treatment. While its theories had begun to seep into the broader culture, as a therapeutic tool it remained the province of an overwhelmingly white cultural elite.

Many blacks undoubtedly associated humanistic psychology with the larger field of psychology, for which they had acquired a well-founded distrust. The history of American psychology and psychiatry was woven into the history of racism in both the American medical establishment and the American government. In the past, doctors had hypothesized that the black brain was "smaller and less developed" than the white brain, thus explaining why blacks were "not capable of managing a high degree of civilization."[50] They had also identified genetic predisposition in some racial stocks as an explanation for mental inferiority in blacks.[51]

For many blacks, seeking assistance from psychological institutions was also incompatible with their cultural and religious beliefs. The horrific legacy of slavery and segregation had instilled in many black Americans a sense that they were capable of and expected to endure "superhuman" levels of psychological and physical suffering. Problems in daily life or relationships, including the experience of anxiety or depression, appeared trivial in comparison to the obstacles their ancestors had overcome.[52]

One black psychiatrist has argued that the belief in superhuman strength produced a cultural imperative that blacks stay strong in the face of extraordinary psychic and physical obstacles. This mentality was reinforced by various mediums of black culture—music, poetry, and literature—and was perpetuated in black churches, where ministers delivered sermons designed to arm parishioners against difficulty.[53] In aggrandizing the values of self-denial and self-sacrifice, though, ministers tended to prevent blacks from admitting to mental distress.

The concept of a healing God to whom believers could pray for the abatement of mental distress solidified the construction of psychological difficulties as a private, and thoroughly personal, struggle. Trust in religious solutions often precluded the possibility for reliance on a psychological "expert" whose motives were invariably less trust-inspiring than those of God, religious figures, and fellow church members.[54]

The fact that psychology was a predominantly white institution, and that whites were the cause of much of blacks' distress, further prevented blacks from seeking professional help. But this pride, and this stoicism, also proved to be a form of masochism. Black men historically have suffered the highest levels of suicide of any American demographic and have always had a greater likelihood of being diagnosed with serious illnesses when evaluated by clinicians.[55]

While many blacks' distaste for psychology dated back to even the earliest incarnations of American psychology, it became in many ways more acute in the late 1960s, when the ideals of integration were giving way, in large segments of the population, to a more black-centric politics, influenced by black power.[56]

In 1968, sociologist Lewis Killian wrote that "in practice integration had turned out to mean the token integration of a minority of qualified blacks into what remained a white man's society."[57] Another scholar noted that many blacks at the time were characterized by "the experience of bitter disappointment, disgust, and despair over the pace, scope, and quality of social change [and by] the prolonged and direct encounter of certain civil rights workers—especially those connected with SNCC [the Student Nonviolent Coordinating Committee] and CORE [the Congress of Racial Equality]—with the grim and aching realities, the dark and brute actions and deceptions of certain sections of the deep South."[58]

The trajectory of the civil rights movement, from hope and faith in integration to cynicism and anger, had paralleled the evolution of eminent black psychologist Kenneth Clark's sentiments. In 1952, Clark had testified in *Briggs v. Elliott*, one of the five cases combined in *Brown v. Board of Education*.[59] Drawing on the doll studies that he and his wife Mamie Clark had performed on racial prejudice in children in segregated and desegregated schools, Clark's testimony spoke to the necessity of desegregating schools to eliminate racism.[60] By the mid-1960s,

however, his patience had waned as he looked in vain for progress on integration. In 1965 he wrote: "I am tired of civil rights.
Maybe I should develop some ideas concerning the enormous
waste of human intelligence sacrificed to the struggle for racial
justice in America at this period of the 20th century. How long
can our nation continue the tremendous wastage of human intellectual resources demanded by racism?"[61] In the years that
followed, the black power movement took hold, and with it
came a new black psychology.

While those who applied humanistic psychology to race
sought to negate racial differences with humanistic understanding, black power offered both recognition of the unique experiences of racial minorities and symbolic compensation for previous
wrongs they had endured. A splinter group of black psychologists channeled the black power perspective by refusing to enter
into a paternalistic relationship with white-centered movements
like humanistic psychology. Instead, they attempted to construct an alternative psychology, independent of white theory
and inapplicable to white individuals. They drew inspiration
from black nationalists like Frantz Fanon, a psychiatrist from
Martinique who was a physician, scholar, and political militant
in the Algerian revolution, and who identified mainstream psychology with "scientific colonialism."[62]

Ironically, new black psychologists had more in common
with humanistic psychologists than they cared to admit. Many
of their foundational concepts seemed to be drawn directly
from Maslow. Chief among these guiding precepts were "an affirmation of one's own cultural integrity and psychological
strength" and an "elevation of the total person" in the service of
attaining "optimal" mental health.[63] As their perhaps inadver-
tent adoption of humanistic theory suggests, humanistic psy-

chology seemed, in many respects, to be ideally suited to the interests of blacks.

Black psychologist and University of Michigan professor Adelbert Jenkins recognized this affinity and was optimistic about humanistic psychology's ability to appeal to blacks. He believed, as well, that humanistic psychology's reformulated notions of mental distress and of human nature could help overcome blacks' resistance to psychotherapy. Mental distress was, according to humanistic psychologists, not internally derived but a product of an environmental resistance to human potential through the frustration of healthy individual strivings. Individuals, however, were not powerless to rise above environmental oppression. On the contrary, they were inherently health- and growth-oriented and, given the opportunity, would maximize their potential. This formulation implied that the American government, and the culture at large, was still on the hook for the obstacles they had set in the way of blacks (in the form of discrimination and oppression), but that blacks had not been irreparably damaged and would continue to seek greater heights of self-realization.[64]

Jenkins extracted, from humanistic psychologists, a positive program capable of adaptation to the specific concerns of blacks in America. He also identified the applicability of their platform of protest to black psychology. Humanistic psychologists offered a reasoned critique of the ignominious tendency of social scientists to overlook social injustice by focusing on individual dysfunction. They accused psychoanalysis and broader drive theories, for example, of constructing pathological behavior as a product of a flawed psyche, locating the source of pathology within the individual and, in effect, blaming the victim. In all likelihood, argued Jenkins, accepting the psychoanalytic paradigm would have exacerbated the "sense [in blacks] that something inside themselves prevented them from struggling effectively to realize their full psychosocial potential."[65] According to one historian of black psychology, drive theory had also helped to "reinforce what can be referred to as nativist themes by declaring that human differences resulted from causes within people rather than environmental forces in society. Therefore the 'plight' of blackness, including the so-called culture and cycle of poverty, had been blamed on inherent inadequacies of blacks themselves."[66]

Theories of environmental conditioning, which humanistic psychologists also opposed, further reinforced psychology's inclination to "blame the victim" by explaining mental distress and pathological behavior as direct products of small-scale environments, such as the family or the neighborhood, but rarely with reference to larger social forces. Such behavioral theories, which were dominant in the 1940s and 1950s, had the potential to blame black families for the distress of black children, rather than locating black families, and their particular challenges, in the context of the broader culture and its systemic disadvantaging of blacks.

Even as drive theory tended toward psychological determinism, environmental conditioning theory suggested environmental determinism. In both cases, the individual will was denied, leaving the "subject" passive at best and inherently psychologically pathological at worst.[67] Humanistic psychologists, of course, hoped to correct the errors of both psychoanalysis and behaviorism. They criticized these theories for denying individual subjectivity and disempowering will, and in their place offered a theory that, they believed, would inherently align better with black interests. The direct application of their guiding principles to the unique situation of blacks, however, tended to remain at the theoretical level.

Unfortunately, Jenkins's work, which melded humanistic psychology with black concerns and was well respected, was relatively peripheral to the humanistic psychology movement (at least in its early years). More central contributions, like those of Abraham Maslow and Carl Rogers, tended to exclude black issues entirely.

Maslow himself was sensitive to the natural affinity between the goals of humanistic psychology and of black liberation movements, but he felt no particular obligation to forge a connection between the two. In fact, he tended to blame blacks for their lack of attention to the relevance of humanistic psychology. In his personal notes, he wrote, "One sad thing about the whole business is that you can interpret one aspect [. . .] of the Negro rebellion as reaching out for this very humanistic entranced personal ethic and philosophy. They reach out for it as if it didn't exist. And yet it does exist. They just don't know about it. You could call it in a way an answer to their prayers, to their demands. In principle it is something which should satisfy them, because it's a system of values which involves a reconstruction of science as a means of discovering and uncovering values (rather than it being value-free). Not only that, but it includes the beginnings of a strategy in tactics of reaching there. That is, a theory of education, including a philosophy of education including both means and ends of education."[68]

Implicit in Maslow's statement was an awareness that the goals of humanistic psychology, which prioritized the capacity for choice, for freedom, and for self-development, were inherently complementary to the objectives of civil rights. Absent, however, was any identification of humanistic psychology as having a responsibility for connecting with blacks.

In the 1960s, most humanistic psychologists professed their unrestrained support for improving race relations, but were, in reality, unwilling or uninterested in taking race relations to the forefront of their professional lives. The attention paid to racial issues at the annual conferences of the American Association of Humanistic Psychology and in the *Journal of Humanistic Psychology* was scant. In fact, not one article in the first two *decades* of *JHP* explored racial issues.[69]

This combination of personal interest and lack of professional attention tended to come across as racial tokenism; humanistic psychologists seemed superficially willing to endorse the goal of racial equality but not to work for it. The critique blacks lodged against whites in humanistic psychology paralleled their critique of white liberals in general. As sociologist Lewis Killian wrote in 1968, "Much of white support for black rights appears to be lip-service, an approval of rights without a corresponding commitment to do anything to grant them."[70]

In his relatively brief interaction with humanistic psychology, Price Cobbs had identified this racial tokenism. When he raised issues regarding racial dynamics and concerns, other members often responded by saying, "Let's just be human!" Cobbs felt deeply that just saying "I'm liberal and I'm for you" wasn't enough, but that that was all that many humanistic psychologists were willing to offer.[71]

Stanley Krippner shared this view of humanistic psychology's limitations in terms of exploring race. He argued that because they felt race was a social construct, many humanistic psychologists believed a revisionist perspective based on common humanity would erase the societal distinctions between blacks and whites.[72] Krippner observed that whether dangerously naïve or just overly idealistic, humanistic psychologists tended to minimize and even ignore the pervasive nature of the racial prejudice with which the culture was saturated. Further, they tended to alienate racial minorities by homogenizing human experience, and ignoring the individual struggles and psychological scars characteristic of minorities living in a racially divided culture.[73]

Carl Rogers had hoped to do better. Championing the goal of using humanistic psychology to achieve racial understanding, Rogers himself facilitated several black-white encounter groups and celebrated the results. "The outcomes are a gut-level experiential learning [about] racist attitudes on the part of whites, and a rare opportunity on the part of blacks," he later wrote.[74] For blacks, he felt that the "bitterness and rage which exists" could be expressed productively, easing the burden of misunderstanding and isolation. Rogers touted the outcome of racial encounter as "the surprising result [that blacks and whites] tend to become persons to each other and can talk openly and freely without reference to stereotypes or color.[75] But while Rogers harbored high hopes for the integrationist potential of the groups, he tended to view race-based encounter as a side project, and only intermittently gave it his attention.

His approach was typical of humanistic psychology adherents, who tended to express initial excitement about the potential of black-white encounter groups but later became distracted by the numerous aspects of humanistic psychology that competed for their attention.[76] He was concerned about social injustice but not willing to subordinate other concerns in favor of activism. More extreme reactions came from humanistic psychologists like Virginia Satir, who failed to acknowledge any obligation the movement might have to pressing political issues of the time. Satir, when confronted about her lack of political consciousness, replied, "I want to change the family and their interactions. I want to change the communications and I even want to change the way therapists see dynamics and interactions. But I like the world as it is otherwise."[77]

The brand of humanistic psychology that Satir (and others) practiced reflected an extreme personal focus that was a liability for the movement. Although the goal of racial harmony was aligned with their liberal interests and utopian aspirations, humanistic psychologists often reverted to acting like other psychologists, taking comfort in their disciplinary insularity and bowing out of broader cultural conflicts.[78] In the case of civil rights, the AAHP mimicked the shortsightedness of larger organizations like the American Psychological Association (APA), which attended to the needs of black members (and the larger cultural crises they represented) only when forced to do so.

The APA didn't even begin to acknowledge racial concerns until 1969, when at their annual convention twenty-four graduate student members of the newly formed Black Students Psychological Association (BSPA) demanded the APA council respond to their requests. Standing shoulder-to-shoulder in front of the council, the students asked that more black students be recruited to undergraduate and graduate programs in psychology, that blacks receive better representation in the APA, that black students be offered socially relevant experience in programs designed to benefit the black community, and that the credibility of the black power movement be recognized.[79]

This organized protest of black students was typical of the increased pressure facing professional organizations in the late

1960s. The American Sociological Association, for example, faced a comparable "disruption" at its own annual convention in 1969.[80] In these organizations, as in most professional and academic organizations of the 1960s, blacks were underrepresented and their race-specific concerns generally unrecognized.[81] But by the end of the decade, even associations with few black members began to feel internal pressure to confront racial issues.

Black students had grown, over the course of the 1960s, increasingly organized and self-assured in their sense of mission.[82] The civil rights activities of the 1950s, including the *Brown v. Board of Education* decision of 1954, the Montgomery Bus Boycott of 1955, and the University of Alabama riots in 1956, erupted in the form of further protests and riots in the 1960s, infusing racial issues with a sense of undeniable urgency.[83] Beginning with the freedom rides of 1960, the establishment of the Student Nonviolent Coordinating Committee that same year and of the Congress of Racial Equality in 1961, the passage of the Civil Rights Act in 1964, and the subsequent formation of the Equal Employment Opportunities Commission designed to enforce it, civil rights swept through the decade on a swift tide of activity and change.[84]

The response of the APA to the challenge from black graduate students was decidedly mixed. Milton J. Rosenberg, University of Chicago professor and council member, told the students that "the council was 'beyond racism' and was tired of the 'make it hot for whitey routine.' "[85] In frustration APA president George Miller asked, "How can we keep [psychology] a science if we try to solve everybody's goddamn problems?"[86] Other psychologists were more sympathetic to the demands of the black students, but doubtful about their relevance to the mission of the APA. University of Texas professor Sigmund Koch expressed his remorse that "psychology has no answers in respect of the problems [black students] are concerned about."[87]

While these sentiments were typical of psychologists in response to the clash between disciplinary interests and social concerns, they were also common to liberals in other professions, who felt that, though they naturally supported equal rights, racial equality was irrelevant to their professional priorities. Many blacks judged the compromised efforts of predominantly liberal professional organizations toward racial integration to be insufficient and even insulting.[88]

The suspicion of psychologists' racial tokenism compelled blacks to approach even the most earnest attempts of humanistic psychologists as inadequate. The success of Leonard and Cobbs's black-white encounter groups, for example, was compromised by the markers of white liberalism that accompanied them.[89]

Centralized at Esalen, which had earned a reputation as an "upper-middle-class utopia," the groups hardly seemed designed with black interests in mind.[90] The breathtaking location—the cliffside views, the sulfur-infused hot springs, and the rolling hills of organic gardens—suggested a level of luxury and self-indulgence that was estranged from the daily experience of prejudice and struggle familiar even to middle-class blacks, and was unimaginable to the many blacks who lived in rural or urban poverty.[91]

The sexual ethos of Esalen, too, was foreign to many blacks, smacking as it did of the white leisure class.[92] Esalen's baths were clothing-optional during the day and entirely nude at night, and sexual promiscuity (between visitors or between visitors and staff) was rampant. These facts were widely publicized by the media. To many blacks, nudity as a form of protest was a bit frivolous, particularly in comparison to civil rights, the war in Vietnam (which was so costly to minority communities), and women's liberation. It also ran counter to the strong influence of the black church.[93]

When confronted with open nudity at Esalen, black men must have been at least a little wary.[94] Several historians have documented the care with which certain black men held themselves to standards of sexual morality, in the face of entrenched cultural myths that had constructed them as hypersexual predators.[95] Even Cobbs's initial reaction to Esalen reflected his perception of the threatening nature of sexual impropriety at Esalen. "Oh God," Cobbs thought, "what have I gotten myself into? Me, a conventional young black professional, raised to be respectable. The visions of long-haired hippies swimming nude made me wonder what my mother would have thought about us being there."[96]

Cobbs was also particularly concerned about the geographic limitations of hosting black-white encounters in Big Sur, viewing the inaccessibility as an obstacle to the realization of meaningful social change from the groups.[97] Big Sur was a 150-mile trip from San Francisco on the Pacific Coast Highway, a narrow and serpentine roadway of treacherous hairpin curves that was uniquely susceptible to adverse weather conditions, flooding, and falling rocks (like the one that would eventually kill founder Dick Price).[98]

Both Murphy and Leonard were sensitive to Esalen's limitations in this respect. Even before the first interracial encounter group, Murphy had proposed opening a city location that would better suit the needs of black participants. He hoped that it would attract wider community attention and enable people from the city to attend groups. Esalen's San Francisco extension officially opened in 1967.

The new location, modeled closely on the original in terms of workshops and seminars, was initially a great success, with attendance exceeding ten thousand in the first two months of operation.[99] Even with little advertising, the inaugural event alone, a lecture by Abe Maslow titled "The Farther Reaches of Human Nature," had drawn an audience of two thousand people.[100]

Murphy, who became primarily responsible for the San Francisco extension while Price stayed on at Big Sur, brought to the project the same serious intentions he had infused into the original institute. In the first year it attracted serious scholars, including B. F. Skinner.[101] It also honored its intentions to address race issues meaningfully, offering four racial confrontation workshops in the summer encounter series of 1968. The registration form explained that:

> Open racial confrontation is at last a reality, but it has brought bloodshed and death, terror and polarization. Rather than fear a confrontation, we must welcome and embrace it. For only in direct and honest encounter can white racism and black self-hatred be discarded. This series of Racial Confrontations is to allow for bloodless riots where the most dreaded thoughts and emotions may be expressed, where self-delusions that limit can be stripped away. Only when such confrontation has occurred can man expand his blackness and whiteness into creative humanness.[102]

Unfortunately, the San Francisco extension wasn't able to sustain the interest of the leaders, or participants, for very long. Attendance began to drop off after the initial surge of interest. The racial encounter groups were poorly attended by blacks and reflected the same middle-class bias of the initial Big Sur group.[103] Viewing the San Francisco extension as secondary to that of the Big Sur branch, Esalen leaders seemed to have failed to devote the necessary resources to outreach for the center.

The San Francisco office was plagued by internal tensions as well. Faced with staff whose commitment to racial issues differed dramatically from one person to the next, the extension proved as vulnerable to the dividing potential of racial conflict as any other organization. These tensions were most aptly demonstrated in 1969, when an argument erupted between Ron Brown, a black graduate student at the San Francisco wing, and Bill Smith, a white administrator. The argument quickly escalated into shouting, and several things Smith said, including his threat to call the police, struck Brown as being racially loaded. Michael Murphy, George Leonard, and Price Cobbs met with the two to try to ease the conflict, but to no avail. As was typical, Murphy backed away from the confrontation, angering Leonard and Cobbs. Brown later said of Murphy that he "just never understood the racial part of it."[104] This insensitivity drove Cobbs away from Esalen; he never again ran a group there. Leonard, too, kept his distance from Murphy for a while, and Murphy himself lost some of his evangelical zeal for Esalen's mission.[105]

The San Francisco extension was a sinking ship. In spite of early attendance, it had lost money from the start and soon began to tax the Big Sur facility.[106] In the 1972 catalog, Esalen reported in the news section that the San Francisco extension lost $125,822 in 1971. In the same catalog, the San Francisco facility announced its intention to cosponsor its programs with the Gestalt Institute of San Francisco.[107] Eventually, around 1973, the facility's treasurer recommended to Murphy that the extension close. Whether this financial necessity stemmed from a lack of public interest or organizational mismanagement was a matter of some contention, but the outcome was evidence that the San Francisco Esalen never found the groove that the Big Sur Esalen did. "Perhaps Esalen needed that deep black Big Sur soil to thrive," remarked George Leonard, in retrospect.[108]

Leonard's statement suggests the otherworldly quality of the Big Sur Esalen; it was hospitable to the lofty goals of spiritual seekers but ill-suited to the weighty, urban social issues of the time.[109] In recognizing the disconnection between this laboratory of change and the real world, Leonard was admitting, too, the structural limitations of the racial encounter techniques in which he had once invested his hopes for the redemption of society. Even though it would be nice to get the world leaders into an encounter group, the resulting change might be more contained than he'd originally hoped, and a good deal more personal.[110]

Leonard was one of many humanistic psychologists who were beginning to believe, toward the end of the 1960s, that placing the individual in the interpersonal context of encounter was another form of individual therapy. Although it might produce healthier, more fulfilled individuals who, when collected, might reach a critical mass and take society in new and better directions, the basic unit of change was to be the singular person.

11

The Postmortem Years

"One very important aspect of the post mortem life is that everything gets doubly precious, gets piercingly important. You get stabbed by things, by flowers and by babies and by beautiful things—just the very act of living, of walking and breathing and eating and having friends and chatting."

ABRAHAM MASLOW[1]

By the late 1960s, humanistic psychology had moved out of its infancy. Its character felt more solid and defined, and at the same time its weaknesses and limits were better known. It was a player in most major academic circles, and was represented in the departmental course listings and faculty interests of most universities. And though it wasn't the most popular theory in the field, it had its circle of intimates, who were loyal and outspoken. They gathered at a number of institutes in Northern California, but also in intellectual pockets in places as diverse as western Pennsylvania and rural Georgia.

Within certain psychology departments, humanistic psychology actually became the dominant orientation. As early as 1959, Duquesne University in Pittsburgh offered a master's degree in existential-phenomenological psychology, adding a doctoral program in 1962. Sonoma State College established a graduate program in humanistic psychology in 1966. And private institutes like John F. Kennedy University in California and the Union Institute in Michigan both began programs in 1964.[2]

This was just the beginning. Some of the best-known humanistic psychology programs were established in the late 1960s and early 1970s, when the movement was in full swing. Among them was an unlikely candidate for a humanistic emphasis: a small, rural college at the foot of the Appalachians in Carrollton, Georgia.

West Georgia College had become a four-year institution in 1957, as the town was transitioning from its agricultural roots in cotton production to a technological orientation in wire and cable manufacturing. Its students were locals, and the majority were politically conservative. They were insulated, in significant ways, from the student movement and the counterculture. Hippies, in fact, were a foreign element, not seen much before 1969, when the psychology department stirred things up.[3]

Several West Georgia psychologists who had been sifting through as much of the new psychological theory as they could find decided they wanted to refashion the department to be more relevant to students' lives. Because they were impressed by Maslow's work in particular, they decided to call him directly and ask him to recommend a new chairperson to head their program. He sent them his former student, Mike Arons, who immediately got to work hiring like-minded people. Almost overnight, thirty new courses were added, most of which couldn't be found anywhere else in the nation (or the world). They included "Human Growth and Potential," "Holistic Psychology East & West," "Phenomenology of Social Existence," "Phenomenology of Spatiality & Temporality Myths," "Explorations into Creativity Values," "Meaning, & the Individual Will," and "Choice & Belief." When teaching these courses, the faculty tended to use nontraditional resources, like literature, philosophy, art, film, and music, and in certain cases wrote their own texts to supplement the available literature.[4]

West Georgia's unusual new program was alluring, attracting students from all over the world, many of whom were already established in professions ranging from law to bellydancing, and almost all of whom were looking for a change. Established professors found themselves unexpectedly drawn to the small-town Georgia mecca, as well. Brandeis psychologist Jim Klee, for example, left idyllic Waltham, Massachusetts, in 1971 for a sabbatical at West Georgia and never returned. These kinds of moves were even more impressive than the jumps of northeastern and midwestern academics from comfortable academic positions at distinguished universities to comparably suitable positions in California—at institutes like the Western Behavioral Sciences Institute, or the California Institute of Integral Studies, which had opened in 1968—where the better weather and more liberal politics compensated for the lack of prestige.

Regardless of the specific location, though, the centralization of humanistic psychologists at places like West Georgia occurred in part because they found themselves more productive, supported, and stimulated than they did when they were dispersed at larger (and sometimes more reputable) universities where their work was less valued. Humanistic psychologists' project of establishing a base of humanistic research that could compete with the output of other orientations seemed daunting when members were isolated, but more possible when they could feed daily on each other's insights and enthusiasm.

In 1971 Don Gibbons, an Association of Humanistic Psychology member and psychology professor at West Georgia College, gathered enough signatures (the required 1 percent of APA members) to found a division of humanistic psychology within the APA.[5] The first organizational meeting of the new division, known as Division 32, held on September 4, 1971, was attended by fifty-seven individuals and chaired by psychologist Albert Ellis. The division's membership soared in the first few years and came to include a vibrant international contingent.[6] This early success earned the division two seats on APA's Council of Representatives and ensured that its members would have forums for their theory and research, both by forming a connection to *JHP* and creating a new journal titled *Interpersonal Development.*[7]

Also in 1971, a group of humanistic psychologists established a proper intellectual home for the movement. The Humanistic Psychology Institute (HPI, later known as Saybrook University) was the brainchild of Eleanor Criswell, who was then an assistant professor in Sonoma State's humanistically oriented psychology department. Criswell was concerned that there was no real way to become a humanistic psychologist, no specific place devoted to training people to study and research humanistic ideas. Nor was there a place, she believed, where teaching embodied such humanistic ideals.[8] She proposed the idea of a graduate school to the Association of Humanistic Psychology (AHP) in 1970 and became its first director.[9] (The American Association of Humanistic Psychology had changed its name to the Association of Humanistic Psychology in 1969, acknowledging the increased international attention to its theories.[10])

For the first few years, HPI and AHP were literally entwined, sharing a large industrial space in a brick building on Ninth Avenue in downtown San Francisco. Their aims were synergistic; together they searched for ways to bring new people into humanistic psychology and to transmit humanistic ideas to the world. Early on, HPI sought to create, at various universities, programs intended to train people specifically in humanistic psychology's methods and theory. It cooperated with Sonoma State, for example, to found a one-year extension program designed to train people at any level (pre- or postdoctoral) in humanistic psychology. HPI soon turned to its own pursuits, however, establishing its independence from AHP and, beginning in 1972, offering graduate degrees.[11]

In many respects, HPI came to resemble the humanistic psychology movement in miniature. It built on the successes of related programs, but forged its own identity. It struggled to accommodate internal conflict (mainly between academic and experiential interests) productively. It tried to elevate institutional harmony over the individual interests of its faculty. And even when it failed on any of these counts, it kept pressing on.

At the same time that humanistic psychology was coming into its own at institutes and colleges across the nation, its father was beginning to fade. In February 1970, Maslow found himself eye to eye with his own mortality. Gazing at the ocean while driving south from Esalen, he wrote, "Thoughts of death while this will all go on. So impulse to hang on to it, appreciate it, be sure to miss not one single moment of it. It intensifies the *beauty* & the poignancy of it."[12]

For three years, he had suffered intermittent chest pains, heart palpitations, insomnia, "sick exhaustion," general fatigue, feebleness, trembling, and depression. But he had also experienced a new freedom from obligation and expectation, and had discovered new sources of transcendence.

What Maslow called his "postmortem life," which began after his 1967 heart attack, was in his eyes all bonus. It was less planned, less structured, slower, and more relaxed. Periods of work were punctuated with the periods of rest his body required.

He found that the formlessness of this period of his life, and the long intervals of reading and observing, enriched his conscious awareness. His conclusions were better and more integrated, he believed, and his insight was clearer and more assimilated. He was beginning to self-actualize.[13]

He had chosen, during this period, an unlikely model for his personal transformation. His granddaughter Jeannie had been born in 1968. To Maslow, she was the embodiment of "being values." She was "perfect and miraculous in her tiny perfection," nonambivalent, uninhibited in her expression, orgiastic, defenseless, nonmonitoring, nonediting, non-self-observing, utterly amusable. She was free from competitive instincts, sexual hang-ups, and social restraints.[14]

Maslow wrote in his journal of the exhilaration and rapture that Jeannie evoked. Her presence defied the staleness of existence. Each time he saw her, she felt entirely new to him. She was unqualified delight and process-oriented pleasure.[15]

The extent of his enjoyment was, no doubt, a function of the expectation that he would soon die. He would miss seeing her grow up and would never discover the kind of woman she was to become. This realization, he wrote, "was sad & yet also intensified the experience & made me cling to it & suck every bit of juice out of it."[16]

Maslow's professional life, during these postmortem years, was characterized by a comparable degree of intensity. He vacillated between a sense of disappointment—in humanistic psychology, in the human potential movement, and in his own contributions—and a feeling of professional triumph.

In the years just before his heart attack, Maslow expressed, in his journal, a grave sense of self-doubt. While he had generated vital theory, he admitted, he had failed to follow up with the kind of meticulous research that would support and reinforce it.

"As I felt the research impulse drain out of me," he wrote in his journal in 1966, "I guess I must have felt that the right to call myself a psychologist was also draining out of me, & in several kinds of situations I've felt inadequate, not sufficiently trained, etc."[17]

His sense of professional alienation ran deep. "The positivists have so much taken over APA & the elementary texts & graduate education that AAHP is not even known to most," he wrote "& my kind of work is shoved into a corner where I'm a hero to a few & unknown, neglected, despised by most, or simply not defined as a 'scientific psychologist.'"[18] His hurt was a product of decades of representing a minority perspective, of receiving rejections from prestigious journals, of being dismissed by peers for his unconventional views and approaches. Against his optimistic nature, he had begun to internalize some of the harsh criticism he had encountered, and to experience a sense of doubt that made his work feel futile.

He was being too hard on himself. In reality, the cultural fascination with humanistic psychology had given it a boost professionally. The proliferation of courses and academic programs devoted to Maslow's principles was one measure of his success. Another was his election to the presidency of the American Psychological Association. In 1966, near the time when he was fantasizing about being thrown out of the APA, he received word of his nomination.[19]

This was a big moment for Maslow, and for humanistic psychology. "Astonished by being nominated to presidency of APA," Maslow wrote in his journal. "Apparently I've read the situations incorrectly, feeling out of things, alienated from the APA, rejected & rejecting."[20]

The presidency of APA, an organization whose membership would surpass thirty thousand by 1970, was the most distinguished post an American psychologist could occupy.[21] Maslow was flattered by the recognition. His orientation toward the perceived value of his work changed almost overnight. He noted the advantages for AHP, "for adding weight & prestige to my causes, for having a guaranteed hearing for anything I want to say."[22]

At the same time, Maslow privately expressed his vexation at APA's choice, fearing that their endorsement of him represented an attempt at co-optation. What was being affirmed, he feared, wasn't his theory but a neutered interpretation of it that was unthreatening to the values of American academic psychology, which, after all, hadn't departed in any remarkable way from the constraints Maslow and his peers had railed against in the 1950s. His friend Frank Manuel remembers how disturbed he was: "What had he done, he kept asking morosely, what had become of him, when it was possible for those positivistic piddlers to choose him?"[23]

After his heart attack, Maslow judged his obligation to APA to be among the most taxing responsibilities he faced. He lacked the kind of energy, and the kind of interest, that the position required.[24] Prioritizing his health and seeking a reprieve from his "panicky" dreams, Maslow canceled his presidential address.

But no such evasion could quell the tide of interest in his theory that his election to the position signified. By the late 1960s, the success of Maslow's books was a further testament to his preeminence. His work circulated widely. Two hundred thousand copies of *Toward a Psychology of Being*, for example, were sold even before a trade edition was issued in 1968. And terms like "peak experience" and "self-actualization" were on the lips of "legions of admirers," many of whom had never read his work.[25]

The success of Rollo May's books was another indication of the size of the audience with whom the basic theories of humanistic psychology resonated. In fact, May's publications, which included *Psychology and the Human Dilemma* (1967) and *Love and Will* (1969), were among the bestselling books in popular psychology at the time. In a nine-page article, a *New York Times* reporter documented the sales of *Love and Will* in its first year and a half as being in excess of 135,000 copies, and wrote that it was "fast becoming the source book for post-Freudian man."[26]

In *Psychology and the Human Dilemma*, May spoke to individuals in a time of transition, when traditional values were obsolete and viable alternatives hadn't yet emerged to fill their place. The basic human dilemma—that of maintaining a sense of significance in light of one's objecthood, wrote May, was only exacerbated by unsettling cultural changes in sexual mores, religious beliefs, traditional roles, and governmental authority.[27]

In the late 1960s, many Americans were feeling disoriented by cultural flux. In 1968 alone, Martin Luther King, Jr., and Robert Kennedy were assassinated, the My Lai massacre and the Tet Offensive shed new light on the horrific nature of America's involvement in Vietnam, and Lyndon B. Johnson finished his term in shame. The women's liberation movement began to gain steam, while the civil rights struggle raged on and student protests continued. As the election of Richard Nixon suggested, though, many Americans had abandoned the idealistic hopes that had fueled not just the radical movements of the decade but the liberal legislative programs of the Kennedy and Johnson administrations.

Naturally, May's solutions to this cultural upheaval were psychological rather than political. Grounded in his experience providing psychotherapy, May touted the values of heightened personal awareness, freedom and self-determination, responsibility for oneself and others, and an acceptance of the requisite anxiety involved in living.[28] Man was intuitively capable of so much more, May claimed, than psychologists had made him out to be.

Like Maslow, May indicted psychologists for failing to provide the affirmation and validation people so badly needed. He also argued that the discipline of psychology, by its rhetoric and the scientistic philosophy that underlay it, had helped strip people of precisely the inner resources that were needed most in periods of cultural despair. Addressing the mainstream psychologist, he wrote, "You have spent your life making molehills out of mountains—that's what you're guilty of. When man was tragic, you made him trivial. When he was picaresque, you called him picayune. When he suffered passively, you described him as simpering; and when he drummed up enough courage to act, you called it stimulus and response. Man had passion; and when you were pompous and lecturing to your class you called it 'the satisfaction of basic needs' . . ."[29]

In contrast, the psychology May espoused was designed to embolden individuals, to celebrate their complexity and gird them for action. He again used the language of existential psychology to give meaning to their struggles and offer solutions. In *Love and Will*, he normalized neurosis, targeting the culture as its source and thereby freeing individuals from blame for their pathology. He distinguished neurotics from the masses by the fact that the usual cultural defenses didn't work for them; neurotics experienced consciously that of which the unfeeling majority was temporarily unconscious. The solution for societal neuroses, he felt, was the same as the solution for personal neuroses: expanding people's awareness so that specific issues could be illuminated, assimilated, and embraced.[30]

"The microcosm of our consciousness is where the macrocosm of the universe is *known*," he writes. "It is the fearful joy, the blessing, and the curse of man that he can be conscious of himself and his world. For consciousness surprises the meaning in our otherwise absurd acts. Eros, infusing the whole, beckons us with its power with the promise that it may become our power. And the daimonic—that often nettlelike voice which is at the same time our creative power—leads us into life if we do not kill these daimonic experiences but accept them with a sense of the preciousness of what we are and what life is. Intentionality, itself consisting of the deepened awareness of one's self, is our means of putting the meaning surprised by consciousness into action."[31]

• • •

Both May's and Maslow's theories suggested that individual development could counteract social deterioration. But in the final years of his life, Maslow began to see society as more central to self-realization. He recognized that his prior conceptualizations had favored the individual at the expense of groups, and that for an individual to thrive, she would need social nurturing and a sense of belonging.[32] He proposed what he termed the "bodhisattvic path," which integrated individual development with social zeal, arguing that both the self-improver and the social helper had to evolve simultaneously.[33]

In using the Buddhist term for enlightenment (bodhisattvic), Maslow nodded to the other turn his theory had taken in his last years. His sickness didn't make him a religious man, but it pushed him to make room for "small 'r' religion" in his theory.[34] While his concept of self-actualization had assumed that the healthiest individuals experience ecstatic peaks, his later theory of self-transcendence proposed a "high plateau," where transcendence was less intense, but also less fleeting. Plateau was both poetic and cognitive, rather than purely emotional, and replaced the element of surprise with the element of choice. Often attained through hard work, and often brought on more gradually, sustainable transcendence was more appropriate for older people, who were systemically less able to tolerate the violence of peaks.[35]

While humanistic psychology certainly allowed for man's transcendent nature, Maslow felt it necessary to generate theory more specifically focused on topics like unitive consciousness, mystical experience, and cognitive blissfulness. With the help of Anthony Sutich and psychiatrist Stanislav Grof, he founded a subsidiary school of humanistic psychology devoted to these interests, called transpersonal psychology. It began with the first publication of the *Journal of Transpersonal Psychology* in 1969.[36]

That same year he worked, when he had the energy, on a new book titled *The Farther Reaches of Human Nature*. In it, he developed the ideas of his friend and colleague Douglas Mc-Gregor, specifically "Theory Z," a concept that raised the ceiling on his hierarchy of needs. McGregor had first proposed the idea in 1960 in a book called *The Human Side of Enterprise*, which was influential in industrial management. Theory-Z people, Maslow explained, were able to transcend self-actualization (Theory Y).[37] They viewed peak and plateau as the most important things in life, and spoke naturally in being-language (the language of mystics, seers, profoundly religious men). They were holistic, awe-inspiring, responsive to beauty, and they were able to identify the sacred in everyday life. At the same time, though, they were less happy than healthy self-actualizers; they seemed to possess a "cosmic sadness" and were more reconciled to evil.[38] Perhaps he counted himself in this group, or deemed it his ideal, as he sat perched on the precipice of his life, able to see farther but also aware that he had not much farther to go.

Maslow and Bertha had left their home of eighteen years in January 1969 to settle in Northern California. The departure was bittersweet. On the one hand, they felt uprooted and insecure. They were sad to give up their house, and the "blessed river" they lived along. At the same time, they were relieved to escape the more unpleasant aspects of Brandeis, and of Boston.[39]

Maslow's students had grown progressively offensive to him. They were more rebellious than ever (a group of black militant students had recently vandalized scholarly work in protest of institutional racism) and lacked respect for authority.[40] He felt a comparable sense of frustration with his colleagues, whom he perceived as apathetic or unthinking.

The weather had become an issue as well. The cold Boston winters taxed Maslow physically and made him feel like an invalid. California's gentle weather, he hoped, would prove salubrious and possibly even extend his life.

The real allure of California, though, was a fellowship at the Saga Administrative Corporation, a company that managed college cafeterias. As the company grew dramatically, its president developed an interest in humanistic management. He offered Maslow a Mercedes-Benz, a generous salary, and a private office with a secretary. In exchange, Maslow had no duties to the company, but was expected to work on his own writing and maintain his relationship with the company for two to four years.[41]

Abe and Bertha bought a home in Menlo Park, just outside of Palo Alto, and installed a swimming pool, in the hopes of further strengthening Maslow's heart.

Meanwhile, Maslow's outlook improved. He adored the people at Saga and found the plant itself attractive and homey.[42] His journal entries in the few months following the move described his sense of gratitude and privilege, and detailed relief at being released from his duties and schedules. By all reports, he was the happiest he'd ever been.

Although his health wavered throughout 1969 (he reported in late April that he had spent a month on his back), his energy seemed to soar in the early months of 1970. In addition to travel within California, time with his granddaughter, lectures, and parties, he recorded numerous ideas for applying humanistic psychology to race relations, student riots, poverty, and more. He planned a book on humanistic politics.[43]

On June 8, 1970, he experienced his third heart attack while jogging in place beside the pool, and died instantly.

At his memorial service a few months later, his friends, including those who had once affectionately mocked his grandiosity, took serious stock of what it meant to lose Maslow's utopian thinking. It had served an essential function, interrupting them from their daily tasks and redirecting their sights upward. "When utopia dies, the society is spent," warned his friend Frank Manuel.[44] Maslow died certain that this would not be the case. He felt good about himself and proud of the work he had done. And he offered his life as proof of his theory.[45]

Brandeis Professor James Klee was tempted to conclude that "they do not make men like Abe Maslow anymore," but he resisted. That kind of despair went against what Maslow had built. His sense of wholeness and his clarity of vision were themselves models of how hope could win.[46] At his memorial service, his close friend Ricardo Morant explained how both Maslow and Einstein had "sensed a different cadence than the rest of us." Where others saw only change, Maslow saw growth and development. "For our sake," said Morant, "we can only pray that he also sensed more clearly."[47]

Maslow left his legacy on tenuous footing. He hadn't trusted his colleagues to do the work required to elevate humanistic psychology to a higher plane. In 1969 he had counted only himself and Rogers as "among the living." "Fromm has gone downhill," he wrote. "May *may* get to Mt. Olympus but really isn't there yet. And that's it. The younger ones may or may not grow to the B-realm. Can't tell yet. And Fromm & May are just not empirical enough. Also many of the other therapists & philosophers."

He wondered too if Murray would accomplish anything great before he died.[48] And, though he respected Rogers as a researcher, he was continually dismayed at his lack of depth, and his failure to include metaphysical concerns and consider evil.[49]

His cynicism about his peers had likely stemmed, in part, from frustration with himself. Though he repeatedly defended his "freewheeling explorations, affirmations, and hypotheses" as necessary and utterly testable prescientific endeavors, he was aware that in leaving the actual empirical testing to others he was leaving a hole in the movement that might never be filled.[50]

What he *could* entrust his enthusiastic followers to do was to continue to organize and promote the movement. One fortuitous product of his election to the presidency of APA had been an expanded sense of recognition professionally and a wider berth for those with ideological similarities.

12

A Delicious
Look Inward

"Men weren't really the enemy—they were fellow
victims, suffering from an outmoded masculine
mystique that made them feel inadequate when there
were no bears to kill."

BETTY FRIEDAN[1]

Maslow's life had ended with a hope that he had imbued humanistic psychology with a moral and intellectual integrity that
was strong enough to withstand the temptations of its remaining adolescence. He knew, on some level, that he had made
some mistakes in parenting the movement. And while he had
defensively distanced himself in his final years from his progeny
(focusing his attention instead on transpersonal psychology), he
had also tried to impart some final lessons.

Maslow's plea for the value of the bodhisattvic path, and
his admission that his earlier theory had been wrongly dismissive of groups, organizations, and communities, however, was
tucked in the appendix of a posthumous collection of his work.

Even if it had been more prominently featured, it was probably too late to transmit that particular message.

Humanistic psychology, in its varied cultural manifestations, had fallen down on the issue of group identity. Maslow himself had failed to imagine that being black or being female, for example, could have a meaning that was in any way superordinate to being *human*.

The avoidance of collective identity was typical of psychologists in general. Disciplinary specialization had tied them to the study of the individual psyche. But even humanistic psychologists with broader social concerns didn't do much better at affecting professional or social change. Although black-white encounter groups earned some attention in the late 1960s, they failed to make a dent in race relations, or to heal blacks' alienation from psychology.

The trifling numbers of blacks in the Association of Humanistic Psychology suggested that even humanistic theory held little appeal. At AHP's 1979 convention, a mere six of the approximately fifteen hundred participants were black. Carl Rogers expressed his regret, without any intention to act. As his daughter Natalie concluded, "In AHP, race issues just never made it."[2]

In the words of humanistic psychologist Richard Farson, who worked closely with Carl Rogers at Western Behavioral Sciences Institute, "Humanistic psychology, like all of psychology, was dragged kicking and screaming through every liberation movement. It was embarrassing how far behind the curve we were."[3]

In the first decade of the movement, concerns specific to women fared about as well as, or worse than, concerns related to blacks.

But in contrast to blacks, who were only minimally involved in the movement, women were central to humanistic psychology. In failing to prioritize women's liberation, the leaders of humanistic psychology were hurting their own followers, colleagues, and even family members.

When Carl Rogers's daughter Natalie—who was a humanistic psychologist in her own right—chaired a panel on women at an AHP annual convention in the 1980s, she expressed her residual indignation. "I feel like a child who is angry with her parents," she said.[4] For Natalie Rogers, as for most women engaged in feminist struggles, this statement had a literal and figurative meaning. She *was* angry with her father, a founder of AHP, who had been a hypocrite. While he had devoted his professional energy to helping individuals reach their full potential, he had failed to see the constrained nature of his own daughter's existence. For years, Natalie had subordinated her own identity to those of her husband and children.

Natalie Rogers was also angry with AHP, an organization whose goals appeared so harmonious with those of feminism but whose practices had fallen so short in supporting women. As late as 1984, she observed that 90 percent of the speakers at the annual convention were men, though participation figures favored women. She counted six all-male panels and ten panels in which there was one woman and two to five men, and found it ironic that a panel titled "Designing the AHP Future" was an all-male panel. She noted that these figures were a scant improvement on the AHP conferences of the 1960s and 1970s.[5]

For many humanistic psychologists, feminism was a family issue, rooted in their own domestic struggles. Like Rogers, who was forced to grapple with the criticism of his daughter, Rollo May was confronted by several influential woman in his life (most notably his second wife Ingrid) about the necessity of increasing his sensitivity to gender issues.

Feminist concerns crept into the lives of humanistic psychologists in much the same way they had entered the wider cultural consciousness—slowly and subtly at first. In the 1950s, with the postwar United States invested in a domestic ideal of femininity (reflected in advertising rhetoric and in women's declining professional employment), dissatisfaction about the lot of women in American society often manifested as a greater willingness from women to express a sense of unease about their lives in general.[6] In 1956, a writer for *Life* magazine observed: "If there is such a thing as a 'suburban syndrome,' it might take this form: the wife, having worked before marriage or at least having been educated and socially conditioned toward the idea that work (preferably some kind of intellectual work in an office, among men) carries prestige, may get depressed being 'just a housewife.' Even if she avoids that her humiliation still seeks an outlet. This may take various forms: in destructive gossip about other women, in raising hell at the PTA, in becoming a dominating mother. [. . .] In her disgruntlement, she can work as much damage to the lives of her husband and children (and her own life) as if she were a career woman, and indeed sometimes more."[7]

Other early forms of protest were even subtler: beginning in 1957, women began having fewer children and marrying later, and more women in the middle classes began attending college.[8]

Meanwhile, cultural conditions were ripening for a more overt feminist resurgence. In the late 1950s and early 1960s, the sexual liberation movement gave women new freedoms.[9] As early as 1953, scientists began to study and publish on women's sexuality. In 1953, Alfred Kinsey published *Sexual Behavior and the Human Female* (a bestseller), and in 1966 William Masters and

Virginia Johnson published their laboratory studies of human sexual response, debunking myths about female sexuality and facilitating open conversation about female sexual concerns.[10] By 1962, the birth control pill became widely accessible; over a million American women were soon using it for family planning.[11] Literary censorship began to lift as well. Books like Helen Gurley Brown's *Sex and the Single Girl* (an instant bestseller) helped to normalize a more open, less inhibited idea of female sexuality.[12]

In 1963, Betty Friedan offered American women a lens through which to identify their latent dissatisfaction with their roles as housewives. In her bestselling book *The Feminine Mystique*, she argued, "The core of the problem for women today is not sexual but a problem of identity—a stunting or evasion of growth that is permitted by the feminine mystique." For Friedan, the "feminine mystique" was the damaging myth that the only path to fulfillment for an American woman was through the role of housewife-mother.[13]

Friedan drew heavily on psychological theory to inform her conception of women's problems.[14] In fact she credited humanistic psychology, at least in part, with her reconsideration of the female role. Specifically citing Maslow's work, Friedan attempted to demonstrate the humanistic, unselfish nature of women's strivings. She described Maslow's finding that the higher the dominance or strength of self in a woman, the less self-centered she was and the more her concern was directed outward to other people and to worldly concerns. She also credited Maslow with the insight that women who were more conventionally feminine were more focused on themselves and their own inferiorities.[15] Emphasizing self-actualization, potentiality, and self-awareness, Friedan's language throughout the book evoked Maslow's theories.[16]

Friedan, who had been trained as a Freudian at the University of California, Berkeley, had come to oppose Freudianism and behaviorism, concluding that both approaches reinforced rather than challenged cultural imperatives.[17] She wrote that "for years, psychiatrists have tried to 'cure' their patients' conflicts by fitting them into the culture. But adjustment to a culture that does not permit the realization of one's entire being is not a cure at all, according to the new psychological thinkers."[18] What Friedan desired was a theory that, in the image of her memoir-style book, would advance a vision of an improved culture and society through its analysis of highly personal and individual experiences.[19]

Though hardly exclusively responsible for the tide of feminism that swept through and beyond the 1960s, *The Feminine Mystique* gave voice to a set of concerns and anxieties that had been building for years and that would, over the next few decades, change the shape of gender relations in America. Friedan received a flood of responses to the book—some from barely literate women and some written in crayon—that demonstrated the personal resonance of her argument with American women.[20]

In the mid-1960s, these personal concerns grew increasingly overt. And they were, ironically, often exacerbated by heightened legislative attention to women's issues. Despite the passage in 1965 of Title VII (which made it illegal to discriminate against women in hiring and promotions), the creation that same year of the Equal Employment Opportunity Commission (EEOC), and the founding of the National Organization for Women (NOW) in 1966, women remained politically and culturally subordinate to men. President Kennedy's record on female appointments was actually worse than those of his four immediate predecessors, and dramatic pay differentials persisted between men and women, suggesting the ineffectuality of the EEOC.[21] Women were also poorly represented in Congress: in 1966, ten of 435 members of the House of Representatives and two of 100 U.S. senators were women.[22]

The failure of government support to remedy the basic dynamics of gender and power signaled the need for individual action on the part of women. Organization arose from the demographic in which it had resided throughout feminism's dormancy in the 1930s, 1940s, and 1950s: in secular groups of elite, mainly educated, primarily white women. In 1966, NOW was formed by twenty-eight women and men who attended the Third National Conference of the Commission on the Status of Women. The founders included Betty Friedan, the organization's first president, and the Reverend Pauli Murray (the first African American, female Episcopal priest), who jointly drafted the organization's statement of purpose, establishing NOW's commitment to gaining equal participation for women in all domains of society.[23]

In the early 1970s, the rise of consciousness-raising (CR) groups, which bore a striking resemblance to encounter groups, marked the convergence of women's domestic and political discontent. CR groups, fueled in part by the framing ideology of humanistic psychology as advocated by Friedan in *The Feminine Mystique*, began at the grass-roots level, lacking formal structure and organization. Feminist Anita Shreve explained that CR was the "political reinterpretation of one's personal life." Its purpose was to "awaken the latent consciousness [. . .] that all women have about [their] oppression."[24] The embodiment of the renowned motto "the personal is political," CR groups sought to convince women that what they had previously perceived as personal problems were actually social problems that required social rather than personal solutions.

CR groups originated somewhat organically, as groups of radical women began to form "rap sessions" or "bitch sessions" in which they vented their frustrations about their personal struggles, sharing private experiences of oppression by men that ranged from marital struggles to incidences of sexual violence.[25] "The process is simple," wrote one feminist. "Women come together in small groups to share personal experiences, problems and feelings. From this public sharing comes the realization that what was thought to be individual is in fact common; that what was thought to be a personal problem has a social cause and political solution."[26]

Although CR groups originated with leftist activists, they spread more broadly through word of mouth to middle-class women with divergent political interests.[27] By 1970, CR groups were active in every major American city, uniting women over discussions of their cultural victimization, sexual experiences, and innermost desires. In 1973 alone, more than a hundred thousand people nationwide reported membership in a consciousness-raising group. Typical groups remained, for the most part, limited to white women of the middle class, who were more likely to have leisure time to devote to the groups, and whose college experiences gave some intellectual form to their feminist inclinations.[28]

Consciousness-raising relied on the same epiphanic experience that encounter groups so esteemed. Shreve wrote, "The heart of the matter, say the women, was 'the click'—the light bulb going off, the eye-popping realization, the knockout punch. It was the sudden comprehension, in one powerful instant, of what sexism exactly meant, how it had colored one's own life, the way all women were in this together."[29] But while encounter groups conceived of epiphany as the goal, CR viewed the revelatory moment instrumentally—as an invaluable tool that would facilitate personal and political action.[30] Feminist Kathie Sarachild argued that the purpose of CR had always been "social transformation as opposed to self-transformation."[31] And proponents of CR made every effort to differentiate it from therapy, maintaining that the purpose of CR groups was to analyze male supremacy and conceptualize ways to defeat it.

Not everyone bought this explanation. Like encounter groups, CR groups were mocked as being "trivial" and "nonpolitical," and were disparaged as "hen parties," even by other members of the radical left. Betty Friedan referred to CR groups as "navel-gazing."[32] Some perceived the self-absorption they associated with CR to be extremely threatening. Like drug experimentation, which caused people to "tune out," and encounter groups, which obscured social and political concerns with personal catharsis, it was feared that CR participants might "retreat from action into self-indulgent personalism."[33] Proponents of CR argued that the effect would render contrary results, that women would become *more committed* to resisting the system.[34]

CR groups did seem to surpass encounter groups in several respects. To begin with, CR groups implicitly accounted for group-level forces, wove the political into the personal, and offered a sustaining form of intimacy and support that guided women through significant changes. Also, unlike encounter groups, CR groups remained responsive to changes in the culture, evolving as the political climate changed, as career opportunities expanded, and as the priorities of the women's movement shifted.[35] In retrospect, CR groups may have unknowingly drawn on the more moderate and salubrious tenets of humanistic psychology, while many encounter groups exacerbated the excesses and oversights.

Regardless of their cultural value and their obvious alignment with the goals of humanistic psychology, though, the necessity of women's groups eluded most in the movement. In fact, many humanistic psychologists viewed even general feminist considerations as irrelevant to their goals. At worst, they deemed women-specific concerns to be antipathetic to the ideals of universal understanding, and they perceived individual feminists—particularly radical ones—to be threatening.

Even certain women in AHP initially rejected the notion that women's concerns should be considered distinct from men's. Psychologist Maureen O'Hara, for example, initially rejected a feminist analysis, feeling that the common humanistic psychology perspective characteristic of Carl Rogers, with whom she worked closely, "was already big enough to allow space for a subjectivity that was both essentially human *and* gendered."[36]

O'Hara's perspective quickly changed. She soon began to realize that the conversations happening in AHP were occurring absent a recognition of female subjectivity. By treating everyone the same, she sensed, the leaders were unwittingly privileging the white male. In order to recognize women as distinct individuals, it was important to acknowledge the gendered world in which their subjectivity had developed.[37]

In the wake of her efflorescent feminism, O'Hara came to believe that several essential characteristics of women were ignored by humanistic psychologists. Because women tended to be more relationally oriented and interdependent, she felt, viewing the life course as a journey from dependence to independence could prove inhibitory to women's potential. She also noticed that in groups women were more inclined to make statements like "We've been thinking," which would often be admonished by group leaders with the imperative to "think for yourself." The expectation that health was equated with independence and autonomy ignored the reality of women's relational concept of self. In order to foster women's self-actualization, she concluded, it was necessary for facilitators to recognize the range of possibilities for the experience of self and relationships.[38]

The shift in O'Hara's perspective and the mounting frustration that accompanied it was characteristic of AHP women in general, and of American women more broadly. The leaders of humanistic psychology seemed incapable of adequately considering anything beyond the distinct individual; group-level forces seemed to exist in their blind spot. Carl Rogers, for instance, genuinely believed that if you properly nurtured the subjectivity of an individual, gender was irrelevant, and he only slowly began to recognize that something was missing from his writings on the person-centered approach.[39] White males like Rogers, feminist critics felt, could afford to focus solely on individuals, being themselves free of cultural oppression and discrimination. Women, however, had to attend to more pressing material and political deficits before they could have the luxury of self-focus.[40] They would have to fulfill their more basic needs before examining, in the Maslowian sense, their "being" needs.

O'Hara noted that "many of the men at [the Center for Studies of the Person—an institute Carl Rogers founded in 1968] could not understand why there was any necessity for a women's group. They saw it as hostile, and I suppose it was. I mean there were times when it was really bitter, and part of the bitterness had to do with the absolute denial on the part of men of the fact that women's situation was any different from theirs."[41] Natalie Rogers remembers that "you really had to get in their faces to get them to listen."[42] This resistance only exacerbated the animosity many women felt toward the men, who, at least in their minds, represented the male power structure of the country. Natalie remembers herself as "very confrontative, outspoken, and angry." In her intensity about women's concerns, she claims, "I scared the shit out of you."[43]

As frustration mounted, male leaders—particularly liberal, sensitive, and intelligent ones—found it increasingly difficult to ignore feminist concerns. The women's liberation movement was so widespread that it seemed every man (and particularly every white, middle-class man) had a wife, daughter, or friend committed to the cause.

It was through the love and respect for the women in their lives that the founders of humanistic psychology began (slowly) to prioritize women's issues. Carl Rogers's increasing sensitivity to gender issues was hastened by the desperation of his daughter. In 1968, Natalie, who had been a "feisty" child and adolescent but who had "disappeared" into herself during her twenty-year marriage, announced she was divorcing a man whom both her parents liked and valued. Motivated by his strong desire for growth and understanding, Rogers struggled to understand his daughter's perspective, and he listened to her openly. Her experience was certainly one that a humanistic psychologist could appreciate: she felt that her intellect and the wholeness of her being were suppressed by the marriage. The validity of her experience was undeniable to her father, and it began to inform his clinical interactions with women.[44]

Professionally, he began to adjust in simple ways, like noticing that four or five men had spoken in a row and encouraging a woman to speak. Recognizing the ways that groups served as a microcosm of the culture, he began to tackle group forces that influenced the behavior of individual women in his sessions.[45]

Although he grew more sensitive than most to the distinct nature of women's experience, his struggle to integrate gender concerns persisted for decades. Natalie Rogers remembers the continued challenge that feminists presented to her father. At an invited lecture that he gave at Harvard in the early 1970s, she recalls a woman speaking up to criticize his gendered use of pronouns throughout his speech. In Natalie's opinion, her father gave a "wrong answer," and she and her colleagues from Greenhouse, a growth center in Cambridge, Massachusetts, confronted him about it later.[46]

He took this criticism seriously. In the late 1970s, the struggles inherent in his daughter's transformation even penetrated his perception of his fairly traditional marriage to Helen Rogers, a woman who had been an ideal faculty wife, furthering her husband's career with her competence and interpersonal ease, and often subordinating her own passions for painting, reading, and traveling to her husband's needs. As Helen lay on her death bed, nearly paralyzed by arthritis, Rogers wrote, "She is giving up the old model of being the supportive wife. This change brings her in touch with her anger at me and at society for giving her that socially approved role."[47] Fortunately, Helen's daughter Natalie and granddaughter Frances didn't wait so long to embrace this anger. In fact, they co-led feminist workshops for mothers and daughters.[48]

Around the same time, Rogers attempted to express more publicly his support for women's rights. One way he did this was by attending to the "pronoun problem." His 1977 publication of *Carl Rogers on Personal Power* began with "a special note." "I have been greatly perplexed by the pronoun problem, or, more exactly, the 'he-she' issue," he wrote. "I am totally in sympathy with the view that women are subtly demeaned by the use of the masculine pronoun when speaking in general of a member of the human species."[49] He resolved this problem in the book by alternating between chapters in his use of masculine and feminine pronouns.

Rollo May, who wrote more for a popular audience, had attended to the pronoun problem a decade earlier, though perhaps without engaging in the deeper struggles with women's realities that Rogers's 1970s transformation represented.[50] In 1972, feminist Carolyn Morell targeted Rollo May's bestselling *Love and Will* for being "unintentionally sexist," arguing that the book implicitly justified the existing power relationship between men and women and thereby contributed to women's dissatisfaction and dehumanization. "Since he assumes innate behavioral distinctions between sex groups," she stated, "he ignores the crucial social fact that female/male behavior and temperament, along with sex roles, is overwhelmingly conditioned, and that these distinctions have political implications. In essence, he disregards the fact that the female/male relationship is a power-structured one in which the male is dominant and the female subordinate."[51]

She also accused May of reinforcing the patriarchy by writing for a male reader, making statements—like "If you called a lady 'sexy' "— in which the *you* could only sensically be male, or lesbian. Morell described the sexual enlightenment May advocated basing superficial, invoking changes in expression but not in power.[52]

May's response, which was published as an article in the *Journal of Humanistic Psychology*, was typical of the ambivalent way in which the movement grappled with feminism. Initially, he grudgingly conceded that his analysis "does suffer from unintentional sex prejudices. So does practically every other book written by a man (and most of them by women) in that period." He also noted, again a bit defensively, that Maslow and himself were "emphatic" supporters of the feminist movement. A paragraph later, however, May pivoted toward a more positive reaction. He said that he would rewrite certain sections for future editions and would continue to struggle with the "man-woman issue." In the spirit of humanistic psychologists, May wrote, "One *can* learn," and he thanked Morell for her "help" in the revision of his book.[53]

Implicit in Morell's critique of May was the argument that the white male perspective wouldn't intuitively account for the unique position of women. She repeatedly described May's errors as "unintentional" and "unconscious," suggesting that the white male paradigm was itself the problem. Morell's allegations were representative of the bulk of feminist critique of humanistic psychology, which revolved around the contention that humanistic theory arose from the experience of alienated, urban, white men of European descent who, according to one scholar, privileged "the sole self-evolving individual on a solitary and heroic journey of self-discovery [. . .] characterized by subduing nature, overcoming matter, transcending the body, promoting individuation, differentiation, and abstraction."[54]

If humanistic psychologists were guilty of sexism, it tended to be of this more subtle variety, embedded as it was in the very circumstances in which they had been born and bred. Maslow was another example. He was highly educated, urban, and of white European descent, and had, like Rogers, married a woman who never challenged traditional gender roles. Bertha Maslow raised their two daughters, fostered her husband's career, and never worked outside the home. By all reports, she seemed content with these choices, and so his marriage likely strengthened his belief that women were more suited to growing relationally, through their experiences with husbands and children.[55]

Still, in contrast to his peers, Maslow had been interested in women's psychology and sexuality since the 1930s, when he worked with Harry Harlow. In his 1939 paper "Dominance, Personality and Social Behavior in Women," he anticipated 1960s feminists, highlighting common desires in men and women for work, assertiveness, and growth.[56]

His personal papers, too, reflected his ongoing interest in women's issues. His files from the 1950s and 1960s contained a significant number of well-marked and highlighted clippings of magazine and newspaper articles about the changing roles of women.[57] And, in his journal entries from the 1960s, he indicated the pleasure he felt with regard to the sexual emancipation of women, and at the same time contemplated ways to further improve women's cultural circumstances.

Maslow's perspective on women's liberation, though, would have rubbed many feminists the wrong way. The bulk of his personal musings related to what he perceived to be the essential differences between women and men. Although he was well aware of the costs of forcing women into a role that was purely relational, with no room for self-development, and although he noted that self-actualization was hardly possible for American women within the current gender dynamic, he also stressed the danger of ignoring what he believed was the unique relationality of women.[58]

"I think it's the women themselves, like Betty Friedan, who get themselves into derogating & devaluing housework, children, wifehood, etc., feeling it to be not good enough: for them, & generally doing this in a dichotomous way, either-or. So they think of full-time jobs, which of course threatens the home. Why not part-time jobs in flexible time, allowing emergency needs of family to come first, as I did at Brandeis with my Woman-Salvage-Operation? This would need a very profound reorganization of the culture & of its economic structure. The Soviet solution—giving women full-time jobs—is no real, happy solution.[59]

Second-wave feminists diverged on the question of whether to attend to ontological gender differences, like those described by Maslow, or to promote a policy of total equality that disregarded any notion of essential difference, perceiving gender differences to be socially constructed and thus remediable.[60] Equality feminists believed that the emphasis on difference was destructive, and that given the present differentials in social expectations and societal respect for men and women, the perception of immutable differences between genders couldn't help but be contaminated by our prejudices.[61]

Although most humanistic psychologists seemed to be more sympathetic to difference feminists, the basic theory of humanistic psychology wasn't inherently oriented toward either type of feminism. Upon reading the *Feminine Mystique*, for instance, Maslow found himself in conflict. "Humanness," he wrote, "is postpotent to femaleness (*I think!* Now, after reading her book, I'm less sure of this.)"[62]

This type of self-doubt was characteristic of the openness with which many humanistic psychologists approached specific collective or cultural interests—even those that didn't naturally resonate with them. For most, the urgency of women's concerns grew more tangible in the 1970s, when women became more organized in expressing their dissatisfaction. Unfortunately, Maslow never lived to witness these changes.

The relevance of humanistic psychology to women's goals became more palpable as more women from a range of backgrounds (female psychologists included) got involved in the women's movement. In 1971, NOW had over 150 chapters and somewhere between five thousand and ten thousand members. By 1972, it had grown to about thirty thousand members, and feminist ideas were saturating the culture far out of proportion to the numbers of self-identified, active feminists. A 1972 poll, commissioned by Virginia Slims cigarettes (a company that sought to exploit feminist inclinations in order to sell cigarettes) showed that 48 percent of women supported efforts to strengthen and alter women's status in America, while 36 percent opposed it. These figures had been 40 percent and 42 percent respectively in the year prior. Evaluations of the effectiveness of women's organizations had also risen from 34 percent in 1971 to 43 percent in 1972. In response to the pressure of these interests, political opposition to the women's movement grew increasingly hesitant. Congress passed a series of women's rights legislation between 1972 and 1974.[63]

Unsurprisingly, many women who supported feminism found AHP's goals to be complementary to their own. Ilene Serlin, former president of Division 32 (the movement's group within the APA) with Humanistic Psychology Institute founder Eleanor Criswell, wrote about the comfort many women found in the world of humanistic psychology. "Much of humanistic thought," they wrote, "especially in regard to the centrality of personal experience and holistic and tacit ways of knowing, has

was remarkably similar to what Dr. Lowell was always saying. And Keisha, too, come to think of it.

When I got home, I pulled out my notebook and made a
list. This time, it was all about me.

THINGS I AM GOOD AT

- Being a mom.
- Being a daughter. Sometimes.
- Being a friend.
- Talking on the phone.
- Reading.
- Eating. Especially pastries.
- Drinking coffee.
- Loving Stevie Wonder.
- Making puns.
- Dressing in black.
- Making fun of myself.
- Liking myself.
- Loving myself.

The last one was the hardest to write. I took the paper,
folded it twice, and stuck it in my lingerie and sock drawer,
where I kept all of Aidan's cards from birthdays and Mother's
Day over the years. I'd show Dr. Lowell—and probably Keisha, too—when I could look in the mirror and say it all to
myself without hesitation. Especially the last one.

That was something I would do in a million years. Or less,
if I just gave myself a chance.

The Adventures of Huckleberry Pie

This pie might seem to be one thing at first bite, but as you dive deeper, you'll find it is so much more. It's blended with all-American berries, not just the huckleberry—an elusive fruit that takes many forms—but also blueberries and cranberries. It takes a trip down the Mississippi of your taste buds, so delicious it almost makes you want to craft a new word to describe its taste. It's more nuanced than it seems, and it flips the idea of the average pie on its head.

Go beyond what you see on the outside—a plain, average piece of pie—and come to love this new American classic.

20

THAT MORNING, AIDAN DECIDED HE WANTED TO WEAR shorts. In thirty-seven-degree weather. With a slow, steady drizzle of cold rain outside. It took an extra ten minutes to talk him out of it. He succumbed to the combined bribe of Jiffy Pop popcorn for breakfast and a half hour of extra SpongeBob SquarePants after school.

Meanwhile, Mom was wandering around the house picking things up and putting them down again. My book? Up, then down. Aidan's last school picture? Up, down.

"Mom, are you testing gravity, or do you think you could stop that?" My words came out sharper than I meant. She jerked away from the candy cane Christmas candlestick I'd forgotten to put away.

"Sorry, dear. Just . . ." Her voice trailed off. I felt horribly guilty for snapping at her.

"Never mind. Just help me get Aidan's shoes on, okay?"

After Aidan was suitably dressed, Mom walked him to school so I could get ready. I wore a pair of black pants and a crisp white cotton shirt with a black blazer over top. I wrapped a double strand of jet beads around my neck and made sure my hair was smooth, not fuzzy.

I took an extra few minutes with my makeup, too. I

viewed myself in the mirror, almost satisfied with the result. If I turned my head just right, I looked like one of those career women who were always being featured in *O, The Oprah Magazine*.

I dumped the contents of my vintage carpetbag purse on the table and extricated my MetroCard, my wallet, a pack of Kleenex, and my lip salve. I placed them into a slim black clutch I'd bought for Hugh's high school reunion. It was a little fancy for daytime, but it was fairly inconspicuous, and way more professional-looking than my usual purse.

Dressed for success, that was me. And my interior almost matched the exterior.

On the way to John's office, I stopped off at Starbucks and indulged in a tall skim latte. I sipped it as I walked down Twenty-fifth Street. Maybe it would be easy. Maybe the Cooking Channel folks would love my ideas and give me a standing ovation.

And maybe I'd sprout wings and fly around the room.

The first person I saw when I stepped off the elevator was Nick. I smiled, then felt it falter as I caught sight of his face.

"Ms. Hagan." Gone was any hint of friendliness. Nick's eyes shone a frozen blue, his lips creased in a thin line.

"Ni—, Mr. Harrison," I replied. "Am I late?"

He frowned. Or scowled, really, and glanced at his watch. "No. Five minutes early, in fact." He said it as if it were an accusation.

"Oh. Well, then." I straightened the hem of my coat. "Should we go into the conference room?"

"Not yet. Take a seat, please." He gestured toward the reception area sofa. I perched on the edge, feeling myself start to sweat.

"Thank you." He sat down as well and leaned forward, placing his hands on his knees. "Moll— That is, Ms. Hagan. We have a problem."

Ms. Hagan. I looked at him stupidly. "A problem?"

"Yes, and it's a serious one. It seems one of John's competitors knows of our potential marketing plans."

"Is that bad?"

I saw his jaw clench. He cleared his throat. "Yes. Since only you and I know the specifics of the campaign, and I didn't tell anyone . . ."

My throat closed over. "You think I—?" My voice came out in a tiny little squeak, as if Minnie Mouse were on the witness stand.

He looked at me, not saying a word. Ouch, blue ice.

"No. No, I didn't tell anyone about it." Then I got a sick feeling. "Except—oh, God, except I did the presentation in front of these women, these scrapbookers—"

He flipped his hand out in an impatient gesture. "And?"

"And one of them is in advertising, and said she knew Natalie." Fuck. And I'd already known Natalie was trying to get something from me, I just didn't know what. How dumb was I anyway?

His lips tightened even more, if possible. I couldn't be any dumber than what Nick obviously thought of me. Fuck again. "And you thought it would be all right to demonstrate your presentation to a group of people, at least one of whom works in the same field? When you knew how crucial this was?"

Put that way, I'd screwed up bad. Really bad.

"God, I'm sorry."

He leaned back, pulling his hands up his thighs. "Yeah. Well. I wish you had thought before you spoke."

Me, too. "I'm sorry," I repeated.

"Well." He checked his watch. "We might be able to salvage this." His tone was still frosty. He got up and watched me without holding his hand out to help, like he normally would have done.

Totally professional. *I would not cry, I would not cry, I would not cry*. I swung my chin up and stared him in the eye. "Right. I'm going to go knock their socks off."

His lips lifted in what was almost a smile. "You are."

Would he ever trust me again? Worse, would he ever call me Molly?

Still reeling from the encounter with Nick, I slipped into the conference room and clutched my presentation so hard my knuckles turned white. I was determined not to let that slipup make me slip up even more now.

"Thanks to all of you for coming today." John had come to stand next to me, so close I could feel the breeze stir when he waved his hand.

There was a platter full of Simon's products on the conference table. Everything smelled delicious, and all I wanted to do was crawl into the nearest cupcake and dissolve into tears.

But I knew for both my and Aidan's sake I couldn't. I couldn't help, however, taking an extra deep sniff as the sugary, buttery aroma permeated the air.

John waited until he had everyone's attention before he started to speak. "Corning and Associates is embarking on a new direction, one that will bring the company's expertise to the forefront of the consumer experience. And, we hope, revolutionize it." He gestured toward me before I could try to decipher just what he'd said. "I'd like to introduce our creative marketing consultant, Molly Hagan. Molly will be explaining the initial concept of Simon Baxter's exciting new venture. And, we hope, intrigue you so much you'll be interested in featuring Simon's bakery on the appropriate programs. We are"—he leaned forward as though he were confiding in them—"offering you an exclusive look at this ahead of your competitors." He gestured toward me. "Molly?"

There were half a dozen of them, men and women, a range of ages, all with at least ten pounds too many. I guess cooking network execs probably had to eat more than regular people.

John sat down in the chair next to me while Simon was on the other side. Nick leaned against the wall near the door. My eyes kept flicking toward him. No change in his hard, cold expression. I had really done it. Shoot. It hurt way more than it should have.

I dropped my eyes down to the folder John had made to accompany Nick's PowerPoint demonstration. I flipped it open to the first page, drew a deep breath, and started speaking.

There was a full thirty seconds of silence after I stopped. I was really proud of myself that I didn't automatically think they hated it.

The oldest of the execs sat forward. He tilted his head as he spoke. "Food and entertainment. A delightful mix."

It was as if his approval had unleashed some sort of floodgates—the other people in the room all began to smile and talk among themselves. I heard "Anthony Bourdain," "throwdown," and "special" all exclaimed from them at one point or another.

Simon had joined the group, and I heard his accent weaving in and among the other voices: "Yes, this is scalable, and we will be looking to expand, once Vanity Fare is established as the premiere pastry destination in New York City."

Wow. That sounded pretty neat, once I actually thought about it.

Nick remained where he was, near the door, his sharp eyes taking in the scene. I tried not to look at him, I really did, but that still-pathetic part of me wanted to know we were okay. That he thought I'd done okay, and that he knew I hadn't betrayed him. The company.

I wondered if Simon had told him about us, and that we weren't us anymore. I highly doubted it. Simon wasn't the sort to reveal anything that might possibly make him look bad.

"You did great," John said, walking over and placing a hand on my arm. "I think they're gonna bite."

"Thanks." I darted another glance at Nick. "Um, John, did you hear anything about a competitive agency finding out about the marketing plans?"

His face blanched. "No. Why?"

"It's probably nothing, just that Nick said there'd been some talk, and that it seems like it's something I did. That Natalie found out what we were planning."

He frowned and drew me to the far corner of the room. Simon was still going strong, now declaiming a variety of bon mots to the group of enthralled executives.

"How would she have found out? Have you been in touch with her?"

I jerked out of his hold. "I wouldn't do that, even if I liked her. Which I don't," I added, just in case he wasn't clear on that. I sure as hell wasn't going to tell him about my encounters with her—they sounded fishy, even to me, and I knew exactly what had happened during them.

"So what happened?"

"Yes, Ms. Hagan, tell us. What happened?" Nick had uncoiled himself from the wall to join us, the snake.

I felt myself turning red. "It's that I was with this group of ladies, women from my neighborhood, and we got to talking, and they asked me what I was working on, and then they asked me to show them what I was going to present, you know, just for feedback and to see and everything"—boy did I sound lame—"and it turns out that this one woman knows Natalie, and she must've told her the gist of what I'd done." I held my hands out to both of them. "You have to know, I had no idea it was going to cause a problem."

John rushed in before Nick could condemn me with some more coldly spoken words. "I'm sure it'll be fine, Molly, Natalie can't do anything at this point." He gestured toward the still-chatting group of people clustered around Simon. "The presentation is done, the secret is spilled."

"The point isn't whether we are in jeopardy," Nick said, his voice tight and clipped. "The point is why Natalie appears so hell-bent on interfering."

At which point John and Nick both turned and looked at Simon.

And I felt sick.

"I'll speak to him after this," Nick said. It sounded more like a threat than a promise, and I was glad I wasn't Simon.

Eventually the Simon Show ended, and the crowd dispersed. John led them out of the room, and I could tell he was pleased by the response.

And I was able to grab a cookie, something with macadamia nuts and white chocolate. So the day wasn't entirely shot.

Simon came over to me, an intimate gleam in his eyes. Uh-oh.

"I knew you could do it," he said, placing his hand on my arm. "You came through magnificently. I have to admit I was a bit concerned about your ability to make the presentation. Of course there was never any doubt about your fantastic wit." He lowered his eyes to my chest.

"My wit's up here, Simon," I said, tapping my head with my finger.

"Right." He didn't even have the grace to blush. He leaned in closer. "Are you free tonight?" he whispered.

What would it take to make him understand? I had images of pelting him in the head with his own pastries until he finally got it. I shook my head no, then looked up and met Nick's eyes. Something in them made my stomach tighten.

I stared at him for a long moment, drinking in the want I read in his eyes. Want and . . . sadness?

I edged a little farther back from Simon, and met his gaze. "I meant what I said, Simon," I whispered back.

"What about Nick?" he snapped, still in that quiet whisper. I wondered if I should just tell Simon to skip the middleman—me—and date Nick instead.

"What about him? I'm not dating him, either." I glared at him.

"What about that birthday party?" His voice had a self-righteous tone that set my back up.

I began to put my papers into my bag. "See," I said in as calm a voice as I could muster, "this is exactly why it's not appropriate. We can talk when this is all over."

He put his hand on my arm again. "When?"

I turned and looked at him, and was startled by his expression. It was possessive, sulky, and . . . mean. I didn't like it. And I was quickly coming to realize I didn't like him. And I didn't want to go out with him, even when the project was over.

Had I really gotten that strong? I drew my hand away, put the last of my papers into my bag, and walked out, not answering him or myself.

Far from the Fattening Crowd

In a new, carb-obsessed world, it's hard to imagine the old ways, where people ate bread, pasta, and rice without guilt. And enjoyed plenty of flavor. At Vanity Fare, we try to integrate the old, tasty ways with the new diet-conscious ways. Taste our fruit mélange of strawberries, kiwis, bananas, and blueberries melded together with a low-fat custard. Low carbs, low sugar, loads of taste. Eating right to stay fit never tasted so good.

21

"HELLO?"

It was around 10:00 P.M., Aidan had gone to sleep a while ago, and Mom was fussing in the kitchen. It pleased me that she'd taken on some of our domestic tasks—she'd always turned her nose up at mastering any kind of culinary skill as something ordinary women did. I had grabbed a book and was hiding out in the bedroom, waiting for Keisha to call.

My mind, however, refused to concentrate on the feisty heroine and the noble, dangerous hero. Instead I kept replaying that afternoon's conversation with Nick. It kinda broke a bit of my heart that he would even think me capable of that kind of duplicity. And I had to figure out what to say to that scrapbooking she-devil when I saw her again.

"Hi, Molly." Not Keisha. A man's voice. Not John. Definitely not Simon.

"Nick?"

"Yes," he replied in his pompous voice. Then his tone changed. "Listen, sorry to call so late, but I just got back from a dinner meeting. Is it too late?"

I rolled onto my back on my bed, wishing my heart weren't pounding so fast. "No, not too late at all. I stay up later than I should, actually. I always mean to go . . ." I was babbling. "Anyway. What's up?"

"I just wanted to call and say I thought you did a terrific presentation today." His voice was more than professional. Thank goodness. "The network is very excited about the opening. It was a few of their staff I had dinner with tonight, actually."

How high school crush-ish of me was it that I was happy he hadn't just had a date?

"Thanks for calling. I'm really sorry about practicing in front of those women, I had no idea—I was nervous as hell, actually." Even more when I thought you didn't trust me.

"Natalie's a bitch," he said bluntly. "It's over, you told me what happened, and it's fine." Men. Always able to move on while women chewed discontent like a bone. "I knew you were nervous, which is why I wanted to call and let you know how well you did. And—"

He stopped. I waited a heartbeat, two, then spoke. "What?"

I heard him take a deep breath. "I just wanted to explain about before. About saying no. It's just . . . well, it wouldn't be right right now."

I assumed my cheeriest, doesn't-bother-me-at-all voice. "No problem. Really."

He gave a dry chuckle devoid of humor. "No, it is a problem. But I just wanted to tell you, it's not you. It's not that I don't— That is, I wish things were different."

"Oh. Okay. Thanks." Different? Different how? Like I was taller? He wasn't so picky about who he dated? He didn't want to mix business with pleasure?

He exhaled so hard I could almost feel the breeze in my ear. "Is Aidan free this weekend? I want to take him to that place again."

"Are you sure?"

"Of course. I promised. Plus I like him, he's a cool kid."

I tried to swallow the lump in my throat. "Thanks. Yeah, he's free anytime. No birthday parties this weekend, thank goodness."

"Okay. How's Saturday? Around one? I figured we could grab some pizza and then I could take him over."

"Saturday's great."

"Okay. I'll see you then. Bye."

"Bye."

I hung up, then stared at the phone for a while. He had called me. At home. At ten o'clock at night. To tell me I did well. After I'd screwed up royally. And that he wished things were different.

And that he wanted to hang out with my son.

I was all gooey inside. I mean, I knew the end result was the same, but he thought well enough of me to make the effort to reach me. That meant something, at least. My quick success with Simon might have made me a little cocky, if such a thing were possible. Maybe it was enough that Nick was my friend, had my back, liked Aidan. Maybe he even trusted me. Heck, he'd gotten my mother to listen to advice, and that was something I had never been able to do.

It wasn't that bad being turned down. Although I wished I could've kissed him, just once, to see if his lips felt as good as they looked.

Ah, but what would an about-to-be divorced romance reader be without an unattainable fantasy?

Luckily, the phone rang again before I could answer that question.

"Hello?"

"Hey, babe. How'd it go?" It was Keisha. She'd been my cheerleader throughout the preparations, so I knew she'd want to hear all about it.

"Good. Actually," I said, trying to sound casual, "Nick just called to tell me the network is really excited. Seems like they might do something on the shop."

"Nick, huh?" Leave it to Keisha to find the crucial nugget of information in there. "So what else did *Nick* say, hm?"

"That he wished things were different."

"Different how?"

"He said he had to say no to my asking him out, not because of me, but because things aren't different, somehow."

"Well, that's fairly cryptic. What do you think he means?"

I shrugged, then realized she couldn't see me. "I don't know. I'm guessing it has something to do with the whole church and state thing—a while ago, John mentioned I shouldn't say anything to Nick about Simon."

"Whoa, slow down. I feel like I need a diagram."

"Well, basically, I think Nick is the watchdog for the finances and all that—"

"And the dog better not be sniffing around any other bitch's butt, right?"

"Oh, I love your way with a metaphor. Yeah, that's it in a nutshell."

"Or a kibble."

"You'd better stop or I'm going to have to smack your nose with a newspaper."

"Only if you leash me first, Mistress. Hey, that's an idea: phone sex!"

"Um . . . I love you, Keisha, but not that way."

She giggled. "No, silly, I mean you. To make extra money."

"Oh, yeah, that'd be great: *Are you sure I don't look fat like this? Oh, okay, go ahead and do your thing, I'll wait. Are you done yet? Oh, you are? Sorry, I didn't notice.* Um, I don't think me doing phone sex is a long-term, or even a short-term, solution to my financial problems."

"But if Nick called . . . ," she said in a teasing voice.

I glared. Of course she couldn't see me. "How come I don't say a thing, and you still know I've got a mad crush on him?"

"You asked him out, didn't you?"

"Well, yeah, but—"

"And have you asked anyone out? Ever?"

"Well, no, but—"

"Ergo, you have a mad crush."

"Hey, why didn't you become a lawyer? You probably would've done a lot better than Hugh."

"Hmph, no thanks. I'd rather show old movies than wear a suit and get litigious all day."

"Good point. What was playing tonight?"

"*Wuthering Heights.*"

"Which one?"

"The one with Laurence Olivier. Look, I know you have a mad crush on Timothy Dalton, but that version sucks ass."

"You're right, Miss Film Major. But damn, he's gorgeous."

"Does Nick look like *him*? Then I could understand all your fussing."

"Not really. Except maybe in the dark, dangerous way. Oh, and he has black hair."

"What color eyes?"

"Blue. Dark, stormy blue."

"Hold on, honey, you've got to check yourself. I hate to be the bearer of bad news, but he turned you down, right?"

I sighed. "Yeah. But, man, is he foxy."

"So now the bakery thing is done, what's next?"

"Oh, besides developing my love of scrapbooking?"

"Look, honey, I know you're white, you don't have to rub my face in it."

I cackled. "That's where you're wrong. Next to me? With dreads hanging down her back? A woman named Tamsin. Wearing kente cloth, no less."

"Ouch. Okay, I'm toast. I might as well be dating the Irish carpenter if my sisters are pasting photos into albums with some weird-ass confetti and shit."

"And next you'll be following NASCAR." She snorted. "Next up," I continued, "I think John has some more work for me. I really can't do much until I hear from the Teaching Fellows, which'll be in late May. Hugh sent me the rent money, and I canceled my cell phone. Mom's been doing some of the cooking—"

"God help you," Keisha muttered.

"—and she's kept the foreclosure folks at bay while she tries to figure out her finances. Nick gave her some advice on that, too." I continued speaking over her snort. "She's been picking up a few things here and there, which is nice. Not enough to live on, certainly, but I think I can make it until I hear."

"And then what?"

"Well, if I get in, I start training—and getting paid—a few weeks after that. If I don't? I have no frigging clue."

"It's sort of a plan."

I sighed, and looked out the window. "I don't know, Keish. I really don't. I know I have to do something, but I don't know what."

"What's up with the divorce proceedings?"

There I knew I was on solid ground. "Well, I was going to do it all amicably, back when Hugh had a job, but when he lost his job, and told me he couldn't pay that much, I lost it. He shouldn't be able to just tell me he can't support our child and have that be okay."

She cheered. "You go! I told you not to go down easy. Can I be blunt?"

"Um, like you never have been before?"

"Yeah, right. Well, Hugh is a lazy fuckhead. But, and this is the good part, he's also a pussy. See, he'll cave on the whole divorce agreement thing, and you can move forward knowing Aidan will always be okay."

"If Hugh doesn't pussy out and become a deadbeat dad."

"If he does, I *am* getting a law degree so I can sue his ass."

"Thanks, Keish. It's nice to know you have my back."

"Always, honey. Always."

"So?"

Dr. Lowell pushed her glasses back up on her nose. She was wearing her most intimidating therapist's outfit: a tasteful plaid suit with a double strand of pearls wrapped around her throat. If I saw her on the street, I would assume she was smarter than me, richer than me, and happier than me. All right, maybe I shouldn't be going there.

"Well, let's see. I did that big presentation, and I didn't fall on my face. Or have lettuce in my teeth. I went to somebody else's house to do scrapbooking—"

She raised her eyebrows in a question.

"—I'll explain in a minute. I made a lunch date with some new friends, I asked a man out, an absolutely stunning man wants me but I don't want him, my mother is *not* driving me crazy, Aidan is a sweetheart, Hugh is a jerk, and Keisha still lives three thousand miles away."

She leaned back, resting her hands on her knees. Her manicure was perfect. "Sounds like you've had a busy week."

I laughed. "Yeah, you could say that."

"You sound good." She sounded pleased.

"I am." Now I sounded pleased.

"Want to tell me about it?"

"Sure. I mean, besides the list?"

She nodded.

"I don't know if I can explain it." She wrinkled her nose at me. I held my hand up before she could speak. "Okay, I know, that's why I'm here. To explain. Okay. Well, with Simon, the thing is—he's gorgeous, but he knows it. And honestly, I'm not sure how much we have in common, besides both of us thinking he's beautiful. He doesn't read, he's a total go-getter business guy, and Aidan doesn't like him."

"Has Aidan told you so?"

I grimaced. "He asked me if foreign people—Simon's British, remember—were supposed to be here because we got our freedom from his country. And was there someone we should call to tell on him so he'd have to leave."

"Okay, then. So you'll dump him. That must feel—"

"Weird. Yeah, it is. I did dump him already, actually. And I mean, it's not like I've ever dumped anyone before. Not really. Especially not someone I'd usually be gnawing on my arm to get."

"But it's not right. And you know it. So you did the right thing and stopped it before either one of you gets hurt." She gave an approving nod.

"Mm."

"How's the financial situation?"

I heaved a sigh. "Bad. Not as bad as I'd first thought, but pretty bad. I'm checking into alternate insurance plans, and Mom and I are cooking, but—well, you know, I haven't paid you in a while." I knotted my fingers together and leaned forward on her couch. She waved her hand in dismissal.

"Don't worry about it. Let's worry about getting you on your feet first and then paying me. I'll survive." Good, because without her, I couldn't have survived myself this long.

"Do you really think I'll be able to make it?" I watched my hands clench each other.

"Look at me, Molly." I looked up and met her gaze. It was kind and warm. Immediately my insides relaxed a tiny bit. This was why she was worth every penny I didn't have. "I have confidence in you. *You* have to have confidence in you. And I know you can do this, and be happy."

"Funny, a lady at a bar told me the same thing," I said in a reflective tone. I flapped my hands. "But never mind. Really, that's all I've ever wanted. I mean, Hugh always talked about getting things, and buying stuff, and eating fancy meals—me, I just want enough to be able to give Aidan some of the toys he wants, have seafood once in a while, and buy new jeans in the fall. That's it. It doesn't take much."

"And you're more than capable of managing it. I know you are. Do you know you are?"

I exhaled. A big, life-affirming sigh that seemed as if it could sweep away all my doubts and insecurities. "Yes. I know I am."

She smiled and leaned back in her chair. "See? And once you know that, you can do anything."

"Now you sound like Helen Reddy."

She looked puzzled.

"'I Am Woman?' Australian pop singer from the 1970s? Don't tell me you never heard that song."

She chuckled. "Yes, of course. And speaking of which, how are things going with Hugh?"

I stretched my legs out in front of me and clasped my hands behind my head. "He's going to regret my going all Helen Reddy on his ass. I've asked my lawyer to try to get sufficient child support, to put everything down in writing. Thank God I paid him in advance. Originally, we had a gentleman's agreement without official documentation, but since he's no gentleman, I'm not going to leave it up to chance. Of course, it could take longer this way, but that doesn't matter to me."

She beamed at me. "Roar away, Molly. You are Reddy for life." She emphasized the word so I'd know she was making a pun. A really, really bad pun.

• • •

It was a little later than usual when I finally left Dr. Lowell's office. I'd gotten stuck in the elevator with a messy kid who just had to press all the buttons on the way down. From the forty-third floor. His smile reminded me of Aidan's. His baby-sitter shot me a thankful look as I told him it had always been my dream to do the same thing. It was about fifteen minutes later when I emerged from the double glass doors onto the sidewalk. The subway was a few blocks away, and it was fairly balmy, for March, at least.

I was just reaching into my bag for my MetroCard when I slammed into him. The impact sent my purse flying out of my hands, and I stumbled a little.

"Molly?" A firm arm held me by the elbow. Nick's blue eyes held a look of concern. I guess they should, given my legs were akimbo and my purse was upside down on the ground. If I wasn't mistaken, a tampon was making its slow escape from the depths of my bag. I eased my foot around and stomped on it, then bent over and quickly stuck it back into the bag.

"Are you okay?" he asked, his voice all rumbly and gruff, as if he hadn't spoken in a while.

I nodded, zipping my bag closed. "Yeah, sorry, I wasn't watching where I was going." I looked up into his face. It was very close to mine. "What are you doing here, anyway?"

He loosened his grip on my arm a bit and stepped backward, looking down at the sidewalk as he did so. I did, too, hoping something else hadn't rolled out of my purse. Thank goodness, there was just some old gum and an empty Snapple bottle, neither of which was mine.

"Doing here?" He actually sounded—nervous.

"Yes. Doing here. You. What are?" I repeated.

"Um. I have an appointment." He gestured toward Dr. Lowell's building.

Interesting. As far as I knew, the only professional offices were therapists' offices. And if Nick—professional, smart, and all that—needed help, what hope was there for the rest of us?

But of course I didn't say any of that. Although I couldn't resist throwing out a line to see if he bit. "Really? What a coincidence. I'm just coming from my therapist's."

The expression on his face grew even more anxious, if possible. "Nice to see you, Molly, see you soon," he said, walking off with the stride of a man who did not want to explain anything else.

I wondered if his session was actually with Dr. Lowell. I chuckled as I walked away from the building. It was good to know even the most intently intimidating man needed help sometimes.

I pulled a Helen Reddy and roared as I headed toward the subway.

Pies-Fed Revisited

The day-old section at your local bakery has never been so . . . glamorous. Or so regally approachable. Take refuge here and reflect on yesterday's freshness. Still delicious, just slightly past their prime. Half price, too. An economic way to save an outdated baked good.

22

THE BUZZER RANG RIGHT AROUND TWELVE FORTY-FIVE. I'D
been glancing at the clock for the last hour, wondering just
when he'd arrive. Aidan was all packed and dressed, wearing
his special Justice League T-shirt, even though I told him
he'd have to wear a sweatshirt over it. He groaned but felt
better when I said he could wait until Nick saw his shirt to
put the rest of his clothes on.

I opened the door, smoothing my suddenly damp hands
on my thighs. I'd chosen my clothes carefully that morning
also—I wore my favorite pair of jeans, the slightly stretchy
bootcut Calvin Kleins, and a light pink top with a rose-
colored cardigan on top. The cardigan had little sparkles all
over it. I liked it because it looked so girly.

"Good afternoon," he said as he strode into the apart-
ment. He must've just gotten his hair cut—again—since it
was shorter than a few days ago. A few specks of hair had
settled on his shoulders, and I reached up to brush them
away.

He reacted as if I'd tried to grab his ass or something. He
ducked, his cheeks got flushed, and he swallowed hard.

"Sorry. I mean, I just thought I'd help you get that hair—"
I flapped my hands in the air like a chicken.

He looked down at his shoulder and frowned. "Oh. Right. Sorry." He brushed the hairs off, and I watched them float to the ground. I quelled the impulse to pick them up and put them under my pillow or something.

"So. How are you?" I asked brightly, clasping my hands in front of me. He looked rumpled, newly shorn, and delicious.

"Good." He cleared his throat. "The shop's soft launch is coming up. Simon's coordinating for the opening event." A pause. "And nearly all of my work here is complete. Just tying some things up, and then . . ." His words trailed off.

Oh. He'd be leaving soon, then, I could figure that much out on my own.

Aidan bounded up, holding his Pokémon backpack. "Hi, Nick. Did you see my T-shirt?"

Nick squatted down and gave Aidan a piercing stare. "Pretty sharp, sport. Did you see *my* T-shirt?" He pulled open the button-down shirt he was wearing and showed his chest to Aidan. I'd never envied my son so much in my entire life. Nick wore a black Batman shirt with a yellow bat logo.

"Cool." Aidan exhaled, his eyes wide. Nick straightened and rebuttoned his shirt.

"Should we go?"

Aidan headed for the door, Nick looking back at me for one long moment. "I'll have him back in a few hours," he said, pulling the door closed behind him.

"Take your time," I said to the empty air. It was funny, I hadn't known Nick that long, but I trusted him implicitly. So much so that I let him take my son out alone. Heck, I'd always felt a moment of panic when Hugh took Aidan off for a boys' day out, and yet here I was, trusting someone with the most important thing in my life.

I wandered back to the kitchen and touched the coffeepot. Still warm. I opened the cupboard and took out my favorite mug, a wide, fat-bottomed cup with gay tulips painted all over it. Aidan had picked it out for me a few Mother's Days ago.

As I splashed in the milk, I wondered when Nick would be leaving. And if he'd be going straight back to England. It bothered me I knew so little about him—I knew he had a sister, but was he going to visit her first? Did he still have family in New York? It shouldn't bother me, but it did.

I wished things were different. I wished I could figure out why he didn't feel comfortable dating me. And even if the reason was because of work, the point was moot, because when the job was done, he'd be gone, it sounded like. Darn. Darn, darn, *damn*.

The coffee did a little bit to bolster my spirits, thank goodness. It was strange, not having anything pressing to do. My day was usually filled with tons of errands: work on copy, clean the house of stray Lego parts so no one would lose a limb, laundry, dishes, grocery shopping, Mom's finances, my worries.

Mom's off-key warblings reached me in the kitchen. How many times had I heard her singing Gilbert and Sullivan lyrics? And every time, she got them wrong. I walked down the hall, smiling to myself. She was gaining volume as I entered the living room. It looked like she was in the midst of organizing her finances. Had Nick actually persuaded her to take charge of them? If so, I was really going to miss him when he left.

"It's not 'sinful economy,' it's 'singular anomaly,' Mom."

She looked up and gave me a wry smile. "Oh, yes, it is sinful economy, Molly, my love." She took her reading glasses off and placed them on top of the biggest pile. "Where did all my money go?"

"To some guy on the trading-room floor?"

She wrinkled her nose. "No, I mean before that. I mean, yes, there, too, but even before that, I spent money so foolishly." She gestured toward the papers. "Spa visits, books, the expensive car, the trip to Morocco, the pool, for God's sake. I didn't need any of that. All I needed was to pay the mortgage, the taxes, and eat. Maybe buy a book once in a while. It all seems so . . . meaningless."

I patted her hand. "Why do you think you did it, then, Mom?" I asked softly. She shrugged, and I could see the tears beginning to form in her eyes.

"I thought I could make enough money from the stock market so I could stop worrying. So you could stop worrying about me."

I looked at her in surprise. "Worry about you? I didn't worry about you until you showed up on my doorstep wearing that old sweatshirt. Why, did I say something?"

"Not you. Hugh."

I felt myself stiffen. "What did he say?"

"One time when you were over, and you and Aidan were out by the pool, Hugh told me you guys weren't as solvent as he'd like."

My mouth dropped open in amazement. "What the—?" Then a nasty suspicion entered my mind. "When was this?"

"Last summer."

"The bastard." She raised her brows at me. I felt myself zoom from zero to sixty in 4.3 seconds. "He was already planning to leave. I was wondering where our savings had gone. I bet he squirreled it away before he told me, and now he's crying poverty." I stood up, shoving my chair behind me. "I'm going to call him now."

Mom held my arm. "Molly, are you really sure you want to talk to him now when you're so upset? I mean, what if you're wrong? Maybe he was genuinely concerned."

I sat back down again, shrugging her hand off my arm. "Mom, I know Hugh. And, forgive me for saying this about your favorite son-in-law—"

"My only son-in-law," she said drily.

"—but he's out for himself. And only himself. Even Aidan comes second to Hugh's desires. Bastard," I repeated, allowing her to take my hand again.

"Sweetie. You've got your lawyer working on this, right? And if you call and tell him you suspect Hugh's buried some assets, he should be able to find them, right?" For once she wasn't defending him—had someone challenged her to that "never in a million years" thing, too?

"Yeah. Although I'd love to give him a piece of my mind and find out if he really is that kind of lowlife. Grrr," I growled.

Her eyes widened. "I've never seen you so—aggressive, Molly. You're acting completely unlike yourself." Her tone implied she didn't like the change. "I mean, calling Hugh to yell at him is something you would never have done before. At least, before all this."

I felt my lips start to smile, despite my anger. "I wouldn't do it in a million years, would I? Sounds like a challenge."

techniques. For years he had rued the way many Americans read *Love and Will*, taking it as a justification for self-focused personal liberation, premised on materialism and hedonism, without the requisite emphasis on individual responsibility.[7] In 1981, he rebroadcast this message to his readers in the publication of *Freedom and Destiny*, arguing that freedom had too often been defined negatively (as freedom *from* political oppression, cultural conformity, etc.) and that true freedom was "the possibility of development, of enhancement of one's life; or the possibility of withdrawing, shutting oneself up, denying and stultifying one's growth."[8] It was a choice to throw your weight behind growth or despair, an endeavor to balance your destiny (your existential, cultural, environmental, and personal liabilities and assets) with your creative will.

In 1971, not long after the publication of *Love and Will*, May had been the subject of a curious, forward-looking profile in the *New York Times*. "Listening to May in public you get the same feeling you get reading *Love and Will*—the feeling that you are swimming out to sea with him at your side," wrote the *Times* reporter. "You know you are getting in over your head; indeed, you suspect that he is, too. But there is a reassuring buoyancy underneath, a sense that if you just keep on swimming everything will be all right."[9]

When *Freedom and Destiny* was published, a decade later, the *Times* still showed respect for May's intellectual prowess, but he was no longer treated as a herald of the future. He was more of a cultural relic. "*Freedom and Destiny* is a piece for trombone," wrote the reviewer for the *Times*. "If it sometimes wails, this is not altogether Dr. May's fault. If we keep on making the same mistakes, what choice has he but to point them out yet again? What can one do with people who fear their freedom, refuse their anxiety and can't appreciate despair? Like an analyst whose patient won't move to the next crisis, Dr. May can only sit back in his chair and re-cross his legs."[10] As he did at the 1975 theory conference, Rollo May held his ground, doggedly communicating his "humanistic" psychology, harping on the same points, sometimes seeming more of a nagging parent than a visionary. May's audience for these 1980s books predictably shrank.

Meanwhile, the mainstream American media sounded the death knell for humanistic psychology. Many declared the utopian dreams of Maslow, Rogers, Murphy, and others dead and buried. In 1981, May's reviewer described his rhetoric as "tired." "He needs a new vocabulary," he wrote, "for even truth needs a change of clothes now and then."[11]

In 1985, a journalist for the *New York Times* wrote that although "in its heyday, in the late 1960s and early 1970s, Esalen was a cultural landmark, the point at the continent's edge from which a stream of new ideas and methods emanated . . . the encounter group movement, for which Esalen was a mecca, is moribund today."[12] The writer described the "graying" Esalen of the 1980s as being faced with the possibility of a "lasting irrelevance." Most growth centers modeled on Esalen, of which there were over a hundred at the movement's peak, had closed; by the decade's end there were no more than a handful.[13] The terms "human potential movement" and "humanistic psychology" disappeared from popular magazines and newspapers.

Many Americans had, no doubt, grown impatient with an approach that had failed to yield the kind of personal and cultural change for which they'd been hoping. A Gallup poll in 1980 found that 45 percent of Americans felt family life had gotten worse over the past decade; only 37 percent thought it had improved.[14] They were pressed upon by rising divorce rates (which increased by 40 percent from 1970 to 1975 alone), economic stagnation, soaring crime rates, and energy shortages.[15]

A number of literary critics depicted the 1970s as a decade of hopelessness. John Updike wrote that "the American ride" had run out of gas.[16] Norman Mailer complained that "it was the decade in which image became preeminent because nothing deeper was going on."[17]

Even for still-hopeful human potentialists, the decade's culmination in Reagan's 1980 election was depressing. Reagan capitalized on the 1970s dissatisfaction, drawing attention to the excesses of civil rights, women's liberation, and sexual freedom, and exploiting the anxiety that many felt when confronted even (or primarily) by the most liberatory aspects of those movements.[18] He spoke to those who wanted to turn the clock back, as well as to many who'd been supportive of political reform and grateful for the personal freedoms it afforded, but who'd grown tired of the sense of centerlessness and disorder that had come to seem characteristic of the seventies. Facing the longest period of inflation in American history, the highest interest rates, a crushing energy crisis, and the legacy of the nation's defeat in Vietnam, many Americans latched onto his rhetoric of strength and individual responsibility.[19]

American psychologists, too, seemed happy to move on. As Rogers himself noted, academics had been ambivalent at best about humanistic psychology. Although they awarded him numerous honors, including three awards for scientific achievement and elections to the presidency of both the American Association of Applied Psychology and the American Psychological Association, he felt they simultaneously perceived him as an embarrassment—"softheaded, unscientific, cultish, too easy on students, full of strange and upsetting enthusiasms about ephemeral things like the self, therapist attitudes, and encounter groups."[20] He described the impact of humanistic psychology as being largely absent from the textbooks, classrooms, and laboratories that academic psychology comprised.

Psychotherapy in the 1980s took a conscious step away from humanistic psychology, as well. A 1983 *New York Times* article identified new trends, including increased demand for short-term interventions, new interest in cognitive-behavioral therapies focused on isolated mental problems, and a preponderance of diagnosis-based treatment reimbursable by insurance companies. Citing a survey of four hundred clinical psychologists and four hundred counseling psychologists, the author reported that the majority (about 41 percent) called themselves "eclectic," while 10 percent self-identified as "cognitive-behavioral," 11 percent described themselves as "psychoanalytic," and 7 percent said they were "behavioral." "Humanistic" had been subsumed under "eclectic" but, as the author notes, had actually come to inform all categories. Contemporary therapists were described as warm, active, supportive, less detached, and more human.[21]

Out of the spotlight, and in diminished numbers, both the human potential movement and humanistic psychology kept kicking. Esalen responded to decreased cultural interest with a renewed commitment to scholarship and expanded social awareness. In contrast to programming in the 1960s and 1970s that relied heavily on encounter, and in the style of Rogers's own work, ventures of the 1980s reached beyond the individual and into the wider world. A prime example was the Soviet-American exchange program that the institute launched in 1982, based on a model of citizens' diplomacy and a desire to forge open communication between the nations.[22]

As of 1985, Esalen offered five hundred seminars per year, drawing about four thousand total participants.[23] Michael Murphy, described in a 1995 *New York Times* article as a "somewhat marginalized figure," remained vital and continued to refine Esalen's program, to publish on human potential, and to advance new theories.[24]

Humanistic psychology pressed on, as well. Although conference attendance declined and courses at mainstream universities grew scarce, hundreds of practitioners continued to define themselves as "humanistic psychologists," defending the significance and enduring relevance of their theory and principles.[25] Even in the twenty-first century, humanistic psychology boasts an active association (with frequent, if not annual, conferences), and Division 32 maintains an energetic presence at APA conventions.[26]

Academic psychologists, however, no longer feel compelled to acknowledge the current, or historical, impact of humanistic psychology. One academic analysis of trends in psychology from 1950 to 1999, for example, tracks only the cognitive, behavioral, psychoanalytic, and neuroscientific schools.[27] And while most introductory psychology texts devote entire chapters to these perspectives, humanistic psychology is often handled in a paragraph, if at all.

This lack of recognition, though, is a poor measure of the movement's impact. The greatest testaments to humanistic psychology's enduring significance are the numerous ways in which American mental health professionals have adopted the leading concepts of prominent humanistic psychologists; the way that later movements in mainstream psychology have subtly replicated its values and reproduced its goals; and the way that the American vernacular, and American ideas of self, have incorporated its language and ideas.[28] If anything, it's the utter pervasiveness of the humanistic perspective that has made evidence of its influence so elusive.

The most tangible indicator of humanistic psychology's legacy might be the frequency with which, upon walking into any psychotherapeutic situation, Americans now encounter some hybrid of the humanistic perspective. Individual counseling, social work interventions, and pastoral counseling all reflect strains of early humanistic theory.[29] They tend to be nondirective, privileging meaningful subjective input from patients and relying on their active involvement in the counseling process. Modeled, in part, on Carl Rogers's client-centered (now termed person-centered) approach, they employ theories of empathic understanding, present-orientation, and self-direction.[30]

Contemporary therapeutic interactions are also premised on a personalized and humanized concept of professionalism. Grounded in humanistic psychologists' view of patients as fully human participants in the therapeutic process, this approach has supplanted prior concepts of professionalism that relied heavily on hierarchical distinctions, experimental control, and notions of a value-free, objective science in interactions between psychologists and patients or study participants.[31] Backed by research that supports the efficacy of self-disclosure, therapists, who used to act as blank slates onto which patients could project their inner conflicts, are now more likely to share personal information.[32]

Social workers, even more than clinical psychologists, now tend to employ methods that draw directly from Rogers's client-centered theory. The "core conditions" of effective social work practice are commonly thought to include empathy, warmth, and genuineness on the part of the therapist.[33] And everything from the standard social work interview, intended to establish an effective therapeutic relationship based on affirmation of the client's worth and dignity, to the content of longer-term interventions, which regard as their cornerstone the therapist's continued encouragement of and positive regard for the client, reflects Rogers's style and leading concepts.[34]

Rogers's theory has also made an indelible mark on pastoral counseling. In a turn from moralism and in opposition to mass culture, pastoral theologians have adopted a Rogerian "ethic of self-realization which define[s] growth as the primary ethical good," elevating individual improvement over competing priorities.[35] Pastoral counseling, in fact, was ahead of its time in adopting this theory. As early as the 1940s, Rogers's *Counseling and Psychotherapy* became a standard text in theological seminaries, and his techniques proved a staple in seminary training, effective even in a brief introductory format.[36]

While Rogers may have had a greater impact on the mental health field than his fellow founders, he was certainly not the only humanistic psychologist to provoke theoretical change in therapeutic realms. Maslow's theory, for example, has encouraged psychologists to consider the positive aspects of human nature, as evidenced in the strengths and health of clients.[37]

Rollo May's theory has also been widely applied within counseling. Considered to be "the father of American existential psychology," May attuned psychotherapists and lay readers to the productive value of anxiety and conflict.[38] In constructing fears and conflicts as fodder for effective treatment, rather than as mere obstacles to overcome or symptoms to eliminate, May helped balance the psychoanalytic and behaviorist approaches that preceded his own. Like Rogers, he also helped to convince psychotherapists (and pastoral counselors) of the value of empathy.[39] Finally, his consideration of the social responsibility of the therapist, as expressed in 1978 in *Psychology and the Human Dilemma*, influenced psychologists to reconsider their role in the cultural problems of their time.[40]

In addition to informing a modern conceptualization of counseling, the techniques of humanistic psychology laid a foundation for practices outside of the realm of individual psychotherapy. Bodywork, like yoga and meditation, for example, has its roots in the holistic approaches of humanistic psychology and the human potential movement.[41] Built in part on the Rogerian ideas of "organismic wholeness" and the Maslowian idea of self-actualization, these practices incorporate mind, body, and spirit in the service of healing. In valuing an active therapeutic process, emotional integration, and self-awareness, bodywork has also integrated the guiding principles of active participation, transcendence, and present-orientation.[42]

Many of humanistic psychology's principles and techniques blended seamlessly, and almost unnoticeably, with American practice. As historian Christopher Lasch wrote of Carl Rogers's approach, it was in many respects "as American as apple pie." It tapped into American ideas of free will, human perfectibility, and personal responsibility.[43]

Given the resonance of humanistic psychology with American interests, it's not surprising that the supposedly defunct movement has come back in other forms—even within the field of academic psychology itself.[44]

The most obvious derivative is the positive psychology movement that sprang up in 1998, quickly gaining adherents in the United States and around the world. Articulated by founders Martin Seligman and Mihalyi Csikszentmihalyi in 2000 as "the study of strength and virtue," positive psychology combined the interests of humanistic psychology and the scientific goals of academic psychology.[45] Seeking to operationalize virtues, values, and strengths in a way that would allow for their empirical identification and measurement, positive psychologists agreed with humanistic psychologists' rejection of a pathology-oriented discipline that focused on weakness and damage while attempting to expand psychological study to realms of well-being, contentment, and optimism.[46]

The similarities between humanistic psychology and positive psychology are numerous. Comparing Seligman to Maslow, one scholar notes the shared desire to "create an optimistic psychology, one that sees the human personality as more than just a collection of neuroses and tics."[47] In opposition to mainstream psychology's post–World War II focus on pathology, Seligman directed an initiative toward "the empirical study of flourishing individuals and thriving communities."[48] His theoretical basis for such work was strongly reminiscent of Maslow's contributions. For example, in developing a "manual of the sanities," which he called the Values in Action (VIA) Classification of Strengths manual, Seligman, with Christopher Peterson, identified virtuous character traits that replicated Maslow's being values (B-values) and included wisdom, transcendence, temperance, and justice.[49]

Yet despite their extensive similarities, positive psychologists have conspicuously failed to acknowledge the tradition of humanistic psychology that preceded them by nearly four decades. In fact, when confronted directly with this apparent debt, positive psychologists have disavowed any connection. Martin Seligman, in particular, has distanced his theory from those of the founders of humanistic psychology and belittled the movement's impact.[50]

For Seligman and Csikszentmihalyi an essential component to the program for a positive psychology is a commitment to the scientific method, which they presume humanistic psychologists to have lacked. In an implicit critique of humanistic psychology, Seligman and Csikszentmihalyi explained that "in this quest for what is best, positive psychology does not rely on wishful thinking, faith, self-deception, fads, or hand-waving; it tries to adapt what is best in the scientific method to the unique problems that human behavior presents to those who wish to understand it in all its complexity."[51]

Reducing humanistic psychology to its least scholarly elements, Seligman and Csikszentmihalyi wrote in 2000 that "one legacy of the humanism of the 1960s is prominently displayed in any large bookstore: the 'psychology' section contains at least ten shelves on crystal healing, aromatherapy, and reaching the inner child for every shelf of books that tries to uphold some scholarly standard."[52] Statements like these earned the ire of humanistic psychologists and generated a flood of letters to the *American Psychologist* demanding that the founders of positive psychology acknowledge the obvious origins of their ideas in the humanistic psychology movement. One respondent wrote, "It was 99.6% pure rejection of their so-called ancestors (even purer than Ivory soap!)."[53]

Regardless of the justifiable indignation of humanistic psychologists, positive psychologists, seeking to forge empirically testable theories within the boundaries of scholarly respectability, couldn't risk being associated with a movement that had become disassociated from academic psychology. Tactfully responding to humanistic psychologists' allegations, Seligman and Csikszentmihalyi wrote, "We do not wish [. . .] to blur the boundaries completely between the positive psychology we hope to see emerge and these worthy traditions. We are, unblushingly, scientists first."[54] And Csikszentmihalyi graciously wrote the preface to the 2001 *Handbook of Humanistic Psychology*, describing his own intellectual debt to Maslow and Rogers and acknowledging the value of the therapeutic contributions of humanistic psychology.[55]

In addition to seeking to evade association with the perception of humanistic psychology's unscientific bases, the founders of positive psychology have tried to distance themselves from the movement's reputation for being overly individualistic and encouraging of narcissism. Instead, positive psychologists have been pragmatic, advocating the inculcation of specific skills to overcome negative thought patterns and to promote socially harmonious action.[56] Positive psychologists have also sought to move beyond the study of inner-oriented virtues, extending their study to civic virtues, which include altruism, responsibility, nurturance, tolerance, civility, work ethic, and moderation.[57]

Similar reincarnations of humanistic psychology emerged within social work theory in the 1980s and 1990s, reflecting the themes of self-actualization, striving, and health-seeking. Specific approaches that incorporated these themes included "solution focused therapy," a form of brief therapy that is thoroughly client-directed and present-focused, and "assets-based community development," a method of identifying and employing a community's strength to sustain its development.[58] Another approach, the "strengths" perspective, even more tangibly reflected many of the goals of the founders of humanistic psychology.[59]

Based on theoretical and ethical objections to an illness-orientation and the hierarchical therapist-client distinctions found in some sectors of the field, the strengths perspective construes healing as an innate capability and values the social worker primarily as a catalyst in the client's self-determined change.[60] It takes as its goal the identification of individual, family, and community strengths, primarily in realms of dialogue and communication, membership, resilience, healing, and wholeness.[61] The strengths perspective's elevation of inborn individual drives toward health, rather than illness-oriented explanations of individual pathology, echoes the priorities both of humanistic psychology and positive psychology.

But, like positive psychologists, advocates of the strengths perspective have made only scant reference to their intellectual predecessors in humanistic psychology. In fact, they claim the emergence of therapeutic perspectives explicitly oriented toward applying a positive view of clients' innate potential is a fairly recent phenomenon.[62] While strengths-perspective advocates haven't directly criticized humanistic psychology or expressed a need for ideological distance from it, the differences between the movements are implicit in their theory. The consideration of social-political forces, for example, is primary among the priorities of strengths-perspective social workers, most of whom would take issue with the assumption of humanistic psychologists that social change is a direct result of self-actualization.[63]

Outside of mental health fields, though, professionals found it easier to appreciate, and acknowledge, their debt to humanistic psychology. "Professionals from education, religion, nursing, medicine, psychiatry, law, business, government, public health, law enforcement, race relations, social work—the list goes on and on—all came to feel that here, finally, was an approach which enabled them to succeed on the previously neglected human dimensions of their jobs, to reach the people for whom they felt responsible but were often unable to help," wrote Richard Farson.[64] Humanistic psychology offered these diverse professionals a way to conceive of their employees, their clients, their constituents, and their patients that was compassionate and optimistic. In many cases it moved them from seeing their charges as responsibilities, or even problems, to seeing them as the vessels of their highest ambitions.

This happened in business, too, where humanistic psychology's theories and techniques found their widest, and most overt, application. Major corporations used humanistic psychology to make their workers more efficient, more productive, and happier.[65] Common applications in this setting ranged from employee retreats to seminars on sensitivity training that derived directly from the work of humanistic psychologists like Maslow and research institutions like National Training Laboratories. For some business owners, like Andrew Kay of Non-Linear Systems, Maslow's work took on biblical proportions, while for others, his management theory was a key resource. The journal Maslow kept during his summer with Kay went through several printings—it was published in 1962 by NLS as a pamphlet titled "Summer Notes on Social Psychology of Industry and Management," and more formally in 1965 as *Eupsychian Management*.[66]

Of this legacy, some humanistic psychologists are proud, interpreting this application to be evidence of the humanization of business that resulted from the movement.[67] Others question the motives of corporations in employing humanistic psychology principles and techniques within management strategies.[68]

"The history of our work," wrote Farson, "is dotted with [. . .] examples of our unwittingly serving the interests of the more powerful against the less powerful." As in the case of union leaders, who "intuitively knew that 'communication' cools out the oppressed worker, making it possible for management to maintain something approximating the status quo," Farson argued, many business leaders have used humanistic theory for corporate profit, without any real interest in the contentment of their workers.[69] Another scholar suggests that in valorizing the use of the movement's theory by corporations, humanistic psychologists confused a first-order change with a second-order change, that is, they mistook a mere change of form for a more radical change of structure.[70]

In extracting the concepts of humanistic psychology at the expense of the overarching orientation, everyone from corporate leaders to academic psychologists and psychotherapists may have ultimately undermined, and even debased, the founders' intentions.[71] Maslow, Rogers, May, and others had hoped not only to empower individuals to realize the full extent of their potential and to revise psychology's pathology orientation, but also to to reorient psychological science and oppose the damaging effects of the cultural imperatives of conformity and adjustment in favor of a complex selfhood based on wholeness and self-determination. Perhaps predictably, they fell far short of these lofty goals.

Although a humanized conception of management came to dominate business theory in the 1960s and 1970s, it did little, if anything, to eradicate the baser profit motives of corporate leaders. Likewise, though a client-centered approach came to pervade psychotherapy, it did little to offset the field's reliance on diagnosis and pathology. It was in 1980, in fact, that the third edition of the *Diagnostic and Statistical Manual of Mental Disorders* committed clinicians to the discrete categorization of mental illness. While the first two editions of the *DSM* had relied on a "biopsychosocial" model, in which individual problems were dynamic and ranged on a continuum, the third edition adopted a research-based medical model, with discrete and clear-cut categories for diagnosis.[72]

In a recent polemic against modern diagnosis, psychologist Gary Greenberg lamented the descriptive nosology that has dominated the field since the 1980s. "The trick with the descriptive approach to diagnosis," writes Greenberg, "is to keep your eye on the loose-leaf notebook and not the patient."[73] Disregarding the patient's account of his interior life, his personality, and the circumstances in his life, the clinician as diagnostician, according to Greenberg, is anything but humanistic. "The industry is working hard to eliminate the human element from psychiatry," he writes, "but for now the best it can do is to circle the answers in notebooks and train practitioners to ignore what's in front of their eyes."[74]

Although positive psychology promises a fuller treatment of the individual, at least in terms of balancing pathology with strength, it also replicates many of the tendencies that humanistic psychologists originally railed against. While pathology-based interventions left the good life undefined (health as the absence of symptoms), the bulk of the work conducted under the heading "positive psychology," and its derivative "happiness research," arbitrarily presupposes a subjective sense of satisfaction as the ultimate goal.[75] A 2010 article in the *New York Times*, for example, took for granted that such happiness should be the supreme measure of whether things are working in our society. Reviewing the work of Derek Bok's *Happiness Around the World*, the critic asks why we should worry about growing inequalities in wealth distribution when lower-income people are not less happy.[76]

As psychologists Frank Richardson and Blaine Fowers and philosopher Charles Guignon point out in *Re-envisioning Psychology*, current marital research suffers from a similar evaluative error; in determining the success of a marriage, most studies equate marital success with personal happiness. "The whole idea that personal happiness or well-being is of primary concern," they argue, "is part of the overweening contemporary emphasis on the individual," where individual success is equated with the emotional experience of personal satisfaction.[77] Conspicuously absent from these studies is an inquiry into communal and relational values, individual experiences of meaning, definitions of the good life, and reasonable ideas about the constituents of effective marriages.

Marriage is just one of many topics of psychological research that Richardson, Fowers, and Guignon perceive to be representative of psychology's current problems. In fact, contemporary psychology as they conceive it doesn't seem to differ substantially from the psychology of the 1950s that humanistic psychologists found to be so oppressive. Academic psychology still continues to claim value neutrality. Psychotherapy still encourages individuals "to think of themselves in too narrow a way." And committed students and colleagues, they note, question the intellectual worth and social significance of contemporary research, worrying that it amounts to nothing more than a "manipulative behavioral technology."[78]

Worse than perpetuating this narrow focus, though, the authors argue that psychotherapy actually exacerbates modern social ills by placing the inner self above all else. This individualistic emphasis compounds the erosion of communal feeling, individual alienation, and emotional disconnection, and fuels a sense of meaninglessness. Instead of seeing this as a pattern that developed in spite of, or in opposition to, humanistic psychology, though, the authors suggest that the work of humanistic psychologists might have unwittingly fueled the problem. Rooted in the excesses of the human potential movement in the 1960s and 1970s—encounter groups and est retreats—our current obsession with self-fulfillment, inner selves, individuation, and individuality, they claim, are now some of the most toxic elements of American psychology.[79]

In *We've Had a Hundred Years of Psychotherapy and the World Keeps Getting Worse*, James Hillman and Michael Ventura make a similar claim. They see modern psychotherapy as solipsistic and worry about the ways in which it redirects inward individual energies that could serve social, political, and environmental ends.[80] The humanistic psychology movement, of course, was saddled with these concerns from the start. While many battled against them, the flow of cultural energy to and from the movement, and the short-sightedness of certain members of the movement, meant that humanistic psychologists were themselves implicated in these offenses.

To conclude that humanistic psychology failed because of its inability to smooth out its implicit paradoxes and propel American psychology to utopian heights, though, would be reductionist. Because of the entrenched nature of humanistic psychologists' ideas within psychology and within the culture, in fact, the results of the movement are exceedingly difficult to evaluate. Whether you consider humanistic psychology a success, a failure, or a little of both depends on your perspective.

If we measure the extent to which the leading concepts of humanistic psychology have pervaded our culture, in fact, we might deem the movement a whopping success. The language of humanistic psychology is everywhere: humanistic ideas of self, growth, health, individual potential, and relation are now woven into the very fabric of our thoughts and perceptions.[81] The fundamentals of "humanistic" communication, encounter, and expression populate our interactions with our spouses, our employees and bosses, our friends and children. They ring from the lips of our talk show hosts, and they populate our self-help shelves.

If we examine contemporary criticism of American psychology, like that of Richardson, Fowers, and Guignon or Hillman and Ventura, however, we might conclude that the movement failed. The field seems hamstrung by the same scientific constraints that characterized it in the 1950s, and many researchers and practitioners display a comparable resistance to conducting interdisciplinary work (asking philosophical questions, exploring social concerns, considering cultural context). While cognitivism and neuropsychology have largely displaced behaviorism and psychoanalysis, these newly dominant approaches seem to have replaced the narrow interpretive frames of the past with comparably narrow frames of their own.

From a hermeneutic perspective, though, the "humanistic" dialogue that crystallized in the humanistic psychology movement in the 1960s and 1970s continues. A 2010 article in the *New York Times* harks back to Rollo May's belief in the value of anxiety and existential struggle. The author, Jonah Lehrer, considers the "upside" of depression, exploring specifically its creative value and enumerating several cases in which it might represent a healthy response to troubling circumstances.[82]

In a similar vein, several contemporary books question our culture's haste to medicate "illnesses" like depression without adequately considering the possibility of nonpathological sadness. Just as Maslow described self-actualizers as wisely unwilling to adjust to a sick system, Gary Greenberg (author of *Manufacturing Depression*) argues that many healthy individuals are being treated for individual problems that represent a healthy response to problematic cultural conditions. According to Greenberg, both psychotropic medications and cognitive-behavioral interventions attempt to adjust the sane individual to an insane society, rather than the reverse. Likewise, Jerome Wakefield and Alan Horowitz (*The Loss of Sadness*) complain that our categories of pathology have expanded to encompass even normal and understandable emotional reactions to negative events.[83]

For decades, Carl Rogers argued for the necessity of an affirming and growth-producing environment in the individual experience of health. But pathology-oriented interventions undermine these conditions. Frank Furedi argues in *Therapy Culture* that by assuming negative outcomes (even before they occur), our culture has produced an environment more conducive to victimhood than growth. He makes specific reference to the aftermath of September 11, when thousands of therapists were mobilized to support New Yorkers who were expected to have pathological reactions to the trauma. No one considered the possibility that they'd be able to cope with it in healthy ways.[84]

Malcolm Gladwell points out in his article "Getting Over It" that people are actually quite resilient in the face of trauma. He cites the estimate that 85 to 95 percent of individuals will cope with trauma remarkably well, not even requiring psychotherapeutic intervention.[85] Why, then, is a positive orientation to human nature still so foreign to psychologists? Why do the numbers of diagnoses continue to skyrocket?

While a range of critics from Lehrer to Gladwell make plain that the American culture we now inhabit isn't any more "eupsychian" than the one that produced the humanistic psychology movement in the 1950s, suffering as it does from a pervasive pathology orientation, the continuity of their critique with that of seminal humanistic psychology figures suggests a form of victory. In the 1950s, the writings of humanistic psychologists were relegated to remote academic journals and small presses, whereas now articles that take up these themes appear in *The New Yorker* and the *New York Times*, and books on these issues are published by major presses like Simon & Schuster, Routledge, and Harper Perennial. For now, the humanistic (and humanistically oriented) psychologists who remain can find comfort in the continued presence of this kind of critique, and in the hope that the tide within psychology will again shift toward a fuller, more positive, and more contextualized treatment of human experience.

Acknowledgments

I'd like to thank the following people (in alphabetical order) for their contributions to the book, either in the form of providing interviews, furnishing material, editing, offering feedback, or emotional support: Robert Abzug, Walter Anderson, the Archives of the History of American Psychology in Akron, Price Cobbs, Eleanor Criswell, George Dickey, Jennifer Percy Dowd, Jackie Doyle, Mallory Farrugia, Richard Farson, Bonnie Foster, Tom Greening, Shirley Grogan, the Harvard Archives, John Heider, the Humanistic Psychology Archives in Santa Barbara, Jeffrey Kripal, Stanley Krippner, George Leonard, John Levy, Kerry Moustakas, Nina Murray, Maureen O'Hara, Joanne and Tim Oppenheimer, Rebecca Paauwe, Donadrian Rice, Frank Richardson, Natalie Rogers, Robert Shilkret, Eugene Taylor, Deborah Von Husen, and Art Warmouth.

I'd also like to thank my toughest critic and most tireless supporter, Daniel Oppenheimer, for his patience and love, as well as his enduring commitment to the project, and my editor, Cal Morgan, for being excited about the project from the start, and for being the kind of careful editor who's hard to find these days.

Notes

Introduction

1. Abraham Maslow, "October 5, 1966," *The Journals of A. H. Maslow*, vol. 2., ed. Richard J. Lowry (Monterey, CA: Brooks/Cole, 1979), 672.

Chapter 1: The Problem of Psychological Health

1. Abraham Maslow, "June 7, 1963," *The Journals of A. H. Maslow*, vol. 1, ed. Richard J. Lowry (Monterey, CA: Brooks/Cole, 1979), 378.
2. Edward Hoffman, *The Right to Be Human* (Los Angeles: Jeremy P. Tarcher, 1988), 305.
3. Maslow, "December 23, 1967," *Journals,* vol. 2, 866.
4. Robert L. Tonsetic, "The Bloodiest Day: December 6, 1967," *California Literary Review*, http://calitreview.com/188.
5. Abraham Maslow, *Abraham H. Maslow: A Memorial Volume*, ed. B. G. Maslow (Monterey, CA: Thomson Brooks/Cole, 1973), 35–36.
6. Ernest Havemann, "The Age of Psychology in the US," *Life* 42, January 7, 1957, 68–70+, quotation from 72.
7. Ellen Herman, *Romance of American Psychology: Political Culture in the Age of Experts* (Berkeley: University of California Press, 1995), 2.
8. E. Brooks Holifield, *A History of Pastoral Care in America: From Salvation to Self-Realization* (Nashville, TN: Abingdon Press, 1983), 262.
9. Herman, *Romance of American Psychology*, 259.
10. Ibid., 262.
11. Ibid., 262.
12. Havemann, "The Age of Psychology in the US," 68.

13. See Alfred Kazin, "The Freudian Revolution Analyzed," *New York Times Magazine,* May 6, 1956, 22–40.

14. Nathan G. Hale, Jr., *The Rise and Crisis of Psychoanalysis in the United States: Freud and the Americans, 1917–1985* (New York: Oxford University Press, 1995), 280.

15. Ibid., 282.

16. Ibid., 299.

17. Nathan G. Hale, Jr., in Sandler Gilman, Edward Shorter, Nathan G. Hale, Jr., Mervyn Jones, and Joseph Schwartz, "The Listener: United States of Analysis," *Independent on Sunday* (London), October 31, 1999.

18. Hale, *Rise and Crisis,* 280.

19. John R. Seeley, "The Americanization of the Unconscious," *Atlantic Monthly,* July 1961, 70.

20. Dan P. McAdams, *The Redemptive Self: Stories Americans Live By* (New York: Oxford University Press, 2006), 133.

21. Russell Jacoby, *The Repression of Psychoanalysis: Otto Fenichel and the Political Freudians* (New York: Basic Books, 1983), 23.

22. Sigmund Freud and Josef Breuer, "Studies on Hysteria," *Standard Edition of the Complete Psychological Works of Sigmund Freud,* vol. XVII (London: Hogarth Press, 1955), 305.

23. Sigmund Freud as quoted in Yiannis Gabriel, *Freud and Society* (New York: Routledge & Kegan Paul, 1983), 93.

24. Ernest Havemann, "Where Does Psychology Go from Here?" *Life,* February 4, 1957, 68–88, quotation from 88.

25. Seeley, "The Americanization of the Unconscious," 70.

26. Colin Wilson, *New Pathways in Psychology: Maslow and the Post-Freudian Revolution* (Chapel Hill, NC: Maurice Bassett, 2001), 166.

27. Abraham Maslow, "Self-Actualizing People: A Study of Psychological Health," in *The Self: Explorations in Personal Growth,* ed. Clark E. Moustakas (New York: Harper & Brothers, 1956), 160–94. This article was originally published as Abraham Maslow, "Self-Actualizing People: A Study of Psychological Health," *Personality Symposia: Symposium #1 on Values* (New York: Grune & Stratton, 1950), 11–34.

28. Ibid., 161–62.

29. Ibid., 161.

30. Ibid., 160–94.

31. Ibid., 177.

32. Ibid., 180.

33. Ibid., 176.

34. Ibid., 187–88.

35. David Riesman with Nathan Glazer and Reuel Denney, *The Lonely Crowd: A Study of the Changing American Character* (New Haven, CT: Yale University Press, 1950), 9.

36. See William H. Whyte, *The Organization Man* (New York: Simon and Schuster, 1956).

37. Paul Goodman, *Growing Up Absurd: Problems of Youth in the Organized System* (New York: Random House, 1960), 10–11.

38. Most work of this kind never received enough attention to have an impact on cultural understanding. These critics proved to be exceptions. In 1950, Yale University reluctantly published 2,000 copies of Riesman's *The Lonely Crowd*. Within three years, Doubleday had licensed paperback rights, and within the decades that followed, the book sold well over a million copies—unheard of for an academic publication. Whyte's book, though originally picked up by Doubleday, was also expected to be "a bust." (Its first run was a "tiny" printing.) But just after its 1956 release, it hit the bestseller list and stayed there for seven months. Goodman's *Growing Up Absurd* earned comparable popular attention, as did economist John Kenneth Galbraith's 1952 *American Capitalism* and journalist Vance Packard's 1957 *The Hidden Persuaders* (a book about media manipulation of the populace). Edwin McDowell, "Sometimes a Best Seller," *New York Times*, May 10, 1981, Sunday Late City Final Edition; Robert J. Samuelson, "'Organization Man' Lives," *Washington Post*, January 7, 1987; Michael T. Kaufman, "William H. Whyte, 'Organization Man' Author and Urbanologist, Is Dead at 81," *New York Times*, January 13, 1999.

39. McDowell, "Sometimes a Best Seller."

40. See Clark E. Moustakas, ed., *The Self: Explorations in Personal Growth* (New York: Harper & Brothers, 1956).

41. The collection compiled writings by well-known psychologists (Gordon Allport, Carl Rogers, and Abraham Maslow), psychoanalysts (Carl Jung, Karen Horney, and Erich Fromm), and philosophers

(Jean-Paul Sartre). Also included were the writings of psychiatrists, anthropologists, and education professors.

42. Clark E. Moustakas, "Explorations in Essential Being and Personal Growth," in *The Self*, 279.

43. Maslow, "Self-Actualizing People: A Study of Psychological Health," in *The Self*, 160–94.

44. Maslow, "Personality Problems and Personality Growth," in *The Self*, 235.

45. Ibid., 237.

46. Ibid., 234.

47. Sloan Wilson, *The Man in the Gray Flannel Suit* (New York: Simon & Schuster, 1955), 109.

48. Abraham Maslow, *Toward a Psychology of Being* (New York: Van Nostrand, 1962), 5.

49. Abraham Maslow, "Creativeness, Autonomy, Self-Actualization, Love, Self, Being, Growth and Organismic People (Mailing List)," December 1959 (Maslow Papers, Box 449.19, "Miscellaneous #2" folder, Archives of the History of American Psychology, Center for the History of Psychology, University of Akron).

50. Hoffman, *Right to Be Human*, 208–09.

51. Erich Fromm, *The Sane Society* (Greenwich, CT: Fawcett Publications, 1955), 15.

52. Ibid., 28.

53. Ibid., 23.

54. Ibid., 33–66.

55. Ibid., 22.

56. Erich Fromm, *Man for Himself* (Greenwich, CT: Fawcett Publications, 1947), 15–16.

57. Daniel Burston, *The Legacy of Erich Fromm* (Cambridge, MA: Harvard University Press, 1991), 164–86.

58. Fromm, *Sane Society*, 22.

59. Gordon W. Allport, *The Nature of Prejudice* (Reading, MA: Addison-Wesley, 1954), 425–40.

60. Ibid.; Gordon W. Allport, *ABC's of Scapegoating* (New York: Anti-Defamation League of B'nai B'rith, 1948).

61. Allport, *Nature of Prejudice*, 12.

62. Ibid., 427–28.

63. Gordon W. Allport, *The Individual and His Religion* (New York: Macmillan, 1950), 58.

64. Fromm, *Man for Himself,* 97.

65. Rollo May, *Man's Search for Himself* (New York: Dell, 1953), 44.

66. Ibid., 14.

67. Ibid., 17.

68. Ibid., 26.

69. Ibid., 22.

70. David Riesman with Nathan Glazer and Reuel Denny, *The Lonely Crowd: A Study of the Changing American Character* (New Haven, CT: Yale University Press, 1967 reprint), xliii.

71. Fromm, *Sane Society,* 242.

72. Ibid., 312.

73. Sidney Jourard, *Personal Adjustment: An Approach Through the Study of Healthy Personality* (New York: Macmillan, 1958).

74. Ibid., 427.

75. Ibid., 433.

76. Ibid., 433–34.

77. Herman, *Romance of American Psychology,* 64–65.

78. Carl R. Rogers and John L. Wallen, *Counseling with Returned Servicemen* (New York: McGraw-Hill, 1946).

79. Ibid., 17.

80. Ibid., 6.

81. Carl R. Rogers, *Client-Centered Therapy: Its Current Practice, Implications and Theory* (Boston: Houghton Mifflin, 1951), 276.

82. Ibid., 218. Rogers further developed this idea in "Facilitation of Personal Growth," *School Counselor* 2, no. 1 (January 1955).

83. Gordon W. Allport, *Becoming: Basic Considerations for a Psychology of Personality* (New Haven, CT: Yale University Press, 1955), 1.

84. Ibid., 36.

Chapter 2: Common Ground

1. William James, "The Will to Believe," *The Will to Believe, and Other Essays in Popular Philosophy* (New York: Longmans, Green, 1897), 7.

2. Abraham Maslow, *Abraham H. Maslow: A Memorial Volume*, ed. B. G. Maslow (Monterey, CA: Thomson Brooks/Cole, 1973), 68.

3. Henry Murray, notes (Henry A. Murray Papers, Conference Reports and Papers, early 1960s, Notes, "Psychology: advantages, values, disadvantage" folder, HUGFP 97.41, Box 2, Harvard University Archives).

4. Ibid.

5. Duane P. Schultz, *A History of Modern Psychology* (New York: Academic Press, 1969), 102.

6. See William James, *Principles of Psychology* (New York: Henry Holt, 1913).

7. William James, *Psychology* (London: Macmillan, 1892), 4.

8. Ibid., 1.

9. Mental philosophy held a position of esteem in American universities (courses on the subject had been considered essential to a proper education). Alfred H. Fuchs, "Contributions of American Mental Philosophers to Psychology in the United States," in *Evolving Perspectives on the History of Psychology*, eds. Wade E. Pickren and Donald A. Dewsbury (Washington, DC: American Psychological Association, 2002), 79–99.

10. Edward Shorter, *A History of Psychiatry: From the Era of the Asylum to the Age of Prozac* (New York: John Wiley & Sons, 1997), 15. Nineteenth-century psychiatric understandings were typically framed in physiological terms, often referring to the nervous system or to brain structures, but were heavily tinged with religious ideas. Explanations of mental illness ranged from the concept of bad humors or bad blood to the notion of satanic possession. Likewise, some psychiatric treatments of the nineteenth century reflected Puritan ideas of asceticism and redemption through suffering. Bloodletting, leeching, and mercury poisoning were common treatments for mental illness until the mid-nineteenth century. Lesser-known treatments included malaria fever therapy, insulin shock therapy, clitoral cauterization, sterilization, and hydrotherapy, which involved either continuous baths or tight wrapping in wet sheets. Malaria fever therapy was administered either by subcutaneous injection or by mosquitoes and was intended to cure syphilitic insanity through a course of

106-degree fevers. Insulin shock therapy brought patients to the brink of death and (ideally) back through fifty to sixty days spent in a coma. Charles E. Rosenberg, "The Therapeutic Revolution: Medicine, Meaning, and Social Change in Nineteenth-Century America," in *The Therapeutic Revolution: Essays in the Social History of American Medicine,* eds. Morris J. Vogel and Charles E. Rosenberg (Philadelphia: University of Pennsylvania Press, 1979), 3–22; Shorter, *A History of Psychiatry,* 17, 39, 56, 165–68; Joel T. Braslow, *Mental Ills and Bodily Cures: Psychiatric Treatment in the First Half of the Twentieth Century* (Berkeley: University of California Press, 1997), 96–98.

11. In 1844, the Association of Medical Superintendents of American Institutions for the Insane was formed. In 1894, it changed its name to the American Medico-Psychological Association. In 1921, it became the American Psychiatric Association, which exists today. For a complete history of the American Psychiatric Association, see Walter E. Baron, *The History and Influence of the American Psychiatric Association* (Washington, DC: American Psychiatric Press, 1987).

12. Louis D. Cohen, "The Academic Department," in *History of Psychotherapy: A Century of Change,* ed. Donald K. Freedheim (Washington, DC: American Psychological Association, 1992), 731–33. For an in-depth exploration of the American transition from the open university system, in which "truth" was broadly conceived, to the modern university system, in which "facts" and "values" were divided, see Julie A. Reuben, *The Making of the Modern University: Intellectual Transformation and the Marginalization of Morality* (Chicago: University of Chicago Press, 1996). American psychology departments were also shaped by German theoretical models. A number of the leading psychologists at the turn of the century—including G. Stanley Hall, James McKeen Cattell, and Lightner Witmer—had studied in the laboratory of Wilhelm Wundt, and others, including William James, had studied more broadly in Europe. Early American psychology took shape under the direct influence of European immigrants like Hugo Münsterberg and E. B. Titchener, who had been recruited to permanent posts at American universities for their expertise in scientific methods. Helmut E. Adler, "The European Influence on American Psychology: 1892 to 1942," *Annals of the New York*

Academy of Sciences, 727, no. 1 (1994): 113–20; Cohen, "Academic Department," 734–36.

13. Ralph Barton Perry, *The Thought and Character of William James* (Boston: Little, Brown, 1935; Nashville, TN: Vanderbilt University Press, 1996), 228. Citations refer to the Vanderbilt edition.

14. Frank McAdams Albrecht, "The New Psychology in America, 1880–1895" (PhD diss., Johns Hopkins University, 1960), 59–61.

15. Duane P. Schultz, *A History of Modern Psychology,* (New York: Academic Press, 1969), 118. Though the date of psychology's birth as an academic discipline is at issue, most link it to the creation of Wilhelm Wundt's psychological laboratory in Leipzig, Germany, in 1880. This date represents a break from the religiously and morally informed psychology that preceded it. Rand B. Evans argues, however, that academic psychology actually began decades earlier, as evidenced by the proliferation of psychology textbooks in the 1820s through the 1860s and in the inclusion of standard psychology courses even at the smallest colleges by the 1870s. Instead of marking the creation of a distinct discipline, Evans contends, the 1880s saw a dramatic shift in the philosophy and curriculum underlying academic psychology. Rand B. Evans, "The Origins of American Academic Psychology," in *Explorations in the History of Psychology in the United States,* ed. Josef Brožek (Lewisburg, PA: Bucknell University Press, 1984), 48–56.

16. It was actually a difficult task to break away from philosophy. There were only four universities with independent psychology departments by 1904, although thirty-four were created in the following ten years. Geraldine Jonçich, *The Sane Positivist: A Biography of Edward L. Thorndike* (Middletown, CT: Wesleyan University Press, 1968), 68.

17. Michael Sokal, "Origins and Early Years of the American Psychological Association: 1890 to 1906," in *The American Psychological Association: A Historical Perspective,* eds. Rand B. Evans, Virginia Staudt Sexton, and Thomas C. Cadwallader (Washington, DC: American Psychological Association, 1992), 43–71.

18. John D. Buenker, John C. Burnham, and Robert M. Crunden, *Progressivism* (Rochester, VT: Schenkman, 1986); Maureen Flanagan, *America Reformed: Progressives and Progressivisms, 1890s–1920s* (New York: Oxford University Press, 2007); Samuel Haber, *Efficiency and*

Uplift: Scientific Management in the Progressive Era, 1890–1920 (Chicago: University of Chicago Press, 1964), 656.

19. William James (1909) as quoted in Margaret Donnelly, introduction to *Reinterpreting the Legacy of William James*, ed. Margaret Donnelly (Washington, DC: American Psychological Association, 1992), 2.

20. Robert D. Richardson, *William James: In the Maelstrom of American Modernism* (Boston: Houghton Mifflin, 2006), 110. Neurasthenia was a psychological illness named by George Miller Beard in 1869. Its primary symptoms were fatigue and anxiety, which were thought to be associated with the stresses of the modern existence, namely increasing competition in the marketplace and the chaos of urbanization.

21. William James as quoted in Joseph Jastrow, "Has Psychology Failed?" *American Scholar* 4 (1935), 261.

22. Richardson, *William James*, 412–15; James's writings on the intersection of religion and psychology include William James, *The Will to Believe, and Other Essays in Popular Philosophy* (New York: Longmans, Green, 1897); William James, *Human Immortality: Two Supposed Objections to the Doctrine* (Boston: Houghton Mifflin, 1898); William James, *The Varieties of Religious Experience: A Study in Human Nature* (New York: Longmans, Green, 1902).

23. James, *Varieties of Religious Experience*.

24. Gordon Allport, "William James and the Behavioral Sciences," Remarks at the installation of the Ellen Emmet Rand portrait of William James in Harvard's William James Hall, November 5, 1965 (Papers of Gordon W. Allport, HUG 4.118.50, Box 5, Folder 154, Harvard University Archives).

25. Dorothy Ross, *G. Stanley Hall: The Psychologist as Prophet* (Chicago: University of Chicago Press, 1972), 233.

26. Hall met his share of opponents, including colleagues like George Trumbull Ladd, whose recognition of philosophical questions infused his own empiricism. Ibid., 313. Ladd (1842–1921) was an American philosopher, schooled at Andover Theological Seminary, who taught at Yale and worked primarily in experimental psychology. He founded the psychology laboratory there and wrote several books, including *Elements of Physiological Psychology* (1887) and *Knowledge, Life, and Reality* (1909).

27. John A. Mills, *Control: A History of Behavioral Psychology* (New York: New York University Press, 1998), 9–10.

28. Jonçich, *Sane Positivist*, 72, 87.

29. Edward L. Thorndike, *Elements of Psychology* (New York: A. G. Seiler, 1905).

30. Edward L. Thorndike, *Animal Intelligence: Experimental Studies* (New York: Macmillan, 1911).

31. Thomas Hardy Leahey, *A History of Psychology: Main Currents in Psychological Thought*, 6th ed. (Upper Saddle River, NJ: Pearson Prentice Hall, 2003), 388.

32. John B. Watson, "Psychology as the Behaviorist Views It," *Psychological Review*, 20 (1913): 158–77, http://psychclassics.yorku.ca/Watson/views.htm. Dating the emergence of behaviorism to Watson's manifesto is contentious within the history of psychology. Max Meyer's theory of behaviorism in *The Fundamental Laws of Human Behavior* (1911) predated the essay. And, in 1935, Jastrow wrote that "in any meaningful sense substantially all American psychologists were behaviorists long before 1912." Mills, *Control*, 40; Jastrow, "Has Psychology Failed?" 264.

33. Watson, "Psychology as the Behaviorist Views It," http://psychclassics .yorku.ca/Watson/views.htm.

34. Ibid., 40.

35. Thorndike, *Animal Intelligence*, 4.

36. Jonçich, *Sane Positivist*, 436.

37. John B. Watson, *Psychological Care of Infant and Child* (New York: Norton, 1928), 5–6.

38. John B. Watson, *Behaviorism*, rev. ed. (Chicago: University of Chicago Press, 1930), 82.

39. H. L. Philp, *Freud and Religious Belief* (New York: Pitman, 1956), 129.

40. Peter Gay, *A Godless Jew: Freud, Atheism, and the Making of Psychoanalysis* (New Haven, CT: Yale University Press, 1987), 42.

41. James, *Varieties of Religious Experience*, 519.

42. Gay, *Godless Jew*, 30.

43. Referenced in Gerald E. Myers, "James and Freud," *Journal of Philosophy* 87, no. 11 (November 1990): 593–99.

44. Jonçich, *Sane Positivist,* 422.

45. Howard Kirschenbaum, *On Becoming Carl Rogers* (New York: Delacorte, 1979), 54.

46. Nathan G. Hale, Jr., *The Rise and Crisis of Psychoanalysis in the United States: Freud and the Americans, 1917–1985* (New York: Oxford University Press, 1995).

47. Ibid., 75.

Chapter 3: Higher, Better Leaders

1. Rollo May, *The Courage to Create* (New York: Norton, 1975), 100.

2. Kirschenbaum, *On Becoming Carl Rogers,* quote from 246.

3. Maslow, "November 8, 1964," *The Journals of A. H. Maslow,* vol. 1, ed. Richard J. Lowry (Monterey, CA: Brooks/Cole, 1979), 568.

4. Maslow, "May 19, 1962," *Journals,* vol. 1, 162.

5. Edward Hoffman, *The Right to Be Human* (Los Angeles: Jeremy P. Tarcher, 1988), 96–106.

6. Kirschenbaum, *On Becoming Carl Rogers,* 54.

7. Mary Harrington Hall and Abraham Maslow, "Overcoming Evil: An Interview with Abraham Maslow, Founder of Humanistic Psychology," *Psychology Today* (1968, reprinted January, 1992): 4, http://www.psychologytoday.com/articles/199201/abraham-maslow.

8. Ibid., 2.

9. For an exploration of the applications of Harlow's work to humans, see: Deborah Blum, *Love at Goon Park: Harry Harlow and the Science of Affection* (Cambridge, MA: Perseus Publishing, 2002).

10. Harry Harlow, Harold Uehling, and Abraham Maslow, "Delayed Reaction Tests on Primates from the Lemur to the Orangutan," *Journal of Comparative Psychology* 13 (1932): 313–43.

11. Maslow published several articles from this work, including, but not limited to: Abraham Maslow, "Appetites and Hungers in Animal Motivation," *Journal of Comparative Psychology* 20 (1935): 75–83; Abraham Maslow, "Self-Esteem (Dominance-Feeling) and Sexuality in Women," *Journal of Social Psychology* 16 (1942): 259–94.

12. Hoffman, *Right to Be Human,* 49–62.

13. Hall and Maslow, "Overcoming Evil," 6.

14.   Ibid., 6.

15.   Maslow as quoted in Mildred Hardeman, "Dialogue with Abraham Maslow," in *Politics and Innocence: A Humanistic Debate*, ed. Thomas Greening (Dallas: Saybrook Publishers, 1986), 75.

16.   Brett King and Michael Wertheimer, *Max Wertheimer and Gestalt Theory* (New Brunswick, NJ: Transaction Publishers, 2005), 300; Hoffman, *Right to Be Human*, 92.

17.   Anne Harrington, *Reenchanted Science: Holism in German Culture from Wilhelm II to Hitler* (Princeton, NJ: Princeton University Press, 1996), xvi. Vitalism asserts that the life of an organism is partially self-determining and that life processes are not explicable by physio-chemical laws. Hans Driesch published his main work on vitalism in 1905. See Hans Driesch, *The History and Theory of Vitalism* (London: Macmillan, 1914).

18.   Although the translation of key Gestalt texts into English was slow in coming, Gestalt psychology reached America directly through the immigration of several key scholars who fled political instability in the 1920s and 1930s—namely, Wertheimer, Köhler, Kurt Koffka, and Kurt Goldstein. Koffka developed his theory of Gestalt psychology in Kurt Koffka, *Principles of Gestalt Psychology* (1935; reprint, London: Routledge, 1999). For a first-hand look at Köhler's theory of Gestalt psychology, and an account of his opposition to behaviorism, see: Wolfgang Köhler, *Gestalt Psychology: An Introduction to New Concepts in Modern Psychology* (1947; reprint, New York: Liverwright, 1970).

19.   Herbert Spiegelberg, "Phenomenology in Psychology and Psychiatry: A Historical Introduction," *Northwestern University Studies in Phenomenology and Existential Philosophy*, ed. John Wild (Evanston, IL: Northwestern University Press, 1972), 67.

20.   Wertheimer, "Experimental Studies," 1037. Max Wertheimer laid the foundation for Gestalt psychology in his 1912 article "Experimental Studies on the Seeing of Motion," in which he advanced a theory of apparent motion, focused on holistic human visual perception, in which the parts of an image were automatically incorporated into an understanding of the whole. Impressed by the psychical phenomena behind

visual perception, Wertheimer wrote, "One sees motion. [. . .] One does not merely see that the object is now some place else than before, and so knows that it has moved [. . .], rather one [actually] sees the motion." Max Wertheimer, "Experimental Studies on the Seeing of Motion," reprinted in *Classics in Psychology*, ed. Thorne Shipley (New York: Philosophical Library, 1961), 1032, 1037. Wertheimer, "Experimental Studies in the Seeing of Motion," 1032.

21. Mary Henle, preface to Molly Harrower, *Kurt Koffka: An Unwitting Self-Portrait* (Gainesville, FL: University of Florida Press, 1983), iii.

22. Abraham Maslow as quoted in King and Wertheimer, *Max Wertheimer & Gestalt Theory*, 300.

23. Kurt Koffka, *Principles of Gestalt Psychology* (1935; reprint, London: Routledge, 1999), 13–18, quotation from 18. Despite his apparent disdain for American science, Koffka traveled to the United States in 1924, serving as a visiting professor at Cornell University and lecturing. He maintained intellectual connections with Wertheimer and Köhler through his returns to Europe for lectures and through Köhler's sabbatical year spent teaching at Clark University, also in 1924–25. In 1927, Koffka permanently settled in the U.S., accepting a professorship at Smith College, in Northampton, Massachusetts. King and Wertheimer, *Max Wertheimer*, 233–37.

24. Hall and Maslow, "Overcoming Evil," 6.

25. Ibid., 5.

26. Harrington, *Reenchanted Science*, xx.

27. Ibid., 114.

28. Ibid., 145–51.

29. Jastrow, "Has Psychology Failed?" 264.

30. Ibid., 264–65.

31. Maslow, "August 25, 1969," *Journals*, vol. 2, 1059.

32. Abraham Maslow, *Abraham H. Maslow: A Memorial Volume*, ed. B. G. Maslow (Monterey, CA: Thomson Brooks/Cole, 1973, 7–19.

33. Ibid., 7, 19.

34. Edward Hoffman, *The Right to Be Human* (Los Angeles: Jeremy P. Tarcher, 1988), 13.

35. James Klee as quoted in Maslow, *Abraham H. Maslow*, 11.

36.   Maslow as quoted in Hoffman, *Right to Be Human*, 123.

37.   Ibid., 187. The article was originally published as: Abraham Maslow, "Self-Actualizing People: A Study of Psychological Health," *Personality Symposia: Symposium #1 on Values* (New York: Grune and Straton, 1950), 11–34.

38.   Hoffman, *Right to Be Human*, 161.

39.   Maslow was finally promoted nine years after taking a position at Brooklyn College.

40.   Hoffman, *Right to Be Human*, 161.

41.   Ibid., 196.

42.   Ibid., 194–96.

43.   Ibid., 196.

44.   Ibid., 201.

45.   Abraham Maslow, *Motivation and Personality* (1954; reprint, New York: Harper & Row, 1970).

46.   Abraham Maslow, "Eupsychia—The Good Society," *Journal of Humanistic Psychology* 1, no. 2 (1961): 1–11.

47.   Kurt Goldstein, *The Organism: A Holistic Approach to Biology Derived from Pathological Data in Man* (1939; reprint, New York: Zone Books, 1995), 162.

48.   Abraham Maslow, "Theory of Human Motivation," *Psychological Review* 50, no. 4 (1943): 370–96, quotation from 383.

49.   Maslow, *Motivation and Personality*, 149–80, quotation from 155.

50.   Hoffman, *Right to Be Human*, 266.

51.   Maslow, "October 10, 1961," *The Journals of A. H. Maslow*, vol. 1, ed. Richard J. Lowry (Monterey, CA: Brooks/Cole, 1979), 123.

52.   Hoffman, *Right to Be Human*, 205–7.

53.   Eugene T. Gendlin, foreword to *Carl Rogers: The Quiet Revolutionary, An Oral History*, by Carl R. Rogers and David E. Russell (Roseville, CA: Penmarin Books, 2002), http://www.focusing.org/gendlin_foreword_to_cr.html.

54.   Howard Kirschenbaum, *On Becoming Carl Rogers* (New York: Delacorte, 1979), 59.

55.   Ibid., 67.

56.   Carl R. Rogers, "Personality Adjustment Inventory" (New York: As-

sociation Press, 1931). This is a slightly revised form of "A Test of Personality Adjustment," also created in 1931.

57. Kirschenbaum, *On Becoming Carl Rogers*, 75.

58. Carl R. Rogers, *Counseling and Psychotherapy: Newer Concepts in Practice* (Boston: Houghton Mifflin, 1942), 87–90.

59. Ibid., 273.

60. Kirschenbaum, *On Becoming Carl Rogers*, 137.

61. Ibid., 154–55.

62. "Medicine: Person to Person," *Time*, July 1, 1957.

63. Thomas Greening, "Reflections on the Depressed and Dying: The Case of Carol," in *Existential-Integrative Psychotherapy: Guideposts to the Core of Practice*, ed. Kirk J. Schneider (New York: Routledge, 2008), 343.

64. Thomas Greening, telephone interview with author, April 15, 2011.

65. Ibid.

66. Thomas Greening, e-mail to author, June 22, 2011.

67. Myron Sharaf, *Fury on Earth: A Biography of Wilhelm Reich* (Cambridge, MA: Da Capo Press, 1994), 234–35.

68. Hellmuth Kaiser, "Emergency," *Psychiatry* 25 (1962): 97–118.

69. Theodor Reik, *Listening with the Third Ear* (New York: Farrar, Straus, 1949), 145.

70. Greening, interview, April 15, 2011.

71. Robert H. Abzug, *Rollo May and the Meaning of Life: An American Epic* (New York: Oxford University Press, forthcoming). Page numbers refer to manuscript.

72. Rollo May, *The Meaning of Anxiety* (1950; reprint, New York: Norton, 1977), 331–37.

73. Abzug, *Rollo May*, 290.

74. Ibid., 314.

75. Rollo May, *Man's Search for Himself* (New York: Dell, 1953), 35.

76. Ibid., 80.

77. "February 9, 1950: 'Communists in Government Service,' McCarthy Says," United States Senate history website, accessed July 8, 2012, http://www.senate.gov/artandhistory/history/minute/Communists_In_Government_Service.htm.

78. Murrow proclaimed, "We will not walk in fear, one of another. We will not be driven by fear into an age of unreason, if we dig deep in our history and our doctrine, and remember that we are not descended from fearful men." Edward R. Murrow, transcript of "A Report on Senator Joseph R. McCarthy," *See It Now*, CBS-TV, March 9, 1954, http://www.lib.berkeley.edu/MRC/murrowmccarthy.html.

79. May, *Man's Search for Himself*, 36–37.

80. Rollo May, "Contributions of Existential Psychotherapy" in *Existence: A New Dimension in Psychiatry and Psychology*, eds. Rollo May, Ernest Angel, and Henri F. Ellenberger (New York: Basic Books, 1958), 37–68.

81. May, introduction to *Existence: A New Dimension in Psychiatry and Psychology*, eds. Rollo May, Ernest Angel, and Henri F. Ellenberger (New York: Basic Books, 1958), 7.

82. Scientism, the idea that natural science has authority over all other interpretations, was often used pejoratively to indicate the inappropriateness of prioritizing the scientific method over all other approaches to the study of man. Gregory R. Peterson, "Demarcation and the Scientistic Fallacy," *Journal of Religion and Science* 38, no. 4 (2003): 751–61.

83. May, introduction to *Existence*, 8–9.

84. Phenomenology was broad and dynamic, and the father of phenomenology, Edmund Husserl, himself reportedly passed through three stages of subtheoretical orientation to the philosophy. Husserl's first phase has been classified as descriptive phenomenology (what he also terms "prephenomenology"), his second phase as transcendental phenomenology, and his third phase as the radicalization of his transcendental phenomenology. Although Husserl's phenomenology progressed through three stages, his transcendental phenomenology, stage two, proved most influential on the application of phenomenology to psychology and psychiatry and later to the practice of humanistic psychology. Thaddeus E. Weckowicz, "The Impact of Phenomenological and Existential Philosophies on Psychiatry and Psychotherapy," in *Humanistic Psychology: Concepts and Criticisms*, eds. Joseph R. Royce and Leendert P. Mos (New York: Plenum Press, 1981), 57.

85. May, introduction to *Existence*, 8.

86. Herbert Spiegelberg, *Phenomenology in Psychology and Psychiatry: A Historical Introduction*, Northwestern University Studies in Phenomenology and Existential Philosophy, ed. John Wild (Evanston, IL: Northwestern University Press, 1972), 195.

87. May, introduction to *Existence*, 8.

88. Ibid., 7.

89. Henri F. Ellenberger, "A Clinical Introduction to Psychiatric Phenomenology and Existential Analysis," in *Existence: A New Dimension in Psychiatry and Psychology*, eds. Rollo May, Ernest Angel, and Henri F. Ellenberger (New York: Basic Books, 1958), 119.

90. Viktor Frankl, *Man's Search for Meaning: An Introduction to Logotherapy* (New York: Washington Square, 1963), 104–9.

91. Friedrich Nietzsche as quoted in Viktor Frankl, *The Doctor and the Soul: From Psychotherapy to Logotherapy* (New York: Knopf, 1955), 54.

92. May, introduction to *Existence,* 12.

Chapter 4: Self, Being, and Growth People

1. Maslow, "November 26, 1960," *Journals*, vol. 1, 81.

2. Richard Farson, "Carl Rogers: Quiet Revolutionary," in *Carl Rogers: The Man and His Ideas*, ed. Richard I. Evans (New York: E. P. Dutton, 1975), xxxiii.

3. Abzug, *Rollo May*, 306–9.

4. Hoffman, *Right to Be Human*, 211.

5. Maslow, "July 11, 1966," *Journals*, vol. 2, 746.

6. Ibid.

7. Abraham Maslow, *Abraham H. Maslow: A Memorial Volume*, ed. B. G. Maslow (Monterey, CA: Thomson Brooks/Cole, 1973), 8.

8. In spite of his lack of higher education, Sutich was grandfathered into the APA and became a licensed therapist in the state of California. He ultimately completed the requirements for a PhD at the Humanistic Psychology Institute of San Francisco (later Saybrook Graduate School) a day before his death on April 9, 1976. "Anthony 'Tony' Sutich: 1907–1976," Transpersonal Psychology Pioneers, http://www.atpweb.org/pioneers/pioneerssutich.html.

9. Anthony Sutich, "Proposed Improvement in Terminology in Relation to Personal Psychological Problems," *Psychological Records* 4 (1941), 375–87.

10. Anthony Sutich, "The Growth-Experience and the Growth-Centered Attitude," *Journal of Psychology* 28, no. 2 (1949), 293–301.

11. Ibid.

12. Peggy Granger, "Another View of Tony Sutich," *Journal of Humanistic Psychology* 16 (July 1976), 7–12, quotation from 8.

13. Anthony Sutich, introduction to *Readings in Humanistic Psychology*, eds. Anthony Sutich and Miles A. Vich (New York: Free Press, 1969), 4.

14. Granger, "Another View," 8.

15. Maslow as quoted in Hoffman, *Right to Be Human*, 263.

16. Will Hardy, *Greater Greater Detroiters: They Light Up Our Life* (Detroit: Hardywill Group, 1983), 50–65.

17. Association for Humanistic Psychology, "Humanistic Psychology Overview," Association of Humanistic Psychology website, accessed December 15, 2010, http://www.ahpweb.org/index.php?option=com_k2&view=item&layout=item&id=14&Itemid=24http://www.ahpweb.org/aboutahp/whatis.html.

18. Roy José DeCarvalho, *The Founders of Humanistic Psychology* (New York: Praeger, 1991), 7–15.

19. Sutich, "Introduction," *Readings in Humanistic Psychology*, 8.

20. Gordon Allport, notes, "Conference on Humanistic Psychology: Old Saybrook, Conn., Nov 27–29," November 30, 1964 (Papers of Gordon W. Allport, Humanistic Psychology Conference folder, HUG 4118.50, Box 4, Harvard University Archives).

21. Eugene Taylor, interview by author, Cambridge, MA, September 29, 2005.

22. Maslow, "May 26, 1963," *Journals*, vol. 1, 312.

23. "Cumulative Contents, 1961–1990," *Journal of Humanistic Psychology*, vol. 30, no. 4 (Fall 1990), 70–112. For examples of early explorations of sensitivity training, see: James V. Clark, "Authentic Interaction and Personal Growth in Sensitivity Training Groups," *Journal of Humanistic Psychology*, vol. 3, no. 1 (Spring 1963): 1–13; James. F. T. Bugental and Robert Tannenbaum, "Sensitivity Training as Being Motivation," *Journal of Humanistic Psychology*, vol. 3, no. 1 (Spring 1963): 76–85.

24. See "Cumulative Contents, 1961–1990."

25. Sutich, introduction to *Readings in Humanistic Psychology*, 7.

26. DeCarvalho, *Founders of Humanistic Psychology*, 7–15.

27. Sonoma State College (now Sonoma State University) was originally an offshoot of the California State College system designed specifically for the education of teachers and founded on principles uniquely compatible with those of the still-embryonic humanistic psychology movement.

28. Association of Humanistic Psychology, "A Chronology of AHP's Annual Conferences," Association of Humanistic Psychology website, accessed May 1, 2008, www.ahpweb.org/aboutahp/ahpcronology .html.

29. DeCarvalho, *Founders of Humanistic Psychology*, 7–15.

30. Abraham Maslow, "June 15, 1959," *The Journals of A. H. Maslow*, vol. 1, ed. Richard J. Lowry (Monterey, CA: Brooks/Cole, 1979), 26.

31. Eugene Taylor, *Shadow Culture* (Washington, DC: Counterpoint, 2000), 271.

32. Edward Hoffman, *The Right to Be Human* (Los Angeles: Jeremy P. Tarcher, 1988), 184.

33. Robert H. Abzug, *Rollo May and the Meaning of Life: An American Epic* (New York: Oxford University Press, forthcoming), 256. Page numbers refer to manuscript.

34. Ibid., 266.

35. Victor Yalom, "An Interview with James Bugental," *Existential-Humanistic Psychotherapy*, http://www.psychotherapy.net/interview/ James_Bugental.

36. Gordon Allport, *Personality and Social Encounter* (Boston: Beacon, 1960), 282.

37. Mitchell G. Ash, "Psychology and Politics in Interwar Vienna: The Vienna Psychological Institute, 1922–1942," in *Psychology in Twentieth-Century Thought and Society*, eds. Mitchell G. Ash and William R. Woodward (Cambridge, UK: Cambridge University Press, 1987), 157.

38. Ibid., 151.

39. Charlotte Bühler, "Humanistic Psychology as a Personal Experience," *Interpersonal Development* 4 (1973–74): 197–214, quotation from 199.

40. See Charlotte Bühler and Marianne Marschak, "Basic Tendencies of Human Life," in *The Course of Human Life: A Study of Goals in the Humanistic Perspective*, eds. Charlotte Bühler and Fred Massarik (New York: Springer, 1968), 92–102.

41. Maslow, "November 4, 1969," *Abraham H. Maslow*, 65.

42. U.S. Department of Energy, "United States Nuclear Tests July 1945 through September 1992," December 2000, accessed June 24, 2012, http://www.nv.doe.gov/library/publications/historical/DOENV_209_REV15.pdf.

43. Maslow, *Abraham H. Maslow*, 38.

44. For more on Americans' response to the Cuban Missile Crisis, see Alice L. George, *Awaiting Armageddon: How Americans Faced the Cuban Missile Crisis* (Chapel Hill: University of North Carolina Press, 2003).

45. See Charles W. Eagles, *The Price of Defiance: James Meredith and the Integration of Ole Miss* (Chapel Hill: University of North Carolina Press, 2009).

46. Pressured by civil rights activists to squash insidious prejudice and to liberate its victims, the government finally began to enforce court orders to end segregation and started to correct injustices. (For example, Executive Order 11063, which Kennedy issued in November 1962, mandated an end to discrimination in housing based on race, color, creed, or national origin.)

47. Carl R. Rogers, *Carl Rogers: Dialogues*, eds. Howard Kirschenbaum and Valerie Land Henderson (Boston: Houghton Mifflin, 1989), 83.

48. Martin Luther King, Jr., "Towards Freedom," transcript of speech, Dartmouth College, May 23, 1962, http://www.dartmouth.edu/~towardsfreedom/transcript.html.

49. Students for a Democratic Society, "Port Huron Statement," 1962, http://www.h-net.org/~hst306/documents/huron.html.

50. Maslow, "September 20, 1966," *Journals*, vol. 1, 668.

51. Gordon Allport, "Psychiatry in Neurotic America" (unpublished notes), Law School Forum December 1950 (Papers of Gordon W. Allport, HUG 4118.50, Box 5, Folder 177, Harvard University Archives).

52. Gordon Allport, *Personality and Social Encounter*, 234.

53. Gordon Allport, *Pattern and Growth in Personality* (New York: Holt, Rinehart & Winston, 1961), 275–307.

54. Maslow, "April 16, 1959," *Journals*, vol. 1, 52.

55. Maslow, "December 16, 1961, *Journals*, vol. 1, 239.

56. Maslow, "November 5, 1961," *Journals*, vol. 1, 130.

57. Sidney Jourard, *Personal Adjustment: An Approach Through the Study of Healthy Personality* (New York: Macmillan, 1958), 1–6. Jourard published several significant texts in humanistic psychology in the 1960s and 1970s. These included *The Transparent Self* (1964), *Disclosing Man to Himself* (1968), *Self-Disclosure* (1971), and *Healthy Personality* (1974, the year of his death). For a full bibliography of his professional publications, see Anne C. Richards, Tiparat Schumrum, and Lisa C. Sheehan-Hicks, "Chronological Bibliography of the Professional Publications of Sidney M. Jourard," http://www.sidneyjourard.com/sidbib.htm.

58. Sidney M. Jourard, "Notes on the Quantification of Wellness," prepared for meeting of the Subcomittee on the Quantification of Wellness of the United States Department of Health and Human Services' National Committee on Vital and Health Statistics, Washington, DC, November 18, 1958 (Murphy Papers, Box 1076, Sidney Jourard folder, Archives of the History of American Psychology, Center for the History of Psychology, University of Akron), 4.

59. Ibid., 11.

60. Jourard, *Personal Adjustment*, xi.

61. Maslow, "January, 13, 1961," *Journals*, vol. 1, 90.

62. Carl R. Rogers, "Toward Becoming a Fully Functioning Person," in *Perceiving, Behaving, Becoming: A New Focus for Education*, ed. Arthur W. Combs (Washington, DC: Association for Supervision and Curriculum Development, 1962), 21–33.

63. Implicit in this interpretation was their notion that human beings possessed a characteristic "nature" that was independent of childhood experiences (as psychoanalysts assumed) and environmental conditions (as behaviorists argued). Roy José DeCarvalho, *The Founders of Humanistic Psychology* (New York: Praeger, 1991), 138–41.

64. Jean-Jacques Rousseau, *Discourse on the Origin and the Foundations of Inequality Among Men*, ed. N. K. Singh (New Delhi: Global Vision, 2006), 54.

65. Bruce Wochholz, "40th Anniversary of the Perspective on ahpweb .org," *AHP Perspective*, August–September 2003, 7. (Original source not cited.)

66. Rollo May, "The Problem of Evil: An Open Letter to Carl Rogers," *Politics and Innocence: A Humanistic Debate*, ed. Thomas Greening (Dallas: Saybrook Publishers, 1986), 12–23, quotation from 13.

67. Maslow, "October 19, 1967, *Journals*, vol. 2, 832–33.

68. Maslow, "May 19, 1962," *Journals*, vol. 1, 162.

69. Ibid., "Problem of Evil," 17.

70. Ibid., 13.

71. Ibid., 18–19.

72. Gordon Allport, unpublished notes, "Conference on Humanistic Psychology: Old Saybrook, Conn., Nov 27–29," November 30, 1964 (Papers of Gordon W. Allport, Humanistic Psychology Conference folder, HUG 4118.50, Box 4, Harvard University Archives).

73. See Sandler Gilman, Edward Shorter, Nathan G. Hale, Jr., Mervyn Jones, and Joseph Schwartz, "The Listener: United States of Analysis," *Independent on Sunday* (London), October 31, 1999. See also Nathan G. Hale, Jr., *The Rise and Crisis of Psychoanalysis in the United States: Freud and the Americans, 1917–1985* (New York: Oxford University Press, 1995).

Chapter 5: Eupsychian Visions

1. B. F. Skinner, *Walden Two* (New York: Macmillan, 1948), 240.

2. C. Wright Mills, "Letter to the New Left," *New Left Review* 1, no. 5 (September–October 1960), http://www.marxists.org/subject/ humanism/mills-c-wright/letter-new-left.htm.

3. Abraham Maslow, *Motivation and Personality* (1954; reprint, New York: Harper & Row, 1970), 277.

4. Abraham Maslow, "April 14, 1969," *The Journals of A. H. Maslow*, vol. 2, ed. Richard J. Lowry (Monterey, CA: Brooks/Cole, 1979), 957.

5. Abraham Maslow, "Self-Actualizing People: A Study of Psychological Health," *Motivation and Personality*, 175–76.

6. Maslow, "April 22, 1968," *Journals*, vol. 2, 962.

7.   Abraham Maslow, *Abraham H. Maslow: A Memorial Volume*, ed. B. G. Maaslow (Monterey, CA: Thomson Brooks/Cole, 1973), 84.

8.   Abraham Maslow, *Eupsychian Management: A Journal* (Homewood, IL: Richard D. Irwin and Dorsey Press, 1965), xi.

9.   Cited in Joyce Milton, *The Road to Malpsychia* (San Francisco: Encounter, 2002), 10; See also Abraham Maslow, "Eupsychia—The Good Society," *Journal of Humanistic Psychology* 1, no. 2 (October 1961), 1–11.

10.   B. F. Skinner, *About Behaviorism* (New York: Knopf, 1974), 11.

11.   Christopher M. Aanstoos, "Cognitive Science and Technological Culture: A Humanistic Response," in *The Handbook of Humanistic Psychology: Leading Edges in Theory, Research, and Practice*, eds. Kirk J. Schneider, James F. T. Bugental, and J. Fraser Pierson (Thousand Oaks, CA: Sage, 2001), 213.

12.   John A. Mills, *Control: A History of Behavioral Psychology* (New York: New York University Press, 1998), 23–24.

13.   Skinner introduced his concept of the air crib to the public with the 1945 article "Baby in a Box." The crib, where Skinner's daughter Deborah was housed for eleven months, reportedly saved his wife time and effort, and decreased her stress. He described Deborah as always cheerful, never sick, and certainly not neglected. She was removed from the crib on numerous occasions throughout the day, when she was fed and changed (a total time expenditure averaging one and a half hours per day). And, as the need for social stimulation developed, he planned to lengthen this time. B. F. Skinner, "Baby in a Box," *Ladies' Home Journal,* October 1945, http://www.uni.edu/~maclino/cl/skinner_baby_in_a_box.pdf.

      Skinner's article, though intriguing, aroused extensive criticism. In 1971, Deborah described the ensuing fallout. "It was spread around," she said, "that because of the box I had become psychotic, had to be institutionalized, and had even attempted suicide." On the contrary, at twenty-seven she was a well-adjusted art student in London. "Behavior: A Skinnerian Innovation: Baby in a Box," *Time*, September 20, 1971, http://www.time.com/time/magazine/article/0,9171,909996,00.html.

14.   Skinner, *About Behaviorism*, 263.

15. B. F. Skinner in Carl R. Rogers, *Carl Rogers: Dialogues*, eds. Howard Kirschenbaum and Valerie Land Henderson (Boston: Houghton Mifflin, 1989), 81. Skinner explained, in his introduction to the 1976 edition of *Walden Two*, that the book was largely ignored until the late fifties, when behavior modifcation gained popularity.

16. Skinner, *Walden Two*, 28.

17. Skinner in *Carl Rogers: Dialogues*, 93.

18. Ibid., 86.

19. Ibid., 118.

20. The debate took place at the University of Minnesota, Duluth, from June 11–12, 1962. *Carl Rogers: Dialogues*, 82.

21. Rogers in *Carl Rogers: Dialogues*, 83.

22. Skinner in *Carl Rogers: Dialogues*, 110.

23. Rogers in *Carl Rogers: Dialogues*, 86.

24. Skinner in *Carl Rogers: Dialogues*, 92.

25. John R. Anderson, *Cognitive Psychology and Its Implications*, 6th ed. (New York: Worth, 2004), 10.

26. John B. Watson, *Behaviorism*, rev. ed. (Chicago: University of Chicago Press, 1930), 5–6.

27. Anderson, *Cognitive Psychology*, 9.

28. George A. Miller, "The Magical Number Seven, Plus or Minus Two: Some Limits on Our Capacity for Processing," *Psychological Review* 63, no. 2 (1956): 81–97.

29. Donald E. Broadbent, *Perception and Communication* (London: Pergamon, 1958).

30. Noam Chomsky, "A Review of B. F. Skinner's Verbal Behavior," *Language* 35, no. 1 (1959): 26–58.

31. Albert Ellis, *Humanistic Psychotherapy: The Rational-Emotive Approach* (New York: Julian, 1973), 1.

32. Michael E. Bernard, *Rationality and the Pursuit of Happiness: The Legacy of Albert Ellis* (Chichester, UK: Wiley-Blackwell, 2011), 6.

33. Ibid., 14; Ellis, *Humanistic Psychotherapy*, 4.

34. Skinner as cited in Aanstoos, "Cognitive Science," 213.

35. Maslow, "April 16, 1959," *Journals*, vol. 1, 52.

36. Maslow, "1965," *Abraham H. Maslow*, 67.

37. Maslow, "Self-Actualizing People," *Motivation and Personality*, 149.

38.   Ibid., 149.

39.   Edward Hoffman, *The Right to Be Human* (Los Angeles: Jeremy P. Tarcher, 1988), 261–63.

40.   Ibid., 267–70.

41.   Carl Rogers as quoted in Howard Kirschenbaum, *On Becoming Carl Rogers* (New York: Delacorte, 1979), 291.

42.   Ibid., 316–17.

43.   Ibid., 317–18.

44.   Richard Farson, telephone interview with author, October 5, 2005; for an example of Koch's work, see Sigmund Koch and David E. Leary, eds., *A Century of Psychology as Science* (New York: McGraw Hill, 1985).

45.   Carl Rogers, "Carl Rogers to Friends, July 22, 1963" (Papers of Gordon W. Allport, Correspondence, Folder Ro-Rz, HUG 4118.10, Box 46, Harvard University Archives).

46.   Richard Farson, "The Case for Independent Institutes," *Voice of San Diego*, April 18, 2005, accessed July 8, 2012, http://www .voiceofsandiego.org/uncategorized/article_002ad7b3-accd-566b -8af5-8a7cf75c1ab9.html.

47.   Ibid.

48.   Rogers, "Carl Rogers to Friends."

49.   Kirschenbaum, *On Becoming Carl Rogers*, 316.

50.   Stanley Krippner, interview with author, San Francisco, June 24, 2005; Stanley Krippner, "Curriculum Vitae," http://www.stanley krippner.com/papers/VITAE.2003.htm.

51.   George Leonard, telephone interview with author, April 5, 2006.

52.   Abraham Maslow, "Some Basic Propositions of Growth and Self-Actualization Psychology," in *The Maslow Business Reader*, ed. Deborah C. Stephens (New York: Wiley, 2000), 31.

Chapter 6: Resacralizing Science

1.   Abraham Maslow, "January 30 1965," *The Journals of A. H. Maslow*, vol. 1, ed. Richard J. Lowry (Monterey, CA: Brooks/Cole, 1979), 452.

2.   Abraham Maslow, *The Psychology of Science: A Reconnaissance* (Chicago: Harper and Row, 1966), xv.

3.   Roy José DeCarvalho, *The Founders of Humanistic Psychology* (New York: Praeger, 1991), 159–216.

4.   Howard Kirschenbaum, *On Becoming Carl Rogers* (New York: Delacorte, 1979), 319–94.

5.   Maslow, "August 21, 1961," *Journals*, vol. 1, 113.

6.   Maslow, "August 30, 1962," *Journals*, vol. 1, 189–90.

7.   Maslow, "May 9, 1966," *Journals*, vol. 1, 730.

8.   Eugene Taylor, "'What Is Man, Psychologist, That Thou Art So Unmindful of Him?': Henry A. Murray on the Historical Relation Between Classical Personality Theory and Humanistic Psychology," *Journal of Humanistic Psychology* 40, no. 3 (Summer 2000): 29–42.

9.   Ibid., 32.

10.   Ibid., 31–32.

11.   DeCarvalho, *Founders of Humanistic Psychology*, 10.

12.   Henry Murray, "A Preliminary Sub-Symposium" (Henry A. Murray Papers, HUGFP 97.45.16, Box 6, Old Saybrook, A Preliminary Sub-Symposium folder).

13.   Ibid.

14.   Henry Murray, "Psychology and the University," *Archives of Neurology and Psychiatry*, 34 (October 1935): 803–17. Quotations are from Murray's archival manuscript. Henry Murray, "Psychology and the University" (Henry A. Murray Papers, Psychology and the University, 1930–1950 folder, HUGFP 97.45.20, Harvard University Archives).

15.   Ibid.

16.   Rollo May, "Intentionality, the Heart of Human Will," *Journal of Humanistic Psychology* 5, no. 2 (October 1965): 202.

17.   Ibid.

18.   Edward Shoben, "Psychology: Natural Science or Humanistic Discipline?" *Journal of Humanistic Psychology* 5, no. 2 (October 1965): 217. Shoben was an academic psychologist best known for his application of learning theory to the processes of psychotherapy. Patrick M. Grehan, "Edward Shoben, Jr.: Overlooked Pioneer of Psychotherapy Integration," *Journal of Psychotherapy Integration* 19, no. 2 (June 2009): 140–51.

19. Shoben, "Psychology," 217.

20. Ibid., 218.

21. Maslow, "April 1, 1963," *Journals*, vol. 1, 297–98.

22. Rogers also affirmed Maslow's view. "We have suffered enough," he said, "from the dogmatism of an unscientific Freudianism which initially enlightened us and then bound us into a rigid straitjacket." He argued that Freud's overelaboration of the subjective was as imprisoning as the confines of an impersonal science-like behaviorism. Carl R. Rogers, "Some Thoughts Regarding the Current Philosophy of the Behavioral Sciences," *Journal of Humanistic Psychology* 5, no. 2 (October 1965): quotation from 184.

23. Ibid., 184.

24. René Dubos, "Humanistic Biology," *American Scientist* 53 (March 1965): 4–19, accessed June 1, 2010, http://www.westga.edu/~psydept/os2/os1/dubos.htm.

25. Carol L. Moberg, *René J. Dubos: Friend of the Good Earth: Microbiologist, Medical Scientist, Environmentalist* (Herndon, VA: ASM, 2005), 121.

26. Dubos is best known for his Pulitzer Prize–winning book *So Human an Animal: How We Are Shaped by Surroundings and Events* (New York: Scribner, 1968).

27. Moberg, *René J. Dubos*, 136.

28. Ibid., 133.

29. Dubos, "Humanistic Biology."

30. Abraham Maslow, "Humanistic Science and Transcendent Experiences," *Journal of Humanistic Psychology* 5, no. 2 (October 1965): 219.

31. Ibid., 219.

32. Ibid., 222.

33. Ibid., 177–78.

34. Ibid.

35. Rogers, "Some Thoughts," quotations from 186 and 189.

36. Maslow, "October 8, 1964," *Journals*, vol. 1, 422.

37. The conference actually concluded with a panel led by Charlotte Bühler. However, no records seem to exist on this dialogue.

38. George Kelly, "The Threat of Aggression," *Journal of Humanistic Psychology* 5 no. 2 (October 1965): 201.

39. Ibid., 199.

40. See George Kelly, *A Theory of Personality: The Psychology of Personal Constructs* (New York: Norton, 1963).

41. Forrest G. Robinson, *Love's Story Told: A Life of Henry A. Murray* (Cambridge, MA: Harvard University Press, 1992), 354.

42. Nina Murray (wife of Henry Murray), interview with author, Cambridge, MA, January 3, 2005.

43. Robinson, *Love's Story Told,* 354.

44. Maslow, "November 27–29, 1964," *Journals,* vol. 1, 436.

45. Gordon Allport, "Psychiatry in Neurotic America" (unpublished notes), Law School Forum December 1950 (Papers of Gordon W. Allport, HUG 4118.50, Box 5, Folder 177, Harvard University Archives).

Chapter 7: Spreading the News

1. Abraham Maslow, *Eupsychian Management: A Journal* (Homewood, IL: Richard D. Irwin and Dorsey, 1965), 247.

2. The EEOC's powers were initially weak, and in the early years they prioritized race-based complaints over matters of discrimination against women.

3. *Public Papers of the Presidents of the United States: Lyndon B. Johnson, 1963–1969,* vol. 1 (Washington, DC: Government Printing Office 1965–70), 704–6, http://www.h-net.org/~hst306/documents/great.html.

4. Lord Taylor, "Deep Analysis of the American Mind," *New York Times,* February 23, 1964, http://query.nytimes.com/mem/archive/pdf?res =F10716F9385F137A8EDDAA0A94DA405B848AF1D3.

5. Ludy T. Benjamin, Jr., "A Brief History of Psychology at Texas A&M University," Texas A&M Department of Psychology website, http://psychology.tamu.edu/TAMUph.htm.

6. "General Catalog for California State University, Fresno: 1964–1965," California State University, Fresno, website, http://www.csufresno.edu/catoffice/archives/oldcourses/6465/psychcrs.html.

7. See Eric Berne, *Games People Play: The Basic Handbook of Transactional Analysis* (1964; reprint, New York: Ballantine, 1996); William Glasser, *Reality Therapy: A New Approach to Psychiatry* (New York: Harper & Row, 1965).

8. For overviews of these techniques, see Richard Fisch, John H. Weakland, and Lynn Segal, *The Tactics of Change: Doing Therapy Briefly* (San Francisco: Jossey-Bass, 1982); Virginia Satir, M. Gomori, John Banmen, Jane Gerber, and Maria Gomori, *The Satir Model: Family Therapy and Beyond* (Palo Alto, CA: Science and Behavior Books, 1991); Nick Totton, *Body Psychotherapy: An Introduction* (Maidenhead, UK: Open University, 2003).

9. Ibid.

10. See Carl R. Rogers, "Significant Learning in Therapy and in Education," *Educational Leadership* 16, no. 4 (1959): 232–42.

11. See Carl R. Rogers, "Psychology and Teacher Training," in *Five Fields and Teacher Education*, eds. D. B. Gowan and C. Richardson (Ithaca, NY: Project One Publications, Cornell University, 1965); Carl R. Rogers, "The Facilitation of Significant Learning," in *Contemporary Theories of Instruction*, ed. L. Siegel (San Francisco: Chandler, 1967); Carl R. Rogers, "A Plan for Self-Directed Change in an Educational System," *Educational Leadership* 24, no. 8 (1967): 717–31; Carl R. Rogers, "What Psychology Has to Offer to Teacher Education," in *Teacher Education and Mental Health—Association for Student Teaching* (Cedar Falls, IA: State College of Iowa, 1967), 37–57.

12. Carl R. Rogers, "Regarding Learning and Its Facilitation," in *Freedom to Learn: A View of What Education Might Become* (Columbus, OH: Charles E. Merrill, 1969), http://www.panarchy.org/rogers/learning.html.

13. See Patricia Albjerg Graham, *Progressive Education from Arcady to Academe: A History of the Progressive Education Association, 1919–1955* (New York: Teachers College Press, 1967).

14. Carl R. Rogers, "Personal Thoughts on Teaching and Learning," in *Freedom to Learn*, http://www.panarchy.org/rogers/learning.html.

15. Carl R. Rogers, "Psychology and Teacher Training," quotation from 60.

16. Ibid., quotation from 62.

17. Ibid., 63 and 77.

18. John Rowan, "Humanistic Education," in *A Guide to Humanistic Psychology*, accessed May 1, 2008, http://www.ahpweb.org/rowan_bibliography/chapter17.html.

19.   See Lucila Telles Rudge, "Holistic Education: An Analysis of Its Ped-
      agogical Application" (PhD diss., Ohio State University, 2008).

20.   Maslow, *Eupsychian Management*, 2.

21.   Ibid., 247.

22.   Edward Hoffman, *The Right to Be Human* (Los Angeles: Jeremy P.
      Tarcher, 1988), 268–70.

23.   Ibid., 268–69.

24.   Maslow as quoted in Hoffman, *Right to Be Human*, 273–74.

25.   Abraham Maslow, *The Maslow Business Reader*, ed. Deborah C. Ste-
      phens (New York: Wiley, 2000), 7.

26.   Hoffman, *Right to Be Human*, 160, 57.

27.   Abraham Maslow, *Religions, Values, and Peak-Experiences* (Colum-
      bus: Ohio State University Press, 1964), 4.

28.   Ibid., xii.

29.   Ibid., 22–23.

30.   "Coast Group Spearheads a Movement Seeking Clue to Human Feel-
      ings," *New York Times*, October 8, 1967.

31.   LeRoy Aden, "On Carl Rogers' Becoming," *Theology Today* 36, no. 4
      (January 1980): 556–59.

32.   David. A. Steere, "Supervising Pastoral Counseling," *Clinical Hand-
      book of Pastoral Counseling*, vol. 3, eds. Robert J. Wicks, Richard D.
      Parsons, Donald Capps (Mahwah, NJ: Paulist Press, 2003), 372.

33.   See Carroll A. Wise, *Pastoral Counseling: Its Theory and Practice* (New
      York: Harper & Brothers, 1951; Paul E. Johnson, *Person and Coun-
      selor: Responsive Counseling in the Christian Context* (Nashville, TN:
      Abingdon Press, 1967).

34.   Joe Boone Abbott as quoted in Allison Buice, "Pastoral Counselors In-
      creasing in Number," *Spartanburg Herald-Journal*, June 27, 1987, B3.

35.   American Association of Pastoral Counselors, "Brief History on Pas-
      toral   Counseling,"   http://www.aapc.org/about-us/brief-history-on
      -pastoral-counseling.aspx.

36.   Chris Mikul, *The Cult Files: True Stories from the Extreme Edges of
      Religious Belief* (Sydney: Murdoch Books, 2008), electronic edition.

37.   Ibid.

38.   Abraham Maslow, "August 13, 1965," *The Journals of A. H. Maslow*,
      vol. 1, ed. Richard J. Lowry (Monterey, CA: Brooks/Cole, 1979), 542.

39. Ibid., 542–43.

40. Mikul, *Cult Files*.

41. Maslow, "January 14, 1966," *Journals*, vol. 1, 586.

Chapter 8: From the Ivory Tower to the Golden Coast

1. Bob Dylan, "Lay, Lady, Lay," *Nashville Skyline*, Columbia Records, April 1969.

2. Edward Hoffman, *The Right to Be Human* (Los Angeles: Jeremy P. Tarcher, 1988), 272.

3. Richard Atcheson, "Big Sur: Coming to My Senses," *Holiday*, March 1968, 22.

4. Jeffrey Kripal, "Mesmer to Maslow: Psychologies of Energy and Consciousness," in *The Enlightenment of the Body: A Nonordinary History of Esalen* (unpublished manuscript, 2005).

5. Ibid.

6. Ibid.

7. Abraham Maslow, "April 30, 1970," *The Journals of A. H. Maslow*, vol. 2, ed. Richard J. Lowry (Monterey, CA: Brooks/Cole, 1979), 1287.

8. Maslow, "September 19, 1967," *Journals*, vol. 2, 828.

9. Maslow, "April 22, 1962," *Journals*, vol. 1, 164.

10. Barclay James Erickson, "The Only Way Out Is In: The Life of Richard Price," in *On the Edge of the Future: Esalen and the Evolution of American Culture*, eds. Jeffrey Kripal and Glenn W. Shuck (Bloomington: Indiana University Press, 2005), 132–64, 150–52.

11. Price's father had abandoned his own mother's Orthodox Judaism and was nonpracticing, while Price's mother—somewhat late in life—decided to baptize the children and join the Episcopalian church to protect the family from the anti-Semitic orientation of their exclusive Chicago neighborhood. Erickson, "The Only Way Out Is In," 134–43.

12. Ibid., 150–52.

13. Ann Taves, "Michael Murphy and the Natural History of Supernormal Human Attributes," in *On the Edge of the Future*, 226.

14. At the time of Murphy's trip, Sri Aurobindo had been dead five years, but his spiritual partner and successor, Mirra Alfassa, known as "the

Mother," remained at the ashram. Murphy had direct connection with Aurobindo's ideas through his writing in *The Life Divine*. According to Kripal, Murphy experienced the religious dimensions of the text he studied in a "classically mystical epistemological structure." Jeffrey Kripal, "Reading Aurobindo from Stanford to Pondicherry," in *On the Edge of the Future*, 108.

15. Sri Aurobindo, "The Human Mind," in *The Hour of God: Selections from His Writings*, compiled and with an introduction by Manoj Das (New Delhi: Sahitya Akademi, 1995), 215.

16. Walter Anderson, *Upstart Spring: Esalen and the American Awakening* (Reading, MA: Addison-Wesley, 1983), 119.

17. Sri Aurobindo, "The Yoga and Its Objects," 1912, http://surasa.net/aurobindo/yoga-obj.html.

18. Kripal, "Reading Aurobindo," 99–131. For a thorough history of Esalen, see Jeffrey Kripal, *Esalen: America and the Religion of No Religion* (Chicago: University of Chicago Press, 2007).

19. Kripal, *Esalen*, 439; Anderson, *Upstart Spring*, 68–72.

20. Despite his background, Harmon had branched out into multidisciplinary study. The seminar was intended to explore conceptual changes in psychology. It included a list of recommended readings in interdisciplinary psychological speculation. Anderson, *Upstart Spring*, 68.

21. Adams had a private practice and Bateson worked for the Veterans Administration hospital, both in Palo Alto, CA. "The Human Potentiality: A Seminar Series," brochure, Big Sur Hot Springs, Fall 1962.

22. Gerald Heard had immigrated to the United States with his best friend Aldous Huxley in 1937. Beginning in 1942, he oversaw Trabuco College, a progressive/visionary experiment in the study of comparative religion. He continued to write and publish extensively, both fiction and nonfiction, into the 1960s. Timothy Miller, "Notes on the Prehistory of the Human Potential Movement: The Vedanta Society and Gerald Heard's Trabuco College," in *On the Edge of the Future*, 86–90.

23. Anderson, *Upstart Spring*, 72.

24. "Human Potentiality: A Seminar Series."

25. Anderson, *Upstart Spring*, 70–71.

26. Ibid., 72.

27. Robert Masters and Jean Houston, *The Varieties of Psychedelic Experience: The Classic Guide to the Effects of LSD on the Human Psyche* (1966; reprint, Rochester, VT: Park Street, 2000), 7–12.

28. Masters and Houston, *Psychedelic Experience*, 7–12.

29. Abraham Maslow, *Toward a Psychology of Being* (New York: Van Nostrand, 1962), 103–14.

30. Albert Hofmann, *LSD: My Problem Child*, trans. Jonathan Ott (1980; reprint, Saline, MI: McNaughton & Gunn, 2005), 47.

31. Ibid., 49–50.

32. Craig S. Smith, "Nearly 100, LSD's Father Ponders His 'Problem Child,'" *New York Times,* January 7, 2006, http://www.nytimes.com/2006/01/07/international/europe/07hoffman.html?_r=1&oref=slogin.

33. Hofmann, *LSD*, 24–25.

34. R. Gordon Wasson, "Seeking the Magic Mushroom," *Life*, June 10, 1957, http://www.imaginaria.org/wasson/life.htm.

35. Hofmann, *LSD*, 11–12.

36. Sidney Katz, "My Twelve Hours as a Madman," *Maclean's*, October 1, 1953, 9–11, 46–55, http://www.macleans.ca/article.jsp?content=20070921_160239_7188.

37. Ibid.

38. Ibid.

39. Hofmann, *LSD*, 27.

40. For examples of this research see Harold A. Abramson, "Psychoanalytic Psychotherapy with LSD," in *The Use of LSD in Psychotherapy*, ed. Harold A. Abramson (New York: Josiah Macy, Jr., Foundation, 1960), 25–80; Arthur L. Chandler and Mortimer A. Hartman, "Lysergic Acid Diethylamide (LSD) as a Facilitating Agent in Psychotherapy," *Archives of General Psychiatry* 2, no. 3 (1960): 286–99; and Humphry Osmond, "A Review of the Clinical Effects of Psychotomimetic Agents," *Annals of the New York Academy of Sciences* 66, no. 3 (1957): 418–34.

41. For more on the research performed in the fifties with schizophrenics and alcoholics, see Edward Baker, "LSD Psychotherapy; LSD Psycho-Exploration:

Three Reports," in *The Use of LSD in Psychotherapy and Alcoholism*, ed. Harold A. Abramson (Indianapolis: Bobbs-Merrill, 1967), 191–207; Humphry Osmond and John Smythies, "Schizophrenia: A New Approach," *Journal of Mental Science* 98 (April 1952): 309–15.

42. Janice Hopkins Tanne, "Obituary for Humphry Osmond," *British Medical Journal*, 328 (March 2004): 713; Abram Hoffer, "Treatment of Alcoholism with Psychedelic Therapy," in *Psychedelics: The Uses and Implications of Hallucinogenic Drugs*, eds. Bernard Aaronson and Humphry Osmond (Garden City, NY: Anchor, 1970), 357–66.

43. Timothy Leary, *High Priest* (Berkeley, CA: Ronin, 1995), 12.

44. Ibid., 13.

45. Hofmann, *LSD*, 94–95.

46. Prior to Leary's research, various studies had established the safety and psychotherapeutic promise of psychedelics. In mid-1960, researcher Sidney Cohen established the feasibility of psychedelic experimentation with his large-scale study of side effects. He documented psychotic episodes as occurring in approximately 1.8 per thousand cases, attempted suicides in 1.2 per thousand, and successful suicides in 0.4 per thousand. Jay Stevens, *Storming Heaven: LSD and the American Dream* (New York: Atlantic Monthly Press, 1987), 173.

47. Ibid., 138–58.

48. Stanley Krippner, "Dancing with the Trickster: Notes for a Transpersonal Autobiography," *International Journal of Transpersonal Studies* 21 (2002): 1–18, http://www.stanleykrippner.com/papers/autobio good.htm.

49. Stanley Krippner, interview with author, San Francisco, June 24, 2005.

50. Krippner, "Dancing with the Trickster."

51. Krippner, interview.

52. Maslow, "December 24, 1961," *Journals*, vol. 1, 242.

53. Abraham Maslow, *Religions, Values, and Peak-Experiences* (Columbus: Ohio State University Press, 1964), 27.

54. Maslow, December 7, 1968, *Journals*, vol. 2, 1092.

55. Rollo May to Charles C. Dahlberg, New York, September 18, 1965 (Rollo May Papers, HPA Mss 45, Box 12:9, Answered Correspon-

dence 1964–1965 folder, Humanistic Psychology Archives, Department of Special Collections, Donald C. Davidson Library, University of California, Santa Barbara).

56. Timothy Leary, "The Religious Experience: Its Production and Interpretation," eds. Timothy Leary, Ralph Metzner, and Gunther M. Weil, *The Psychedelic Reader: Classic Selections from* The Psychedelic Review, *the Revolutionary 1960s Forum of Psychopharmacological Substances* (Secaucus, NJ: Citadel, 1993), 178.

57. Reverend Mike Young as quoted in Jeanne Malmgren, "The Good Friday Marsh Chapel Experiment: Tune In, Turn on, Get Well?" *St. Petersburg Times*, November 27, 1994, http://www.csp.org/practices/entheogens/docs/young-good_friday.html.

58. Emma Harrison, "A Mind-Drug Link to Religion Seen," *New York Times*, August 31, 1963 in ProQuest Historical Newspapers, the *New York Times* (1851–2003), 28.

59. Anderson, *Upstart Spring*, 72.

60. "Human Potentiality: A Seminar Series."

61. Anderson, *Upstart Spring*, 79.

62. Huxley published two books in the mid-fifties that explored psychedelic use: Aldous Huxley, *Doors of Perception* (New York: Harper, 1954) and Aldous Huxley, *Heaven and Hell* (New York: Harper, 1956).

63. Aldous Huxley, *Island* (New York: Harper & Row, 1962), 141.

64. See Huxley, *Doors of Perception*.

65. Kripal, *Esalen*, 132–43; Anderson, *Upstart Spring*, 108.

66. Anderson, *Upstart Spring*, 269.

67. Michael Murphy in Scott London, "The Mysterious Powers of Body and Mind: An Interview with Michael Murphy" (1996), interview conducted in Santa Barbara, CA and adapted from the radio series *Insight & Outlook*, http://www.scottlondon.com/interviews/murphy.html.

68. Maslow, "April 22–23, 1965," *Journals*, vol. 1, 608.

69. Martin A. Lee and Bruce Schlain, *Acid Dreams: The Complete Social History of LSD: The CIA, the Sixties, and Beyond* (New York: Grove, 1985), 81.

70. Robert Greenfield, *Timothy Leary: A Biography*, (New York: Harcourt, 2006), 124.

71. Leary describes the reason for his dismissal from Harvard as due, in part, to the politically risky nature of his research. Timothy Leary, Testimony of Timothy Leary in the Chicago Seven Trial, transcript, http://www.law.umkc.edu/faculty/projects/ftrials/Chicago7/Leary.html.

72. Psychedelic use was legally limited to experimental settings in 1963 and possession became illegal in 1966. Lee and Schlain, *Acid Dreams*, 92, 131.

73. John Osmundsen, "Harvard Study Sees Benefit in Use of Mind Drugs," *New York Times*, May 15, 1965.

74. In spite of his doubts, Maslow remained committed to Leary and Alpert's right to conduct research on psychedelics. In July 1965, Maslow flew to Washington, DC, to testify on behalf of Richard Alpert, whose experimental methods had been called into question by the ethics board of the American Psychological Association. Maslow defended Alpert's right to engage in unorthodox scientific methods and argued that there was potential value in psychedelic experimentation. Maslow, "July 16, 1965," *Journals*, vol. 1, 527.

75. Maslow, "December 10, 1964," *Journals*, vol. 1, 440.

76. Dietrich Bonhoeffer, *The Cost of Discipleship* (New York: Simon & Schuster, 1995), 43–44. First published in 1937 in German as *Nachfolge*.

77. Maslow, "Drugs—Critique," November 29, 1966 (Maslow Papers, Box M 449.7, LSD [drugs] folder, Archives of the History of American Psychology, Center for the History of Psychology, University of Akron).

78. Ibid.

79. Maslow, letter to Paula Gordon, May 11, 1966 (Maslow Papers, Box M 397, Miscellaneous Correspondence folder, Archives of the History of American Psychology, Center for the History of Psychology, University of Akron).

80. Maslow, letter to Rabbi Zalman Schachter, October 24, 1963 (Maslow Papers, Box M 449.7, LSD [drugs] folder, Archives of the History of American Psychology, Center for the History of Psychology, University of Akron).

81. Lee and Schlain, *Acid Dreams*, 82.

82. Ibid., 81.

83. Stevens, *Storming Heaven*, 273–75.

84. Graham B. Blaine, Jr., "Moral Questions Stir Campuses: Sex, Drugs and Psychoses Posing New Problems," *New York Times*, January 16, 1964.

85. Timothy Leary as quoted in Robert E. Dallos, "Dr. Leary Starts New 'Religion' With 'Sacramental' Use of LSD," *New York Times*, September 20, 1966.

86. Leary as quoted in Stevens, *Storming Heaven*, 326. According to Leary, "Turn on means to go beyond your secular tribal mind to contact the many levels of divine energy which lie within your consciousness; tune in means to express and to communicate your new revelations in visible acts of glorification, gratitude and beauty; drop out means to detach yourself harmoniously, tenderly and gracefully from your worldly commitments until your entire life is dedicated to worship and search." Ibid., 326.

87. Maslow, "December 20, 1960," *Journals*, vol. 1, 82.

88. Abraham Maslow, "Resistance to Enculturation," *Journal of Social Issues* 7 (1951): 26–29.

89. Hoffman, *Right to Be Human*, 192.

90. Abraham Maslow as quoted in Hoffman, *Right to Be Human*, 192.

91. Timothy Leary, *Turn On, Tune In, Drop Out* (first published as *The Politics of Ecstasy*, 1968; reprint, Oakland, CA: Ronin Publishing, 1999), 6.

92. William Borders, "LSD Psychologist Arrested Again; Dr. Leary, the ex-Harvard Teacher, Seized in Raid on Dutchess Mansion," *New York Times*, April 18, 1966.

93. "Jury Inquiry Balked by Aide of Dr. Leary," *New York Times*, July 16, 1966, 20.

94. Stevens, *Storming Heaven*, 337.

95. Ibid., 274.

96. Ibid., 273–75.

97. Ibid., 279.

98. "Broken Chromosomes: Some Evidence," *Science News*, November 11, 1967; "Cell Damage from LSD," *Time*, March 24, 1967, 46+; Samuel Irwin and Jose Egozcue, "Chromosomal Abnormalities in

Leukocytes from LSD-25 Users," *Science* 157 (July 21, 1967), 313–14; Maimon M. Cohen, Michelle J. Marinello, and Nathan Back, "Chromosomal Damage in Human Leukocytes Induced by Lysergic Acid Diethylamide," *Science* 155 (March 17, 1967), 1417–19.

99.   "LSD and the Unborn," *Newsweek*, September 18, 1967; "LSD and the Unborn," *Time*, August 11, 1967; E. M. Brecher, "LSD: Danger to Unborn Babies," *McCall's*, September 1967, 70–1+.

100.   "New Reports on Rising Problem: Use of LSD," *U.S. News & World Report*, April 10, 1967; Margaret Mead, "Should We Have Laws Banning the Use of LSD?" *Redbook*, January 1968.

101.   Stevens, *Storming Heaven*, 285.

102.   Lyndon B. Johnson, "Annual Message to the Congress on the State of the Union," January 17, 1968, http://www.lbjlib.utexas.edu/johnson/archives.hom/speeches.hom/680117.asp.

103.   "President Urges a National Drive on Narcotics Use," *New York Times*, July 15, 1969, 1.

104.   Allen Ginsberg, "Graffiti 12th Cubicle Men's Room Syracuse Airport," November 11, 1969, *Collected Poems 1947–1997* (New York: Harper Perennial, 2006), 535.

105.   George Leonard, *Walking on the Edge of the World* (Boston: Houghton Mifflin, 1988), 80.

106.   Stevens, *Storming Heaven*, x.

107.   Leonard, *Walking on the Edge*, 80.

108.   Stevens, *Storming Heaven*, xii.

109.   Joan Didion, "Slouching Towards Bethlehm," *Saturday Evening Post*, September, 23, 1967, vol. 240 (19), 25-94. Reprinted in Joan Didion, *Slouching Towards Bethlehem* (New York: Noonday Press, 1968), quotation from 85.

110.   Leonard, *Walking on the Edge*, 80.

111.   Maslow, "July 9, 1967," *Journals*, vol. 2, 775.

112.   Walter Anderson, interview with author, San Francisco, April 26, 2005.

113.   Jeffrey Klein, "Esalen Slides Off the Cliff," *Mother Jones*, December 1979, 26–45, quotation from 30.

114.   "A Chronology of AHP's Annual Conferences," Association of Humanistic Psychology website, accessed December 15, 2011, http://ahpweb.org/aboutahp/ahpcronology.html.

115. The office doubled as director John Levy's base of operations for San Francisco Venture, an organization devoted to psychospiritually oriented groups and programs with and for the residents of the "ghetto area" in which it was located. John Levy, telephone interview with author, September 20, 2005.

116. Anderson, *Upstart Spring*, 2.

Chapter 9: The Sledgehammer Approach to Human Growth

1. Rick Tarnas, 1978, http://www.esalen.org/air/essays/tarnas_1978.html.

2. John Heider, "HumPot Papers," unpublished manuscript, Esalen 1967–1971, 13.

3. Ibid., 15.

4. Ibid., 14.

5. Ibid., 39.

6. Ibid., 38.

7. George Leonard, telephone interview with author, April 5, 2006.

8. See William C. Schutz, *Joy: Expanding Human Awareness* (New York: Grove, 1967).

9. William C. Schutz as quoted in Peter Friedberg, http://www.esalen.org/air/essays/will_schutz.html.

10. NTL's mission, when established in 1947, was to study and apply group work as a social "technology." NTL hoped "to advance, through improved theories and practices of human relations education, the productivity and quality of human relations in all areas of social life." H. A. Thalen, for the Committee, "Proposed Bylaws of the National Training Laboratories," November 27, 1955 (NTL Papers, Box M226, NTL Historical Documents Folder, Archives of the History of American Psychology, Center for the History of Psychology, University of Akron).

11. "What Is Sensitivity Training?" *NTL Institute Bulletin* 2, no. 2 (April 1968) (NTL Papers, Box M223, NTL Special Reports folder, Archives of the History of American Psychology, Center for the History of Psychology, University of Akron). Focused on will and intention, NTL was premised on the idea that a sense of control over one's des-

tiny was integral to realization of one's "human potential." By connecting individuals more fully to the social experience of their work and improving their group and individual functioning, NTL intended to facilitate self-actualization. Evelyn Hooker, "Theory Session 1: The Meaning of Laboratory Training," June 27, 1955 (NTL Papers, Box M227, NTL in Group Development folder, Archives of the History of American Psychology, Center for the History of Psychology, University of Akron).

12. Abraham Maslow, "Journal Notes on the T-Groups," Bethel, Maine, June 16, 1968 (Maslow Papers, M449.3, T Groups Folder, Archives of the History of American Psychology Center for the History of Psychology, University of Akron).

13. Rogers himself published a book called *On Encounter Groups* in 1970. Carl R. Rogers, *On Encounter Groups* (New York: Harper & Row, 1970).

14. Carl R. Rogers, "Carl Rogers Describes His Way of Facilitating Encounter Groups," *American Journal of Nursing* 71, no. 2 (February 1971): 275–79, quotation from 279.

15. Walter Anderson, *Upstart Spring: Esalen and the American Awakening* (Reading, MA: Addison-Wesley, 1983), 152–56.

16. Heider, "HumPot Papers," 39.

17. Tom Wolfe, "The Me Decade and the Third Great Awakening," in *Mauve Gloves & Madmen, Clutter & Vine* (New York: Bantam, 1977), 126–70, quotation from 135.

18. Abraham Maslow, "September 19, 1967," *The Journals of A. H. Maslow*, vol. 2, ed. Richard J. Lowry (Monterey, CA: Brooks/Cole, 1979), 827.

19. Leo E. Litwak, "A Trip to Esalen Institute—Joy Is the Prize," *New York Times,* December 31, 1967, 8, 28–29, quotation from 8.

20. Ibid., quotation from 29.

21. Jeffrey Kripal and Glenn W. Shuck, eds., *On the Edge of the Future: Esalen and the Evolution of American Culture* (Bloomington: Indiana University Press, 2005), 6.

22. Jeffrey Kripal, *Esalen: America and the Religion of No Religion* (Chicago: University of Chicago Press, 2007), 158–59.

23. Heider, "HumPot Papers," 47.

24. "Seminars," brochure, Big Sur Hot Springs, Winter–Spring 1964.

25. Heider, "HumPot Papers," 9.

26. Laura Perls as quoted in Kripal, *Esalen*, 161; Robert Shilkret, interview with author, South Hadley, MA, September 17, 2005. Professor Robert Shilkret of Mount Holyoke College remembers Fritz Perls's appearance in 1966 as "very California." Addressing a crowd at Boston University's student center, Perls arrived unreasonably late and spoke for a very short time, in spite of the high (five-dollar) cost of admission. Perls announced, "Maybe some of those here tonight are somewhat disappointed. . . . That's right. And now you're learning."

27. Gordon Wheeler, "Spirit and Shadow: Esalen and the Gestalt Model," in *On the Edge of the Future*, 173–74.

28. Kripal, *Esalen*, 163.

29. Maureen O'Hara, interview with author, San Francisco, CA, April 29, 2005.

30. Michael Murphy, afterword to Kripal and Shuck, *On the Edge of the Future*, 308.

31. Jeffrey Kripal, "Esalen Goes to the City: The San Francisco Center (1967–1975)," in *The Enlightenment of the Body: A Nonordinary History of Esalen* (unpublished manuscript, 2005), 12.

32. For Perls's first book on Gestalt, see Frederick Perls, Ralph F. Hefferline, and Paul Goodman, *Gestalt Therapy: Excitement and Growth in the Human Personality* (New York: Dell, 1951).

33. Frederick Perls, *The Gestalt Approach and Eye Witness to Therapy* (Ben Lomond, CA: Science and Behavior Books, 1973), 3–4.

34. For thousands of Americans, "Gestalt psychology" was reduced to Perls's interpretive techniques, to the exclusion of the more comprehensive and empirically validated bases of Gestalt theory as developed in Europe during the early twentieth century. Petruska Clarkson and Jennifer Mackewn, *Fritz Perls* (London: Sage, 1993), 142. One critic, in attempting to distinguish Gestalt therapy from what he termed "Perls-ism," noted that Perls's Gestalt therapy was more accurately a "biological-hedonistic existentialism." He specifically identified three aspects of Perls's theory and practice that were not a part of proper Gestalt therapy: specifically his anti-intellectual attitude, his

view of maturity as "hedonistic isolation," and his "unsupportive stance as a therapist." J. Dublin, "Existential-Gestalt Therapy versus 'Perls-ism,'" in *The Growing Edge of Gestalt Therapy*, ed. Edward W. L. Smith (New York: Brunner/Mazel, 1976), 141–45. Those versed in the Gestalt model also recognized the incompleteness of Perls's brand of Gestalt, which was a "come to your senses" approach, absent of the political and philosophical components that defined the approaches of Gestalt psychologists like Paul Goodman. Wheeler, "Spirit and Shadow," 182. Perls's most purely, and perhaps only truly, Gestalt principles were his focus on the "here and now," present needs and beliefs as syntheses of past experiences, the immediacy of self-expression, and the contention that all perception was interpretation.

35. Anderson, *Upstart Spring*, 133.

36. Ibid., 132–33.

37. Frederick Perls, *Gestalt Therapy Verbatim*, ed. John O. Stevens (Lafayette, CA: Real People, 1969), 4.

38. Anonymous patient as quoted in David Allyn, *Make Love, Not War: The Sexual Revolution: An Unfettered History* (Boston: Little, Brown, 2000), 204.

39. Ibid., 247.

40. In his journalistic coverage of the thirteenth annual AHP convention for the *Mountain Gazette*, Mike Moore describes Esalen as the "proving ground for experiments in the new therapy: encounter, Gestalt, meditation, the healing baths, and the sensuous massage—all that we called 'touchie-feelie' a few years ago." See Mike Moore, "Breaking Free from the Human Potential Movement," *Mountain Gazette*, October 1975, 17–23.

41. Anderson, *Upstart Spring*, 199–202.

42. Abraham Maslow, "Notes on T-groups," unpublished paper (Maslow Papers, Box M449.3, T-groups folder, Archives of the History of American Psychology, Center for the History of Psychology, University of Akron), 7.

43. Perls as quoted in Kripal, *Esalen*, 157.

44. Leonard, interview, April 5, 2006.

45. Kripal, *Esalen*, 167.

46. Leonard, interview, April 5, 2006.

47. See Schutz, *Joy: Expanding Human Awareness*.

48. Leonard, *Walking on the Edge*, 301.

49. Heider, "HumPot Papers," 152.

50. Scott London, "The Mysterious Powers of Body and Mind: An Interview with Michael Murphy" (1996), interview conducted in Santa Barbara, CA, and adapted from the radio series *Insight & Outlook*, http://www.scottlondon.com/interviews/murphy.html.

51. James V. McConnell "Psychoanalysis Must Go" *Esquire*, October 1968, 176+, quotation from 176.

52. Lewis R. Wolberg, introduction to *Inside Psychotherapy: Nine Clinicians Tell How They Work and What They Are Trying to Accomplish*, ed. Adelaide Bry (New York: Basic, 1972), ix.

53. Albert Ellis, *Humanistic Psychotherapy: The Rational-Emotive Approach* (New York: McGraw-Hill Books, 1971), 1.

54. Ibid., 9.

55. Carol Magai and Jeannette M. Haviland-Jones, *The Hidden Genius of Emotion: Lifespan Transformations of Personality* (Cambridge, UK: Cambridge University Press, 2002), 442.

Chapter 10: Such Beauty and Such Ugliness

1. Leonard Cohen, "Bird on the Wire," *Songs from a Room*, Columbia Records, 1969.

2. Carol Magai and Jeannette M. Haviland-Jones, *The Hidden Genius of Emotion: Lifespan Transformations of Personality* (Cambridge, UK: Cambridge University Press, 2002), 184.

3. Ibid., 170.

4. John Heider, "HumPot Papers," unpublished manuscript, Esalen 1967–1971, 161.

5. Ibid., 73.

6. Ibid., 73.

7. Walter Anderson, *Upstart Spring: Esalen and the American Awakening* (Reading, MA: Addison-Wesley, 1983), 145–46, quotation from 145.

8. Michael Murphy as quoted in George Leonard, *Walking on the Edge of the World* (Boston: Houghton Mifflin, 1988), 207.

9. Jeffrey Kripal, *Esalen: America and the Religion of No Religion* (Chicago: University of Chicago Press, 2007), 132–34.

10. Leonard, *Walking on the Edge*, 302.

11. Abraham Maslow, "Politics 3," in *Politics and Innocence: A Humanistic Debate*, ed. Thomas Greening (Dallas: Saybrook Publishers, 1989), 80.

12. Abraham Maslow, "May 9, 1968," *The Journals of A. H. Maslow*, vol. 2, ed. Richard J. Lowry (Monterey, CA: Brooks/Cole, 1979), 920.

13. Abraham Maslow, *Religions, Values, and Peak-Experiences* (Columbus: Ohio State University Press, 1964), 27; Maslow, "February 3, 1965," *Journals*, vol. 1, 452.

14. Maslow, "Jan 18, 1968," *Journals*, vol. 2, 907.

15. Anderson, *Upstart Spring*, 181. Brain researcher Lois Delattre first introduced Michael Murphy and George Leonard at her home in Telegraph Hill in 1965. Leonard, interview, April 5, 2006.

16. Ibid., 181.

17. Ibid., 199–202.

18. Maslow, "August 18, 1968," *Journals*, vol. 2, 981.

19. Maslow, "April 6, 1969," *Journals*, vol. 2, 953.

20. David Dempsey, "Love and Will and Rollo May," *New York Times*, March 28, 1971, SM29.

21. John Levy, telephone interview with author, September 20, 2005.

22. Jeffrey Kripal, "Reading Aurobindo from Stanford to Pondicherry," in *On the Edge of the Future*, 126.

23. George Leonard, telephone interview with author, April 5, 2006.

24. Ibid.; Anderson, *Upstart Spring*, 161.

25. Anderson, *Upstart Spring*, 161.

26. *Look* was a weekly national magazine, published in Des Moines, Iowa, from 1937 to 1971.

27. Leonard, interview with author, April 5, 2006.

28. Ibid.

29. Price Cobbs, interview with author, San Francisco, CA, June 23, 2005.

30. Leonard, *Walking on the Edge*, 266.

31. Anderson, *Upstart Spring*, 162.

32. Cobbs, interview.

33. Leonard, *Walking on the Edge*, 265.

34. Price Cobbs, *My American Life: From Rage to Entitlement* (New York: Atria, 2006), 191.

35. Esalen Seminars Brochure, Summer 1967.

36. Cobbs, *My American Life*, 192.

37. Cobbs, interview.

38. Cobbs, *My American Life*, 194.

39. Ibid., 196.

40. Ibid.

41. Anderson, *Upstart Spring*, 163.

42. Cobbs, *My American Life*, 196.

43. Anderson, *Upstart Spring*, 163.

44. Ibid.

45. Cobbs, *My American Life*, 197.

46. Cobbs, interview.

47. Leonard hoped to extend the lessons of black-white encounter to the highest echelons of American society. He expediently drafted a letter to the president, enjoining Richard Nixon himself to participate in a series of black-white encounter groups to be held at the White House. The letter contained several signatures, including those of top leaders of the Martin Luther King administration, but was never answered by the White House. Leonard, *Walking on the Edge*, 323–24.

48. William H. Grier and Price Cobbs, *Black Rage* (New York: Basic Books, 1968), 179.

49. Ibid., 178–79.

50. Alvin F. Poussaint and Amy Alexander, *Lay My Burden Down: Unraveling Suicide and the Mental Health Crisis Among African-Americans* (Boston: Beacon, 2000), 64.

51. For a comprehensive look at historical racial research, see: William H. Tucker, *The Science and Politics of Racial Research* (Urbana: University of Illinois Press, 1996). The medical establishment's racism had been demonstrated in practice as well as in theory. The Tuskegee syphilis study was the final straw for many blacks who had come to perceive American medical institutions as threatening and authoritarian. Beginning in 1932, government researchers conducted a long-term study (initially intended to extend for six months) of the effects of

syphilis on a group of black men in Alabama. The study continued for forty years, during which time participants were not informed of their diagnosis, but were told they had "bad blood," a vernacular term used to describe a variety of ailments. Participants were also denied penicillin, which had become an acceptable and effective form of treatment around 1945. In July 1972, the Associated Press broke the story, making it public knowledge that 399 syphilitic black men had gone untreated, and many had died, for the purposes of an ad hoc government study that lacked a documented protocol. "U.S. Public Health Service Syphilis Study," Centers for Disease Control and Prevention website, http://www.cdc.gov/tuskegee/; James H. Jones, *Bad Blood: The Tuskegee Syphilis Experiment* (New York, Free Press, 1981), 204.

52. Poussaint and Alexander, *Lay My Burden Down*, 105.

53. Ibid., 110, 105.

54. Ibid., 101–10, quotation from 105.

55. Ibid., 80, 105.

56. The Moynihan report, released in 1965, had increased the alienation that many blacks felt from the social sciences in general with its heavy reliance on damage imagery. In detailing the fragmented self-concepts of black Americans, the report aroused in blacks a pointed suspicion of attempts to address their "pathology." It wasn't until the mid-1970s, when humanistic psychology's cultural power had already begun to decline, that the social sciences began to represent the black psyche in nonpathological ways. Daryl Michael Scott, *Contempt and Pity: Social Policy and the Image of the Damaged Black Psyche, 1880–1996* (Chapel Hill, NC: University of North Carolina Press, 1997), 183. This distrust contributed to the broader frustration that blacks were increasingly experiencing with the white coalition, and caused many to turn away from even the most serious efforts to meaningfully consider race. Although some clinicians attempted, in the 1960s, to formulate a "black psychology," redefining normal black behavior and revising ill-suited language, their efforts received little attention from blacks at the time. Poussaint and Alexander, *Lay My Burden Down*, 74–75.

57. Lewis M. Killian, *Impossible Revolution, Phase 2: Black Power and the American Dream* (Lanham, MD: University Press of America, 1975), 129.

58. Samuel DuBois Cook, "The Tragic Myth of Black Power," *New South* 21 (Summer 1969), 59. Some blacks openly abandoned integrationist efforts, arguing that all-black coalitions would be better able to fully devote themselves to the expedient amelioration of racial inequality. Frustrated with the limited impact of the organization and seeking a novel strategy, SNCC expelled its white members in 1966 and supplanted its integrationist platform with a black power agenda. SNCC's position paper on this decision defends the action by arguing that the intimidating influence of whites had created an "unrealistic" racial atmosphere. SNCC enjoined whites to form their own coalitions in support of racial equality, but justified their exclusive policies as necessary to force social change. Charles V. Hamilton, "An Advocate of Black Power Defines It," in *Black Power: The Radical Response to White America*, ed. Thomas Wagstaff (Beverly Hills, CA: Glencoe Press, 1969), 124–37; SNCC Position Paper (1966), "Who Is the Real Villain—Uncle Tom or Simon Legree?" in *Black Power*, 111–18.

59. L. T. Benjamin, Jr. and E. M. Crouse, "The American Psychological Association's Response to *Brown v. Board of Education:* The Case of Kenneth B. Clark," *American Psychologist* 57, no. 1 (2002): 38–50.

60. The Clark doll studies suggested that black children with low self-esteem tended to prefer white dolls. The findings were published as three articles: K. B. Clark and M. K. Clark, "The Development of Consciousness of Self and the Emergence of Racial Identification in Negro Preschool Children," *Journal of Social Psychology* 10 (1939): 591–99; K. B. Clark and M. K. Clark, "Segregation as a Factor in the Racial Identification of Negro Pre-school Children: A Preliminary Report," *Journal of Experimental Education* 8, (1939): 161–63; K. B. Clark and M. K. Clark, "Skin Color as a Factor in Racial Identification of Negro Preschool Children," *Journal of Social Psychology* 11 (1940): 159–69.

61. Kenneth Clark to Herbert Kelman, January 7, 1965, as quoted in Wade E. Pickren and Henry Tomes, "The Legacy of Kenneth B. Clark to the APA: The Board of Social and Ethical Responsibility for Psychology," *American Psychologist* 57, no. 1 (January 2002), 51.

62. Adelbert Jenkins, "A Humanistic Approach to Black Psychology," in *Black Psychology*, ed. Reginald L. Jones (Berkeley, CA: Cobb & Henry, 1991), 184.

63. William L. Van Deburg, *New Day in Babylon: The Black Power Movement and American Culture, 1965–1975* (Chicago: University of Chicago Press, 1992), 57–60.

64. Jenkins, "A Humanistic Approach to Black Psychology," 79–81.

65. Ibid., 92.

66. Robert V. Guthrie, "The Psychology of African Americans: An Historical Perspective," in *Black Psychology,* 36.

67. Jenkins, "A Humanistic Approach to Black Psychology," 101.

68. Abraham Maslow, "The Unnoticed Revolution 2," February 5, 1969 (Maslow Papers, Box 414, Lectures [AHAP] folder, Archives of the History of American Psychology, Center for the History of Psychology, University of Akron).

69. "Cumulative Contents, 1961–1990," *Journal of Humanistic Psychology* 30, no. 4 (Fall 1990): 70–112.

70. Killian, *The Impossible Revolution*, 78.

71. Cobbs, interview.

72. Krippner, interview.

73. Ibid.

74. Carl R. Rogers, "Some Social Issues Which Concern Me," *Journal of Humanistic Psychology* 12, no. 2 (Fall 1972): 48.

75. Carl R. Rogers, "On No Longer Being Ashamed of America," in *Politics and Innocence*, 23–32.

76. Maureen O'Hara, interview, April 29, 2005.

77. Virginia Satir, interview with Judith Goodman, November 1977 (Virginia Satir Collection, HPA Mss 45, Box 5: 36, Humanistic Psychology Archives, Department of Special Collections, Donald C. Davidson Library, University of California, Santa Barbara).

78. Joyce Milton argues that humanistic psychologists, including Maslow and Rogers, were overly naïve and idealistic when it came to political concerns. Her criticism, though, must be taken in the context of her general disapproval of the humanistic psychology movement and of the negative bias she projects throughout her book. See Joyce Milton, *The Road to Malpsychia: Humanistic Psychology and Our Discontents*

(San Francisco: Encounter Books, 2003). The remarks of Virginia Satir, Stanley Krippner, and Price Cobbs (detailed later in this chapter) suggest that many humanistic psychologists were realistic about the limitations of their theory.

79. Bryce Nelson, "Psychologists: Searching for Social Relevance at APA Meeting," *Science*, New Series 165, no. 3898 (September 12, 1969): 1101–4; David B. Baker, "The Challenge of Change: Formation of the Association of Black Psychologists," in *Handbook of Psychology*, ed. Irving B. Weiner (Hoboken, NJ: John Wiley, 2003), 492–94.

80. Nelson, "Psychologists," 1101; Ida Harper Simpson and Richard L. Simpson, "The Transformation of the American Sociological Association," *Sociological Forum* 9, no. 2, Special Issue: "What's Wrong with Sociology?" (June 1994): 259–78.

81. Lauren Wispe et al. reported that between 1920 and 1966, twenty-five of the nation's largest PhD programs in psychology granted more than ten thousand doctoral degrees, with only ninety-three going to blacks. L. Wispe, J. Awkard, M. Hoffman, P. Ash, L. H. Hicks, and J. Porter, "The Negro Psychologist in America," *American Psychologist* 24, no. 2 (February 1969): 142–50.

82. Clayborne Carson, *In Struggle: SNCC and the Black Awakening of the 1960s* (Cambridge, MA: Harvard University Press, 1981), 153.

83. Numerous sources describe the primacy of racial issues in America in the 1960s. For examples, see August Meier, John Bracey, Jr., and Elliott Rudwick, eds., *Black Protest in the Sixties* (New York: Markus Wiener, 1991); Rhoda Blumberg, *Civil Rights: The 1960s Freedom Struggle* (Boston: Twayne, 1984); and Gene Roberts and Hank Klibanoff, *The Race Beat: The Press, the Civil Rights Struggle, and the Awakening of a Nation* (New York: Knopf, 2006).

84. In 1964, even the House Un-American Activities Committee (HUAC) was preparing to investigate the Ku Klux Klan. Killian, *The Impossible Revolution*, 85. For a contextualization of the 1960s civil rights activity within the events of the 1950s, see Aldon D. Morris, *Origins of the Civil Rights Movement* (New York: Free Press, 1984).

85. Milton J. Rosenberg, as quoted in Nelson, "Psychologists," 1101.

86. George Miller, as quoted in Nelson, "Psychologists," 1103.

87. Sigmund Koch, as quoted in Nelson, "Psychologists," 1103–4.

88. Several sources refer to the phenomenon of racial tokenism, a practice in which "token" blacks are included in an organization, or in which racial issues are paid superficial attention as a token of an organization's commitment to diversity. Yolanda Niemann describes the psychological effects of such tokenism, which include isolation, exaggeration of difference, and general distress in "The Psychology of Tokenism: Psychosocial Realities of Faculty of Color," in *Handbook of Racial and Ethnic Minority Psychology*, eds. Guillermo Bernal, Joseph E. Trimble, Ann Kathleen Burlew, and Frederick T. L. Leong (Thousand Oaks, CA: Sage, 2003), 100–101. Also, several scholars cite racial tokenism as a catalyst in the black power movement. See Stokely Carmichael and Charles V. Hamilton, *Black Power: The Politics of Liberation in America* (New York: Vintage, 1967) and Killian, *Impossible Revolution*.

89. Cobbs, interview.

90. Daryl Scott writes that by the 1960s, "The lower class was becoming increasingly synonymous with black." Scott, *Contempt and Pity*, 144.

91. Historian David Allyn argues that the "unprecedented prosperity" into which adults came of age in the late sixties was responsible for their ability to "put aside practical concerns about the future in order to savor life's pleasures and live according to their ideals." David Allyn, *Make Love, Not War: The Sexual Revolution: An Unfettered History* (Boston: Little, Brown, 2000), 80. Further, Roger Kimball identifies the sexual revolution of the 1960s and 1970s to be fixed to the middle class, in part because of the easier access the middle class had to new forms of birth control, like the pill. Roger Kimball, *The Long March: How the Cultural Revolution of the 1960s Changed America* (San Francisco: Encounter, 2000), 147.

92. David Allyn locates much of the impetus for nudity and toplessness (particularly in the form of topless bars, increasingly revealing swimwear, and nude bathing) in the ennui of the middle class in the early 1960s. Allyn, *Make Love, Not War*, 28.

93. From the late 1960s to the mid-1970s, nudity was mainly being used as a symbolic form of protest in high-culture mediums, namely avant-garde theater on and off Broadway. These displays were intended more as an attack on bourgeois morality than as a defense of civil liberties. Allyn, *Make Love, Not War*, 124.

94. David Allyn describes the heated nature of sexual stereotypes for black men in the late 1960s. He claims that black nationalists tended to exploit, rather than challenge, stereotypes, only heightening the tensions surrounding black male sexuality in white culture. Allyn, *Make Love, Not War*, 91.

95. Several sources discuss the myth of black male hypersexuality and the black male response to the existence of the myth. See Beth Day, "The Hidden Fear," in *The Black Male in America*, eds. Doris Y. Wilkinson and Ronald L. Taylor (Chicago: Nelson-Hall, 1977), 193–206; Grier and Cobbs, *Black Rage;* bell hooks, *We Real Cool: Black Men and Masculinity* (New York: Routledge, 2004).

96. Cobbs, *My American Life*, 192.

97. Cobbs, interview.

98. Anderson, *Upstart Spring*, 15.

99. Leo Litwak, "A Trip to Esalen Institute—Joy Is the Prize," *New York Times,* December 31, 1967, reprinted (with changes) in Gerald Walker, ed., *Best Magazine Articles: 1969* (New York: Crown, 1968), 126.

100. Kripal, *Esalen*, 186.

101. Ibid., 187.

102. "Esalen Encounter Groups, Summer Series 1968: Four Racial Confrontation Workshops," registration forms.

103. George Leonard, telephone interview with author, April 27, 2005.

104. Anderson, *Upstart Spring*, 198.

105. Ibid., 198.

106. David Price, e-mail to author, April 25, 2006.

107. Ibid.

108. George Leonard, interview with author, Mill Valley, CA, April 27, 2006.

109. Cobbs's personal activism strayed quickly from the facilitation of black-white encounter, which he only performed for a couple years. After publishing *Black Rage* in 1968, he found himself in high demand from corporations who sought assistance in addressing the complexity of blacks moving into professional positions. By the early 1970s, Cobbs decided his time could be best spent consulting for nationwide corporations in an effort to increase their sensitivity

to racial issues, and he abandoned both his private psychiatric practice and his involvement in encounter groups. He continued to publish books, including Price Cobbs and Judith Turnock, *Cracking the
Corporate Code: The Revealing Success Stories of 32 African-American
Executives* (New York: American Management Association, 2003).

110.   Leonard, interview, April 18, 2006.

Chapter 11: The Postmortem Years

1.   Abraham Maslow, "1970" in *Abraham H. Maslow: A Memorial Volume*, ed. B. G. Maslow (Monterey, CA: Thomson Brooks/Cole,
1973), 29.

2.   Christopher M. Aanstoos, Ilene Serlin, and Thomas Greening, "History of Division 32 (Humanistic Psychology) of the American Psychological Association," in *Unification Through Division: Histories of
the Divisions of the American Psychological Association*, vol. 5, ed. Donald Dewsbury (Washington, DC: American Psychological Association, 2000), 8.

3.   Donadrian Rice, telephone interview with author, June 2, 2011.

4.   Christopher M. Aanstoos, "The West Georgia Story," *Humanistic Psychologist* 17, no. 1 (1989): 77–85.

5.   Gibson's intention was for the new division to serve as a bridge between AHP and APA, representing the interests of the many individuals who had membership in both organizations. Belief in the
wisdom of this union, however, was not uniform; certain members,
including Mike Arons, argued that the creation of another organization of humanistic psychology would "dilute" the movement. Aanstoos, Serlin, and Greening, "History of Division 32," 9–10.

6.   Division 32 reached a peak of 1,150 members in 1977.

7.   Aanstoos, Serlin, and Greening, "History of Division 32," 21.

8.   Statement by John Levy, Executive Officer, Association of Humanistic Psychology, "The Humanistic Psychology Institute," undated,
from Eleanor Criswell's personal files.

9.   Eleanor Criswell, telephone interview with author, July 30, 2011.

10.   In August 1969 the American Association of Humanistic Psychology
voted to change its name to the Association of Humanistic Psychol-

ogy, out of respect for increasingly evident international interest. The change was officially filed with the State of California in December 1969. Bonnie Davenport, AHP member services, e-mail message to author, February 2, 2007.

11.   Ibid.; "History of the Humanistic Psychology Institute," reported by Eleanor Criswell, Executive Board Meetings, February 9–10, 1974, from Eleanor Criswell's personal files. Criswell never viewed the institute as an intellectual counterweight to the experiential elements, but instead saw it as an umbrella under which all varieties of humanistic work could be sheltered. While HPI was, at times, vulnerable to warring factions of academics vs. experientialists, both sides were supported under the institute's commitment to psychological practices that were relevant to lived experience. Still, the emphases of HPI vacillated between the theoretical and the practical, depending on the leadership at the time. After Criswell stepped down, her husband, Tom Hanna, a philosophy professor and administrator, took over, reinforcing the institute's theoretical and philosophical underpinnings. When he left in 1975, Don Polkinghorne became director. Like Hanna, he considered himself a phenomenologist, but he supplanted Hanna's philosophical interests with a focus on qualitative methods. This track was reinforced by the addition to the faculty of Duquesne psychologist Amedeo Giorgi, who had recently published *Psychology as a Human Science*. In the years to follow, HPI would undergo many such shifts and endure the tumult that came with the range of humanistic interests represented by its board, directors, and faculty. Criswell, interview; Maureen O'Hara, telephone interview with author, July 29, 2011.

12.   Abraham Maslow, "February 12, 1970," *The Journals of A. H. Maslow*, vol. 2, ed. Richard J. Lowry (Monterey, CA: Brooks/Cole, 1979), 996.

13.   Maslow, "March 1, 1969," *Journals*, vol. 2, 947.

14.   Maslow, "December 21, 1968," *Journals*, vol. 2, 942.

15.   Maslow, "February 12, 1970," *Journals*, vol. 2, 996.

16.   Ibid., 997.

17.   Maslow, "May 9, 1966," *Journals*, vol. 2, 730.

18.   Maslow, "May 2, 1966," *Journals*, vol. 1, 620.

19.   Maslow, "September 15, 1966," *Journals*, vol. 1, 664.

20.   Maslow, "May 9, 1966," *Journals*, vol. 2, 730.

21.   "APA History," American Psychological Association website, http://www.apa.org/about/archives/apa-history.aspx.

22.   Maslow, "July 8, 1966," *Journals*, vol. 2, 740.

23.   Frank Manuel, as quoted in Abraham Maslow, *Abraham H. Maslow: A Memorial Volume*, ed. B. G. Maslow (Monterey, CA: Thomson Brooks/Cole, 1973), 5.

24.   Maslow, "January 17, 1968," *Journals*, vol. 2, 1009.

25.   Edward Hoffman, "Abraham Maslow: A Biographical Sketch," in *Future Visions: The Unpublished Papers of Abraham Maslow*, ed. Edward Hoffman (Thousand Oaks, CA: Sage, 1996), 13.

26.   David Dempsey, "Love and Will and Rollo May," *New York Times*, March 28, 1971, SM29. In 1974, *Love and Will* again appeared in the *New York Times*, on a list of books that had received "uncommonly large print orders"—an estimated 400,000 copies—in the prior month. "Paperback Best Sellers," *New York Times*, March 10, 1974, 379.

27.   Rollo May, *Psychology and the Human Dilemma* (Princeton, NJ: Van Nostrand, 1967), 25.

28.   Ibid., 174–75.

29.   Ibid., 4.

30.   Rollo May, *Love and Will* (New York: Norton, 1969), 20 and 308.

31.   Ibid., 324–25.

32.   Abraham Maslow, *The Farther Reaches of Human Nature* (New York: Viking, 1971), 335.

33.   Ibid., 334.

34.   Ibid., 335.

35.   Ibid., 336.

36.   Grahame Miles, *Science and Religious Experience: Are They Similar Forms of Knowledge?* (Portland, OR: Sussex Academic, 2007), 210.

37.   See Douglas McGregor, *The Human Side of Enterprise* (Columbus, OH: McGraw-Hill, 1960).

38.   Maslow, *Farther Reaches*, 273–79.

39.   Maslow, "January 22, 1969," *Journals*, vol. 2, 946.

40.   Maslow, "January 18, 1969," *Journals*, vol. 2, 945.

41. Hoffman, *Right to Be Human,* 316.

42. Ibid., 945.

43. Maslow, "May 5, 1970," *Journals,* vol. 2, 1294.

44. Frank Manuel as quoted in *Abraham H. Maslow: A Memorial Volume,* 4.

45. Maslow, *Abraham H. Maslow: A Memorial Volume,* 29.

46. James Klee as quoted in Maslow, *Abraham H. Maslow: A Memorial Volume,* 12.

47. Ricardo Morant as quoted in Maslow, *Abraham H. Maslow: A Memorial Volume,* 28.

48. Maslow, "July 30, 1969," *Journals,* vol. 2, 980.

49. Maslow, "April 22, 1962," *Journals,* vol. 1, 62.

50. Maslow, *Farther Reaches,* 286.

Chapter 12: A Delicious Look Inward

1. Betty Friedan, *The Feminine Mystique* (1963; reprint, New York: Dell, 1974), 521.

2. Natalie Rogers, telephone interview with author, September 2, 2005.

3. Richard Farson, telephone interview with author, October 5, 2005.

4. "Women in AHP," audiotape of panel proceedings, AHP Annual Convention, 1984, Boston, MA, provided to the author by Natalie Rogers.

5. Ibid.

6. Leila J. Rupp and Verta Taylor, *Survival in the Doldrums: The American Women's Rights Movement, 1945 to the 1960s* (New York: Oxford University Press, 1987), 16. Elaine Tyler May cites McCarthyism, in particular, as contributing to the reassertion of the domestic ideal, as nonconforming women tended to be viewed with suspicion. Elaine Tyler May, *Homeward Bound: American Families in the Cold War Era* (New York: Basic Books, 1988), 13.

7. Robert Coughlan, "Changing Roles in Modern Marriage," *Life,* December 24, 1956, 108–18, quotation from 110.

8. Olive Banks, *Faces of Feminism: A Study of Feminism as a Social Movement* (New York: St. Martin's, 1981), 210.

9. For an overview of the sexual revolution in America, see David Allyn, *Make Love, Not War: The Sexual Revolution: An Unfettered History*

(Boston: Little, Brown, 2000). For a more pointed history of birth control in America, see Linda Gordon, *Woman's Body, Woman's Right: A Social History of Birth Control in America* (New York: Penguin, 1976). For an overview of research on women's sexuality, beginning with the groundbreaking studies of Alfred Kinsey in the 1950s and William Masters and Virginia Johnson in the 1960s, see Kristine M. Baber and Katherine R. Allen, *Women and Families: Feminist Reconstructions* (New York: Guilford, 1992), 61–66.

10.   Allyn, *Make Love, Not War*, 168–70. The Kinsey reports and the work of Masters and Johnson were published as Alfred C. Kinsey, Wardell B. Pomeroy, and Clyde E. Martin, *Sexual Behavior in the Human Male* (Philadelphia: Saunders, 1948); Institute for Sex Research, *Sexual Behavior in the Human Female* (Philadelphia: Saunders, 1953); and William H. Masters and Virginia E. Johnson, *Human Sexual Response* (Boston: Little, Brown, 1966).

11.   Allyn, *Make Love, Not War*, 34.

12.   Allyn, *Make Love, Not War*, 10–14. For the original novel, see Helen Gurley Brown, *Sex and the Single Girl* (New York: Giant Cardinal, 1962). Allyn also describes how Brown's book served as a guide for young women negotiating the waters of sexual experimentation and spawned other nonfiction books offering similar advice. The advice in Joan Garrity's *The Sensuous Woman*, published in 1969 under the pen name "J," explicitly offered itself as a set of instructions that women could use to construct bold new sexual identities. Other manual-style books that followed included Dr. David Reuben's book *Everything You Always Wanted to Know About Sex (But Were Afraid to Ask)*, published in 1969, and Alex Comfort's bestseller *The Joy of Sex: A Gourmet Guide to Love Making*, published in 1972.

13.   Betty Friedan, *The Feminine Mystique* (New York: Norton, 1963), quotation from 77.

14.   Friedan, however, was wary of forging too close a bond between psychology and the political interests of the women's liberation movement. As a former labor union activist, she was conscious of the need to place women's problems in the context of society and the economy, and as a psychology graduate student, she had always been careful to keep politics out of her psychology. In fact, Friedan's motivation for

leaving her graduate program had been her prioritization of the heated struggles occurring in the public arena. Daniel Horowitz, *Betty Friedan and the Making of the Feminine Mystique* (Amherst: University of Massachusetts Press, 1998), 84 and 99.

15. Friedan, *Feminine Mystique*, 319.

16. Joyce Milton credits Maslow, through his influence on Friedan, with shaping the entire women's liberation movement. Maslow's model of self-actualization, she argues, became the dominant view in female psychology (a role that endures to the present). Joyce Milton, *The Road to Malpsychia: Humanistic Psychology and Our Discontents* (San Francisco: Encounter Books, 2003), 210.

17. Horowitz, *Betty Friedan*, 46.

18. Ibid., 311.

19. Ironically, Friedan's representation of her own experience in *The Feminine Mystique* was somewhat inauthentic and contrived, in that she had not been the naïve housewife whose visions were clouded by the feminine mystique, but a political individual whose activist experiences in the 1940s and 1950s yielded her poignant cultural analyses in the early sixties. For more on this see Horowitz, *Betty Friedan*.

20. Ruth Rosen, *The World Split Open: How the Modern Women's Movement Changed America* (New York: Viking, 2000), 6.

21. Kathleen C. Berkeley, *The Women's Liberation Movement in America* (Westport, CT: Greenwood, 1999), 19–20.

22. "Women in Congress," http://www.infoplease.com/ipa/A0801429 .html.

23. Barbara Sinclair Deckard, *The Women's Movement: Political, Socioeconomic, and Psychological Issues* (New York: Harper & Row, 1979), 345–48.

24. Anita Shreve, *Women Together, Women Alone: The Legacy of the Consciousness-Raising Movement* (New York: Viking, 1989), 83.

25. Harriet G. Lerner, *The Dance of Deception: A Guide to Authenticity and Truth-Telling in Women's Relationships* (New York: HarperCollins, 1993), 61–62.

26. Jo Freeman, *The Politics of Women's Liberation* (New York: McKay, 1975), 118.

27. Shreve, *Women Together*, 198.

28. The formal introduction of CR by the women's movement occurred in 1968 at the first national women's liberation conference in Chicago, at which two hundred women from thirty-seven states and Canada met to discuss feminist concerns. Ibid., 6–12.

29. Ibid., 12 and 53.

30. Ibid., 10.

31. Kathie Sarachild as quoted in Alice Echols, *Daring to Be Bad: Radical Feminism in America, 1967–1975* (Minneapolis: University of Minnesota Press, 1989), 87.

32. Echols, *Daring to Be Bad*, 87.

33. Shreve, *Women Together*, 86.

34. The persistent debate over CR was enough to split several feminist organizations, including the New York Radical Women—an early feminist group formed in 1967. In 1969, the feminist group Redstockings became the new home for CR group advocates and actively promoted its use. CR opponents, who frequently defined themselves as socialist feminists, formed the Women's International Terrorist Conspiracy from Hell (WITCH) when the New York Radical Women dissolved. Echols, *Daring to Be Bad*, 86.

35. Ibid., 30.

36. Maureen O'Hara and Gillian Proctor, "An Interview with Dr. Maureen O'Hara: A Pioneer Person-Centred Therapist and Feminist Reflects on 30 Years of Process and Progress," in *Encountering Feminism: Intersections between Feminism and the Person-Centred Approach*, eds. Gillian Proctor and Mary Beth Napier (Ross-on-Wye, UK: PCCS Books, 2004), 60.

37. Ibid., 61.

38. Ibid., 60.

39. Natalie Rogers, telephone interview with author, September 2, 2005.

40. Maureen O'Hara, interview with author, San Francisco, CA, April 29, 2005.

41. O'Hara and Proctor, "Interview," 60.

42. Natalie Rogers, interview.

43. Ibid.

44. Ibid.

45. Ibid.

46. Ibid.

47. Carl R. Rogers as quoted in Milton, *Road to Malpsychia*, 158.

48. Natalie Rogers, interview.

49. Carl R. Rogers, *Carl Rogers on Personal Power* (New York: Delacorte, 1977), ix.

50. According to Stanley Krippner, May had always written exclusively for men, and had failed to consider the unique circumstances and psychological reality of women. When Krippner saw him speak at Sonoma State College in 1966, though, May was struggling to incorporate women in his analyses, mainly by employing nongendered pronouns. The 1967 publication of May's *Psychology and the Human Dilemma* also testifies to May's newfound sensitivity to gender issues: his introduction bears the footnote "Some of these essays were written before the time when we began to realize that 'man' did not embrace 'woman' . . ." Stanley Krippner, interview with author, San Francisco, June 24, 2005; Rollo May, *Psychology and the Human Dilemma* (Princeton, NJ: Van Nostrand, 1967), ix.

51. Carolyn Morell, "*Love and Will*: A Feminist Critique," *Journal of Humanistic Psychology* 13, no. 2 (April 1973): 35–46, quotation from 35.

52. Morell, "*Love and Will*," 42.

53. Rollo May, "Response to Morell's '*Love and Will*: A Feminist Critique,'" *Journal of Humanistic Psychology* 13, no. 2 (April 1973), 47–50, quotations from 47.

54. Ilene Serlin and Eleanor Criswell, "Humanistic Psychology and Women: A Critical-Historical Perspective," in *A Handbook of Humanistic Psychology: Leading Edges in Theory, Research, and Practice*, eds. Kirk J. Schneider, James F. T. Bugental, and J. Fraser Pierson (Thousand Oaks, CA: Sage, 2001), 30.

55. Milton, *Road to Malpsychia*, 210.

56. Abraham Maslow, "Dominance, Personality and Social Behavior in Women," *Journal of Social Psychology* 10, (February 1939): 3–39.

57. Evidence of his persistent interest in feminism can also be found in Maslow's journals, as well as in his archival files. (He often clipped and saved magazine articles related to feminism.) For examples, see Abraham Maslow, "December 27, 1967" and "March 22, 1969," *The*

Journals of A. H. Maslow, vol. 2, ed. Richard J. Lowry (Monterey, CA: Brooks/Cole, 1979), 837, 1139.

58. Maslow did, however, include a few women in his list of self-actualized individuals: he claimed that Jane Addams, Eleanor Roosevelt, and Ruth Benedict (anthropologist and former mentor to Maslow) had achieved self-actualization.

59. Maslow, "March 22, 1969," *Journals*, vol. 2, 1139–40.

60. Deckard, *The Women's Movement*, 386.

61. Naomi Weisstein, "Psychology Constructs the Female," in *Woman in Sexist Society: Studies in Power and Powerlessness*, eds. Vivian Gornick and Barbara K. Moran (1971; reprint, New York: New American Library, 1972), 144.

62. Maslow, "January 8, 1963," *Journals*, vol. 1, 218.

63. Deckard, *The Women's Movement*, 350.

64. Serlin and Criswell, "Humanistic Psychology and Women," 30.

65. Twice there were female and male copresidents. Female presidents post-1976 include Jean Houston, Jacquelin Doyle, Virginia Satir, Peggy Taylor, Lonnie Barbach, Frances Vaughan, Elizabeth Campbell, Maureen O'Hara, Sandy Friedman, Ann Weiser Cornell, M. A. Bjarkman, Jocelyn Olivier, and Katy Brant. Serlin and Criswell, "Humanistic Psychology and Women," 30.

66. Ibid., 32.

67. Jackie Doyle, interview with author, Tiberon, CA, April 28, 2005.

68. Mike Moore, "Breaking Free from the Human Potential Movement," *Mountain Gazette*, October 1975, 23.

Chapter 13: Intellectual Slippage

1. Bob Dylan, "Last Thoughts on Woodie Guthrie," first recited April 12, 1963, New York City's Town Hall, later released in *The Bootleg Series: Volumes 1–3 (Rare and Unreleased) 1961–1991*, Columbia Records, 1991.

2. Bruce J. Schulman, *The Seventies: The Great Shift in American Culture, Politics, and Society* (New York: Free Press, 2001), 161.

3. Terry H. Anderson, *The Movement and the Sixties: Protest in America from Greensboro to Wounded Knee* (New York: Oxford University Press, 1995), 246.

4.   Schulman, *Seventies*, 17.

5.   William J. McKeachie, "Psychology in America's Bicentennial Year," *American Psychologist* 31, no. 12, December (1976): 819–33, quotation from 820; Larry Van Dyne, "For Some Reason, Psychology Is Popular," *New York Times,* November 9, 1975, Op-Ed, 16.

6.   Steven Starker "Self-Help Treatment Books: The Rest of the Story," *American Psychologist* 43, vol. 7 (July 1988): 599; James J. Forest, "Self-Help Books," *American Psychologist* 43, no. 7 (July 1988): 599.

7.   James J. Forest, "Self-Help Books," 599.

8.   Maureen O'Hara, interview with author, August 30, 2011.

9.   Maureen O'Hara, "Oberlin T-group," unpublished personal paper, undated.

10.   Maureen O'Hara, interview, August 30, 2011.

11.   Maureen O'Hara, interview with author, May 13, 2011.

12.   Leo Litwak, " 'Rolfing,' 'Aikido,' Hypnodramas, Psychokinesis, and Other Things Beyond the Here and Now," *New York Times Magazine*, December 17, 1972, 18–38, quotation from 19.

13.   Robert Reinhold, "Humanistic Psychology Shows Its Force," *New York Times*, September 4, 1970, 13.

14.   Tom Wolfe, "The Me Decade and the Third Great Awakening," in *Mauve Gloves & Madmen, Clutter & Vine* (New York: Bantam, 1977), 117–18.

15.   *Bob & Carol & Ted & Alice*, film directed by Paul Mazursky (Los Angeles: Columbia Pictures, released September 17, 1969).

16.   Jane O'Reilly, "Why the Heartland Doesn't Deserve New York," *New York Magazine*, July 10, 1972, 52–53, quotation from 52.

17.   Ibid.

18.   Lawrence Solomon as quoted in Reinhold, "Humanistic Psychology," 13.

19.   Reinhold, "Humanistic Psychology," 13.

20.   David Dempsey, "Love and Will and Rollo May," *New York Times*, March 28, 1971, SM29.

21.   Litwak, " 'Rolfing,' "19.

22.   Ibid.

23.   Richard Farson, telephone interview with author, October 5, 2005.

24.   Maslow, "September 19, 1967," *The Journals of A. H. Maslow*, vol. 1, ed. Richard J. Lowry (Monterey, CA: Brooks/Cole, 1979), 287.

25. Bernard G. Rosenthal, "The Nature and Development of the Encounter Group Movement" (Maslow Papers, Box M449.30, Esalen Crit. folder, Archives of the History of American Psychology, Center for the History of Psychology, University of Akron), 14.

26. Richard Farson, "The Technology of Humanism," *Journal of Humanistic Psychology* 18, no. 2 (1978): 5–35, quotation from 7.

27. Ibid., 16–17.

28. Rosenthal, "Nature and Development of the Encounter Group Movement," 12.

29. Ibid., 27.

30. Ibid., 20.

31. Farson, interview.

32. Eugene Taylor, interview with author, Cambridge, MA, September 29, 2005.

33. May to Massarik, Allen and Levy, November 6, 1971 (May Papers, HPA Mss 46, Humanistic Psychology Archives, Department of Special Collections, Donald C. Davidson Library, University of California, Santa Barbara).

34. Ibid.

35. George Leonard, *Walking on the Edge of the World* (Boston: Houghton Mifflin, 1988), 369.

36. Rollo May, "Remarks to AHP," January 29, 1981 (May Papers, HPA Mss 46, Box 155: 8, Speeches for H. Psych—My Speeches to AHP, Humanistic Psychology Archives, Department of Special Collections, Donald C. Davidson Library, University of California, Santa Barbara).

37. Ibid.

38. Maslow, "August 30, 1962," *Journals*, vol. 1, 189–90.

39. Forrest G. Robinson, *Love's Story Told: A Life of Henry A. Murray* (Cambridge, MA: Harvard University Press, 1992), 354.

40. Farson, "Technology of Humanism," 6.

41. Ibid., 5.

42. Richard Farson to the members of AHP, undated (Association of Humanistic Psychology Papers, HPA MSS1, Theory Conference Folder, Humansitic Psychology Archives, Department of Special Collections, Donald C. Davidson Library, University of California, Santa Barbara).

43. Rollo May to Fred Massarik, Melanie Allen, and John Levy, November 6, 1971 (Association for Humanistic Psychology Papers, Box H9, Correspondence: Rollo May folder, Archives of the History of American Psychology, Center for the History of Psychology, University of Akron).

44. Farson, interview.

45. "Rollo May and Tony Athos in Conversation," typed manuscript, undated (Association of Humanistic Psychology Papers, Box H25, Theory Conference folder, Humanistic Psychology Archives, Center for the History of Psychology, University of Akron).

46. Maslow, "March 3, 1969," *Journals*, vol. 2, 949.

47. Richard Farson to the Members of AHP, undated.

48. Ibid.

49. Ibid.

50. Ibid.

51. Rollo May, opening remarks, "Edited Theory Conference Transcript," Tucson, Arizona, April 4–6, 1975, ed. Rick Gilbert (May Papers, HPA MSS46, Box 155:9, Humanistic Psychology Archives, Department of Special Collections, Donald C. Davidson Library, University of California, Santa Barbara), 5.

52. Participants included: Melanie Allen, Anthony Athos, Gregory Bateson, Kenneth Benne, James Bugental, Arthur Deikman, Joan Grof, Stan Grof, Charles Hampden-Turner, Willis Harmen, Stanley Krippner, Norma Lyman, Fred Massarik, Floyd Matson, Rollo May, Claudio Naranjo, John Perry, Carl Rogers, Jonas Salk, Frank Severin, Elizabeth Simpson, Brewster Smith, Huston Smith, and Nora Weckler. Rick Gilbert, "Edited Theory Conference Transcript."

53. Ibid.

54. Brewster Smith, "Prefaces to a Discussion of Humanism and Science in Humanistic Psychology: Position Paper for the Conference on Theory in Humanistic Psychology" and Melanie Allen, "Toward a Theory of Humanistic Psychology: Keeping the System Open," April 4–6, 1975 (Association for Humanistic Psychology Collection, Box H 13, AHP Theory Conference folder, Archives of the History of American Psychology, Center for the History of Psychology, University of Akron). Brewster Smith provided an important link between

humanistic psychology and mainstream psychology. He served as APA president in 1978, and was the third humanistic psychologist to be president of APA (the first being Rogers in 1947 and the second being Maslow in 1968). Melanie Allen collaborated with her close friend and associate Charlotte Bühler on *Introduction to Humanistic Psychology* in 1972. Her participation in AHP dropped off shortly after the theory meeting. Thomas Greening, e-mail to author, February 10, 2008; "Former APA Presidents," APA website, http://www.apa.org/about/governance/president/past-presidents.aspx. See also Charlotte Bühler and Melanie Allen, *Introduction to Humanistic Psychology* (Belmont, CA: Brooks/Cole, 1972).

55. Smith, "Prefaces to a Discussion of Humanism and Science in Humanistic Psychology."

56. Charles Hampden-Turner, "Sailing Between Scylla and Charybdis or the Equal and Opposite Cop-Out" (Association for Humanistic Psychology Collection, Box H25, Theory Conference, Archives of the History of American Psychology, Center for the History of Psychology, University of Akron). In 1971, Hampden-Turner published *Radical Man*, a key book that related humanistic psychology to human behavior in the realms of business and politics. See Charles Hampden-Turner, *Radical Man: The Process of Psycho-Social Development* (New York: Doubleday, 1971).

57. Willis Harman, "Notes on a Theory of Humanistic Psychology" (Association for Humanistic Psychology Collection, Box H 13, AHP Theory Conference folder, Archives of the History of American Psychology, Center for the History of Psychology, University of Akron). Of this ideal, Rollo May explained, "I prefer not to call what we seek a new subjectivity, for that puts us in the same old dilemma. We make the same mistake then that the people who are devoted to objectivity make, except we use the opposite word. We need to find a dimension in the human being below pure subjectivity and pure objectivity." May, "Theory Conference Transcript," 3–5.

58. Ibid., 3–5.

59. Ibid., 2.

60. Ibid., 3.

61. Ibid., 5.

62. Floyd Matson, "Notes Toward a Theory" (Association for Humanistic Psychology Collection, Box H 13, AHP Theory Conference folder, Archives of the History of American Psychology, Center for the History of Psychology, University of Akron). Matson's key books during the time include: Floyd Matson, *The Broken Image* (New York: Braziller, 1964); Floyd Matson, ed., *Being, Becoming and Behavior: The Psychological Sciences* (New York: Braziller, 1967); and Floyd Matson, *The Idea of Man* (New York: Delacorte Press, 1976).

63. Ibid.

64. Gregory Bateson, "Theory Conference Transcript," 19.

65. "Rollo May and Tony Athos in Conversation."

66. May, "Theory Conference Transcript," 46.

67. Smith, "Theory Conference Transcript," 47.

68. Carl Rogers, "Theory Conference Transcript," 64–65.

69. Carl Rogers to Members of the AHP Theory Conference, memo (Association for Humanistic Psychology Collection, Box H 13, AHP Theory Conference folder, Archives of the History of American Psychology, Center for the History of Psychology, University of Akron).

70. Fred Massarik to Carl Rogers, May 27, 1975 (Rogers Papers, HPA MSS 32, Humanistic Psychology Archives, Department of Special Collections, Donald C. Davidson Library, University of California, Santa Barbara).

71. Farson, interview.

72. Ibid.

73. Richard Farson, "Carl Rogers, Quiet Revolutionary," in *Carl Rogers: The Man and his Ideas*, ed. Richard I. Evans (New York: Dutton, 1975), xx.

74. Ibid., xli.

75. Ibid., 18–19.

76. Ibid., 21.

77. Peter Marin, "The New Narcissism," *Harper's Magazine*, October 1975, 45–56, quotation from 46.

78. Mike Moore, "Breaking Free from the Human Potential Movement," *Mountain Gazette*, October 1975, 21.

79. Ibid., 21.

80. Ibid.

81.   Dempsey, "Love and Will."

82.   Jean Millay, *Multidimensional Mind: Remote Viewing in Hyperspace* (Berkeley, CA: North Atlantic Books, 1999), 95–99.

83.   Tom Wolfe, *In Our Time* (New York: Farrar, Straus and Giroux, 1980), 10.

84.   Paul Bindram in *Inside Psychotherapy: Nine Clinicians Tell How They Work and What They Are Trying to Accomplish*, ed. Adelaide Bry (New York: Basic, 1972), 143-62.

85.   Abraham Maslow, Letter to Paul Bindrim, February 13, 1968 (Maslow Papers, Box M445, Nudity folder, Archives of the History of American Psychology, Center for the History of Psychology, University of Akron).

86.   Webster Schott, "Inside Psychotherapy" (review), *Saturday Review*, August 19, 1972, 61–62, quotation from 62.

87.   "A Chronology of AHP's Annual Conferences," Association of Humanistic Psychology website, www.ahpweb.org/aboutahp/ahpcronology .html

88.   Christopher M. Aanstoos, Ilene Serlin, and Thomas Greening, "History of Division 32 (Humanistic Psychology) of the American Psychological Association," in *Unification Through Division: Histories of the Divisions of the American Psychological Association*, vol. 5, ed. Donald Dewsbury (Washington, DC: American Psychological Association, 2000), 22.

89.   Maureen O'Hara, interview, May 13, 2011.

90.   Aanstoos, Serlin, and Greening, "History of Division 32," 22.

Chapter 14: What Remains

1.   Carl R. Rogers, *A Way of Being* (Boston: Houghton Mifflin, 1980), 49.

2.   William Kessen, "Pastor and Professor," *New York Times*, March 18, 1979.

3.   "Carl R. Rogers, 85, Leader in Psychotherapy, Dies," *New York Times*, February 6, 1987.

4.   Ibid.

5.   Rogers, *A Way of Being*, ix.

6.   "Carl R. Rogers, 85, Leader in Psychotherapy, Dies."

7. Robert Abzug, interview with author, Austin, TX, August 26, 2011.

8. Rollo May, *Freedom and Destiny* (New York: Norton, 1981), 5.

9. David Dempsey, "Love and Will and Rollo May," *New York Times*, March 28, 1971.

10. "Books of the Times," *New York Times*, November 21, 1981, accessed on December 1, 2010, http://www.nytimes.com/1981/11/21/books/books-of-the-times101739.html?scp=5&sq=rollo+may&st=nyt

11. Ibid.

12. Daniel Goleman, "Esalen Wrestles with a Staid Present," *New York Times*, December 10, 1985, Section C, Page 1, Column 1.

13. Ibid.

14. Bruce J. Schulman, *The Seventies: The Great Shift in American Culture, Politics, and Society* (New York: Free Press, 2001), 185.

15. Brian Willats, *Breaking Up Is Easy to Do* (Lansing, MI: Michigan Family Forum, 1995), citing statistics from National Center for Health Statistics, U.S. Department of Health and Human Services.

16. John Updike, *Rabbit Is Rich* (New York: Knopf, 1981), 3.

17. Norman Mailer as quoted in "Mailer on the '70s—Decade of 'Image, Skin Flicks and Porn,'" *U.S. News & World Report*, December 10, 1979, 57.

18. Ronald Reagan as quoted in Haynes Johnson, *Sleepwalking Through History: America in the Reagan Years* (New York: Norton, 1991), 79.

19. Ibid., 28, 34–35.

20. Rogers, *Way of Being*, 51.

21. Bryce Nelson, "Despite a Blur of Change, Clear Trends Are Emerging in Therapy," *New York Times*, March 1, 1983.

22. Jeffrey Kripal, *Esalen: America and the Religion of No Religion* (Chicago: University of Chicago Press, 2007), 331–38.

23. Goleman, "Esalen Wrestles," 1.

24. Bob Morris, "Divine Reinvention," *New York Times*, March 2, 1995.

25. The turn of the century found most humanistic psychologists employed at private institutes and professional schools, most notably the Saybrook Institute (which was founded in 1970 by AHP as the Humanistic Psychology Institute, but later changed its name to heighten its mainstream appeal). Christopher M. Aanstoos, Ilene Serlin, and Thomas Greening, "History of Division 32 (Humanistic Psychology)

of the American Psychological Association," in *Unification Through Division: Histories of the Divisions of the American Psychological Association*, vol. 5, ed. Donald Dewsbury (Washington, DC: American Psychological Association, 2000), 22.

26.   Thomas Greening, e-mail to author, February 3, 2007.

27.   Richard W. Robins, Samuel D. Gosling, and Kenneth H. Craik, "An Empirical Analysis of Trends in Psychology," *American Psychologist* 54, no 2. (February 1999), http://homepage.psy.utexas.edu/homepage/faculty/gosling/reprints/AmPsych99Trends.pdf.

28.   Richard Farson, telephone interview with author, October 5, 2005.

29.   Richard Farson, "Carl Rogers, Quiet Revolutionary," in *Carl Rogers: The Man and His Ideas*, ed. Richard I. Evans (New York: Dutton, 1975), xxx.

30.   Howard Kirschenbaum, introduction to *The Carl Rogers Reader*, eds. Howard Kischenbaum and Valerie Land Henderson (Boston: Houghton Mifflin, 1989), xi–xii.

31.   A. Weick, C. Rapp, W. P. Sullivan, and W. Kisthardt, "A Strengths Perspective for Social Work Practice," *Social Work* 34, no. 6 (1989): 350–54.

32.   See Barry A. Farber, *Self-Disclosure in Psychotherapy* (New York: Guilford Press, 2006).

33.   R. R. Greene, "The Social Work Interview: Legacy of Carl Rogers and Sigmund Freud," in *Human Behavior Theory: A Diversity Framework*, ed. R. R. Greene (New York: Aldine de Gruyter, 1994), 40–41.

34.   Ibid., 37–47.

35.   E. Brooks Holifield, *A History of Pastoral Care in America: From Salvation to Self-Realization* (Nashville, TN: Abingdon Press, 1983), 277.

36.   Ibid., 295–99; LeRoy Aden, "On Carl Rogers' Becoming," *Theology Today* 36, no. 4 (January 1980): 556–59.

37.   George Leonard, *Walking on the Edge of the World* (Boston: Houghton Mifflin, 1988), 326.

38.   James F. T. Bugental, "Rollo May (1909–1994)," *American Psychologist* 51, no. 4 (April 1996): 418.

39.   Holifield, *History of Pastoral Care*, 297. May's ideas of empathy were most clearly articulated in Rollo May, *The Art of Counseling* (Nashville, TN: Abingdon Press, 1939).

40. Rollo May, *Psychology and the Human Dilemma* (Princeton, NJ: Van Nostrand, 1967), x. For a more contemporary exploration of the problems May considers, see James Hillman and Michael Ventura, *We've Had a Hundred Years of Psychotherapy and the World Keeps Getting Worse* (New York: HarperCollins, 1993).

41. Eugene I. Taylor and Frederick Martin, "Humanistic Psychology at the Crossroads," *The Handbook of Humanistic Psychology: Leading Edges in Theory, Research and Practice,* eds. Kirk J. Schneider, James F. T. Bugental, and J. Fraser Pierson (Thousand Oaks, CA: Sage, 2001), 23. Taylor and Martin argue that when humanistic psychology was "absorbed into the psychotherapeutic counterculture," it "fractionated" into three unintegrated streams, all of which existed outside of academia. These included meditation and altered states of consciousness (which became transpersonal psychology); bodywork and group dynamics (which included the encounter groups and corporate interests); and human science (which consisted of political psychology and cultural criticism). The authors attributed this division to Maslow and Sutich's prioritization of the spiritual and their subsequent decision, in 1969, to transfer their loyalties to transpersonal psychology.

42. Gordon Wheeler, "Spirit and Shadow: Esalen and the Gestalt Model," in *On the Edge of the Future: Esalen and the Evolution of American Culture*, eds. Jeffrey Kripal and Glenn W. Shuck (Bloomington: Indiana University Press, 2005), 173–74.

43. Christopher Lasch, *Minimal Self: Psychic Survival in Troubled Times* (New York: Norton, 1984), 211.

44. James Pawelski, "The Promise of Positive Psychology for the Assessment of Character," *Journal of College and Character* 4, no. 6 (2003), http://journals.naspa.org/cgi/viewcontent.cgi?article=1361&context =jcc. Seligman first described "positive psychology" in his 1998 presidential address to the APA. Martin E. P. Seligman, "The President's Address," http://www.positivepsychology.org/aparep98.htm.

45. Martin E. P. Seligman and Mihalyi Csikszentmihalyi, "Positive Psychology: An Introduction," *American Psychologist* 55, no. 1 (January 2000): 7.

46. Martin E. P. Seligman, "Positive Psychology, Positive Prevention, and Positive Therapy," in *Positive Psychological Assessment: A Handbook of*

Models and Measures, eds. Shane J. Lopez and C. R. Snyder (Washington, DC: American Psychological Association, 2003), 3.

47.   Joyce Milton, *The Road to Malpsychia: Humanistic Psychology and Our Discontents* (San Francisco: Encounter Books, 2003), 288.

48.   Pawelski, "Promise of Positive Psychology."

49.   Ibid.; See Christopher Peterson and Martin Seligman, *Character Strengths and Virtues: A Handbook and Classification* (New York: Oxford University Press, 2004).

50.   Milton, *Road to Malpsychia*, 288–89.

51.   Seligman and Csikszentmihalyi, "Positive Psychology," 7.

52.   Ibid.

53.   Stewart Shapiro, "Illogical Positivism," *American Psychologist* 56, no. 1 (January 2001): 82.

54.   Martin E. P. Seligman and Mihaly Cskszentmihalyi, "Reply to Comments," *American Psychologist* 56, no. 1 (January 2001): 89.

55.   Mihaly Csikszentmihalyi, preface to *Handbook of Humanistic Psychology*, xv. At the same time, Csikszentmihalyi also respectfully distanced himself from the "leanness" of the humanistic psychology movement's rigorous cumulative research findings.

56.   Milton, *Road to Malpsychia*, 289.

57.   Seligman and Csikszentmihalyi, "Positive Psychology," 5.

58.   Bill O'Connell, *Solution-Focused Therapy* (London: Sage, 1998), 1; Karen Christensen and David Levinson, eds., *Encyclopedia of Community: From Village to the Virtual World* (London: Sage, 2003), 262–63.

59.   For a good description of the strengths perspective, see Dennis Saleebey, "Introduction: Power in the People," in *The Strengths Perspective in Social Work Practice*, 2nd ed., ed. Dennis Saleebey (New York: Longman, 1997), 3–20.

60.   Ann Weick, "Issues in Overturning a Medical Model of Social Work Practice," *Social Work* 28, no. 6 (1983): 467–71.

61.   Saleeby, introduction to *Strengths Perspective,* 8–9.

62.   Weick, "Issues in Overturning," 467.

63.   Weick et al., "Strengths Perspective," 351.

64.   Farson, "Carl Rogers," xxx–xxxvi, quotation from xxx.

65.   For a good overview of the impact of humanistic psychology in the workplace and the research associated with it, see Alfonso Montuori

and Ronald Purser, "Humanistic Psychology in the Workplace," in *Handbook of Humanistic Psychology.*

66. Because of its continued popularity, *Eupsychian Management* was reprinted with commentary in 1998 as *Maslow on Management.* Many of Maslow's letters and journal entries were published in a 2000 collection *The Maslow Business Reader.* Abraham Maslow, *Eupsychian Management: A Journal* (Homewood, IL: Richard D. Irwin and Dorsey, 1965); Abraham Maslow, *Maslow on Management* (New York: Wiley, 1998); Abraham Maslow, *Maslow Business Reader.*

67. Isaac Prilleltensky, "Humanistic Psychology, Human Welfare and the Social Order," *Journal of Mind and Behavior* 13, no. 4 (1992): 319.

68. Richard Farson, "The Technology of Humanism," *Journal of Humanistic Psychology* 18, no. 2 (1978): 21.

69. Ibid.

70. Prilleltensky, "Humanistic Psychology," 319.

71. At the same time, as Maureen O'Hara points out, the act of giving workers freedom is not necessarily negated by the instrumentality of the act. Even if you give people freedom with the goal of making profit, she argues, you're still giving them freedom, and that inevitably affects the quality of their lives. Maureen O'Hara, telephone interview with author, May 13, 2011.

72. M. Wilson, "DSM-III and the Transformation of American Psychiatry: A History," *American Journal of Psychiatry* 150, no. 3 (1993): 399–410.

73. Gary Greenberg, *Manufacturing Depression: The Secret History of a Modern Disease* (New York: Simon & Schuster, 2010), 63.

74. Ibid., 64.

75. Seligman broadly defines happiness as a sense of satisfaction that derives from pleasure, engagement, and affiliation. Martin E. P. Seligman, *Authentic Happiness: Using the New Positive Psychology to Realize Your Potential for Lasting Fulfillment* (New York: Free Press, 2002), 275.

76. Elizabeth Kolbert, "Everybody Have Fun: What Can Policymakers Learn from Happiness Research?" *The New Yorker*, March 22, 2010, http://www.newyorker.com/arts/critics/books/2010/03/22/100322crbo _books_kolbert?currentPage=all#ixzz0lwgHfkOM; Derek Bok, *The Politics of Happiness: What Government Can Learn from the New Re-*

search on Well-Being (Princeton, NJ: Princeton University Press, 2010).

77. Frank C. Richardson, Blaine J. Fowers, and Charles B. Guignon, *Re-envisioning Psychology: Moral Dimensions of Theory and Practice* (San Francisco: Jossey-Bass, 1999), 157.

78. Ibid., 2–3.

79. Ibid., 4–6.

80. See Hillman and Ventura, *We've Had a Hundred Years of Psychotherapy.*

81. Peggy Rosenthal, *Words and Values: Some Leading Words and Where They Lead Us* (Oxford: Oxford University Press, 1984), 37–38.

82. Jonah Lehrer, "Depression's Upside," *New York Times,* February 25, 2010.

83. See Allan V. Horowitz and Jerome C. Wakefield, *The Loss of Sadness: How Psychiatry Transformed Normal Sorrow into Depressive Disorder* (New York: Oxford University Press, 2007).

84. Frank Furedi, *Therapy Culture: Cultivating Vulnerability in an Uncertain Age* (London: Routledge, 2004), 14–15.

85. Malcolm Gladwell, "Getting Over It," *The New Yorker,* November 8, 2004, http://www.newyorker.com/archive/2004/11/08/041108fa_fact1?currentPage=1#ixzz0mKtwoZn1.

Index